BRIGHTON & HOVE ALBION
ON THIS DAY

BRIGHTON & HOVE ALBION

ON THIS DAY

History, facts and figures
from every day of the year

DAN TESTER

THIRD EDITION

BRIGHTON & HOVE ALBION
ON THIS DAY

History, facts and figures
from every day of the year

All statistics, facts and figures are correct as of 14th July 2024

© Dan Tester

Dan Tester has asserted his rights in accordance with the Copyright, Designs and Patents Act 1988 to be identified as the author of this work.

Published By: Off The Bench Books

Email: info@englishfootballbooks.com
Web: www.englishfootballbooks.com

First edition published 2007 by Pitch Publishing
Second edition, updated and published 2011 by Pitch Publishing

Re-written, revised and republished 2024 by Off The Bench Books

ISBN 978-1-3999-9052-3 third edition (this book)
ISBN 978-1-9054116-5-8 updated edition
ISBN 978-1-9054111-0-8 original edition

Editor – James Halling

Typesetting – Alan Wares

Proofreading – Craig Smith (CRS Editorial)

Cover – Duncan Olner

Printed by Ingrams, Great Britain

Fanzine covers – www.seagullsprogrammes.co.uk

Dan Tester on X – @DJDanteBrighton

For the best football books – www.englishfootballbooks.com

Brighton & Hove Albion On This Day

History, facts and figures from every day of the year

Foreword

It's a pleasure to write the foreword for Dan Tester's third edition of *Brighton & Hove Albion On This Day*, some of which covers my own time as chief executive and deputy chairman.

When I came to the club in 2012, I was aware of the difficult times Brighton had endured in its recent past: nearly surrendering its Football League status; losing the Goldstone Ground and ground sharing at Gillingham; the protracted return to the city; and getting the American Express Stadium built. But I was convinced that one day we would be competing in the Premier League.

Our owner Tony Bloom is fantastic to work for. He's a lifelong Brighton fan who has always had such a strong vision and an unwavering commitment to take the club all the way to the top. It's a pleasure to have been part of that journey alongside him and all the other great people who work at the club and to share some fantastic memories, many of which you will find in this book.

Personal highlights? Where do you start! In my first season we achieved our highest league position for 30 years. Like me, I'm sure you can remember 17th April 2017, when we beat Wigan at the Amex and were promoted to the Premier League for the first time. As I write, we are preparing for our eighth season in the league as a club with an enviable reputation around the world and a bright, stable future.

A few other dates stick out. There is 24th May 2023, when we held the champions Manchester City 1-1 at the Amex to clinch our place in Europe – and Julio Enciso scored the goal of the season to equalise. Or 21st September 2023, when the Amex hosted Europa League football for the first time in our history against AEK Athens.

My favourite is probably 14th December 2023, and the 1-0 win over Marseille which meant we won the group and qualified for the knockout stages. The atmosphere in the Amex that night was unbelievable.

I am sure you have all got your own dates and games etched on your memory – that's what being a fan is all about. Of course, there have been setbacks – the two FA Cup semi-final defeats and Championship play-off losses spring to mind – but whenever we've had a bump in the road, we have always bounced back thanks to the incredible togetherness we have achieved on and off the pitch.

The story of every football club is one of highs and lows. Brighton & Hove Albion has such a rich and varied history going back to its formation in 1901, so it does not surprise me that not only is this Dan's third edition of *On This Day* but that the number of words he has had to write has increased by nearly 30,000, such has been our recent success.

It's a great book for all Albion fans and is full of entertaining facts and anecdotes.

I hope you enjoy reading it as much as I have.

Paul Barber

Introduction

I've supported the club my whole life – over 40 years – and one of my very first memories was the sea of yellow in the north-east corner when we played Oxford United in the FA Cup in 1982.

I've been writing about our blue-and-white-striped heroes since 1997. A year earlier, while studying at the University of Brighton, a lecturer told me I wrote "as if I was talking to someone". Up until that point I'd never considered writing for anything other than applying for jobs or writing birthday cards. A year later I co-founded *Scars & Stripes* and putting pen to 'paper' has been my career ever since.

Since October 2023, I've spent most evenings and weekends writing, re-writing, revising and updating *Brighton & Hove Albion On This Day (2)*, which was published by Pitch Publishing in 2011, just after the new stadium opened its doors. The third edition, which you are now reading, is 27,000 more words than the previous book. As Paul Barber stated in the foreword, the club has provided plenty to write about in the last 13 years!

Up to 2011, the recent history of Brighton & Hove Albion had been a tale of highs, lows, deception (from the former owners), camaraderie, struggle, and a never-say-die attitude; both from those within the club, and the many thousands of supporters who have blue-and-white-striped blood coursing through their veins who simply refused to give up the fight for our home at Falmer. Without their sheer dogged determination and endeavour, there would be no Brighton & Hove Albion – it's as simple as that.

The intervening period has seen a steady progression, pretty much year-on-year, to top-half Premier League finishes and European football – an impossible dream just a few years ago. In many ways, our club is the envy of people throughout the football world. Our recruitment – and simply the way we conduct ourselves – is routinely praised. It's something to be immensely proud of.

This book chronicles facts, figures, statistics, stories and trivia, for each date of the year, going back to the club's Ship Street formation in 1901, to the present day. In bite-sized chunks, important incidents in the club's history are featured; from every promotion, title, cup final appearance, relegation, European match, and big game, to key dates in the stadium fight (and construction), the players, managers and characters that blend together to make Brighton & Hove Albion Football Club what it is.

The last few years have been wonderful, and we've come a very long way since the depressing days of fourth-tier football and 'home' games at Gillingham!

The best is yet to come...

Brighton 'til I die!

Dan Tester

Acknowledgements

I must thank Albion oracle Tim Carder for his invaluable *Albion A-Z: A Who's Who of Brighton & Hove Albion FC* and Albion Results Database. As with my first two editions of *BHAOTD*, writing this book simply wouldn't have been possible without your input. Thanks, mate!

Thanks to Paul Camillin for his support and advice while contemplating whether to write another book, and to our wonderful football club for giving me plenty to write about!

It takes a village to bring up a child and it takes many people to get a book into people's hands. Thank you to Duncan Olner for the beautiful cover, Alan Wares for the great typesetting, Craig Smith for the diligent proofreading, and a special thanks to James Halling (*Dogma* editor) for forensically checking the content. I owe you a pint, mate, and then some!

A big shout out to all the sons – you know who you are.

Huge thanks to the teams at legendary Albion fanzines *Scars & Stripes, The Seagull Love Review, Gull's Eye* and *Dogma* for the use of some of their amazing front covers.

I must also mention Jean Gibbs, who sadly passed away in August 2022. She was my second mum and showed me nothing but love and support in the 32 years I was fortunate enough to have her in my life. I loved her very much and it was fitting – and much appreciated – that I used the money she left me to fund trips to see the Albion in Marseille and Amsterdam. My friends and I raised a glass in her honour in both cities. A fitting memory for an amazing woman.

And last, but by no means least, Honor and Scout. The five years you spent in my life were the absolute highlight of it. I'm eternally thankful for our time together and miss you both each day. You taught me a lot about myself – and loads of things that I need to improve on! You're amazing and I hope the world is ready for you! You'll always be in my heart.

Dan Tester

For Honor and Scout

Gull's Eye – January 1989:
A pessimistic Barry Lloyd ponders life as Albion manager

© *Gull's Eye*

JANUARY

Saturday 1st January 1910

Brighton & Hove Albion's first New Year's Day fixture was a 3-0 victory over Luton Town. The Southern League Division One contest at the Goldstone Ground saw strikes from Bullet Jones (2) and Bert Longstaff. The guesstimated crowd was 7,000.

Saturday 1st January 1994

After signing on Christmas Day 1993, a crowd of 9,753 was at the Goldstone Ground to witness 39-year-old Jimmy Case's second debut for the Albion. Kurt Nogan stole the show with a hat-trick in the impressive 4-1 thumping of Cambridge United with Brighton-born Simon Funnell also on the scoresheet. Future Seagull Steve Claridge – who would make five Albion appearances as a 38-year-old in 2004 – was on target for the visitors.

Tuesday 1st January 2008

Alex Revell grabbed his only Albion hat-trick in the 3-2 victory over AFC Bournemouth at Withdean Stadium. The former Cambridge United forward decided an eventful contest by heading the winner four minutes into injury time. He opened the scoring in the 15th minute from close range and notched again (58th) to make it 2-1. Angry Cherries boss Kevin Bond wasn't happy; "We brought about our own downfall three times. The winning goal was diabolical. We had the ball from a throw-in, needlessly gave it away and for the umpteenth time could not defend a set-piece. It was nothing short of disgraceful." A new tea set was ordered the following day. In a career spanning 20 years, Revell scored 155 goals in 679 appearances for 14 clubs.

Saturday 1st January 2011

Voted the ninth-best match of the Withdean years by Albion fans, Leyton Orient were humbled 5-0. Gus Poyet's men hadn't recorded a league win for two months – three draws and two defeats – but were still top of League One. The 2009 Great Escape leader Russell Slade received a warm, if slightly hungover, welcome from the South Stand, as did former Albion players Dean Cox and Alex Revell. But, the class of 2010/11 were in no mood for sentiment. Glenn Murray dominated proceedings with a classy hat-trick, his third in Albion colours, while on-loan Chris Wood and Ashley Barnes also found the target.

Saturday 2nd January 1909

'Mr Albion' Charlie Webb made his debut, scoring in the 1-1 draw at West Ham United. Born in the Republic of Ireland in 1886, the inside-left scored 79 goals in 275 Albion appearances between 1909 and 1915. Amazingly, Charlie managed the club for nearly 35 years after World War I – a total of 1,215 matches – and eventually retired, aged 60, in 1948 after a year as general manager. Charlie, much-loved and respected throughout the game, passed away in 1973. A tree planted in his honour in Hove Park is still going strong.

Sunday 2nd January 1966

Kevan Brown was born in Hampshire. The right-back played 65 matches for Albion in the late 1980s. He won the FA Trophy three times with Woking, where he once inadvertently caused a match abandonment by falling into a two-feet-deep hole that suddenly appeared in the pitch!

Saturday 2nd January 1993

After disposing of Hayes and Woking in the previous two rounds, Albion entertained south-coast rivals Portsmouth in the FA Cup third round. Lethal strike duo Paul Walsh and Guy Whittingham – who attracted nationwide headlines, such was their potency in front of goal – were sidelined for the visitors through injury. Matthew Edwards scored the only goal of the tie to earn a trip to Manchester United in the next round.

Monday 3rd January 1916

A decade into his 16-year distinguished Albion career, Bert Longstaff received a letter from West Ham United inviting him to 'come and play for us whenever you possibly can on Saturdays'. The Irons helpfully pointed out that their players were insured for £2 per week.

Saturday 3rd January 2000

Brighton-born Darren Freeman scored the first goal of the new millennium in English professional football. The 26-year-old netted after just two minutes into the 4-2 Third Division home victory over Exeter City in the day's early kick-off. The former Gillingham, Fulham and Brentford striker's career was cruelly cut short just two days before his 28th birthday, in 2001, after a succession of hernia injuries.

Friday 3rd January 2020

Albion signed Norway international goalkeeper Cecilie Fiskerstrand. The 23-year-old joined on a free transfer following the end of her contract at LSK Kvinner. Fiskerstrand has represented her country from under-15s all the way through to senior level and was included in Norway's squad for both the 2015 and 2019 FIFA World Cups.

Saturday 4th January 1975

Aldershot and Brentford were dispatched at the Goldstone Ground in the opening two rounds of the FA Cup. Albion were drawn at home again, this time against non-league Leatherhead. Peter Taylor's men were beaten by a Chris Kelly (the 'Leatherhead Lip') strike. The only goal of the contest secured a fourth-round trip to Leicester City for the Surrey side.

Monday 4th January 1982

Íñigo Calderón Zapatería was born in the Basque region of Spain. After seven years in Segunda División B with Alavés B, Alicante and then Alavés, the right-back left his home country to try and make it in England, completing unsuccessful trials at Gillingham, Norwich City and Swansea City, where he'd first flown over to watch his friend Andrea Orlandi in action. Gus Poyet decided to take a punt on the 28-year-old defender in January 2010.

Calde quickly immersed himself in Brighton life, taking an active role in Albion in the Community initiatives, utilising his very unfootball skillset – a qualified teacher with a Master's in sports psychology, and a sports science degree. Over seven seasons, he made 232 appearances for the stripes, scoring 19 times, including eight as Albion romped to the League One title in 2010/11. A wholehearted competitor, Southampton tried to lure Calde away, but he saw sense and remained this side of the south coast. One of a very rare breed of ex Albion players who fans genuinely love – he'll never need to buy a pint anywhere in Sussex for the rest of his life.

Saturday 4th January 1986

St. James' Park – the one in Newcastle – was the venue for a FA Cup third-round tie. Welsh duo Eric Young and Dean Saunders secured a safe passage through, and a trip to Hull City's Boothferry Park.

Saturday 4th January 1992

Second Division Albion hosted Southern Premier Division Crawley Town in an all-Sussex FA Cup third-round encounter at the Goldstone Ground. Goals from Mark 'Smokey' Gall, Clive 'Flash' Walker, 'Free' Raphael Meade and an Ian 'Chappers' Chapman brace set up a fourth-round clash at Bolton Wanderers.

Saturday 5th January 1901

Brighton & Hove Rangers hosted Willesden Town at Withdean. A Gibson, a man of 'exciting credentials', played his part in a 6-2 thrashing of the north Londoners.

Tuesday 5th January 1982

Failure to conquer the famous sloping pitch at Barnet's Underhill meant a FA Cup third-round replay at the Goldstone. It was much less of an uphill struggle this time around as Albion cantered through 3-0 thanks to a Neil McNab penalty and efforts from Mickey Thomas and Jimmy Case.

Monday 5th January 1987

Barry Lloyd was appointed Albion manager. The Middlesex-born former midfielder was on the bench for Fulham in the 1975 FA Cup Final. Alan Mullery, a former team-mate at Craven Cottage, recruited his friend as Albion's reserve and youth team coach before the ex-England captain was sacked eight months later. It took 15 games for the 38-year-old Lloyd to record his first victory – a 2-0 home win over Crystal Palace – on Easter Monday.

Saturday 5th January 1991

The Albion announced that each fan had paid 53 pence towards policing at the Goldstone Ground, putting the club in the top six in the country, for policing costs.

Saturday 6th January 1883

Legendary goalkeeper Bob Whiting was born in West Ham, east London. The six-feet tall custodian impressed the Goldstone Ground faithful with his kicking ability and was once said to have cleared the opposition crossbar from his own area! He made 320 appearances.

Saturday 6th January 1900

Albion predecessors Brighton United entertained Bedminster at the County Ground in Hove. The Greenbacks managed just one goal to the visitors' four. The *Evening Argus* reported; "...from the re-start Baker got away and forced a corner. Taking the kick himself, he placed the leather finely, and (Jock) Malloch, jumping up, headed the ball into the net amid a terrific shout of applause."

Saturday 6th January 2007

After beating Conference sides Northwich Victoria and Stafford Rangers in the FA Cup – 8-0 and 3-0, respectively – Albion's third-round reward was a trip to Premiership West Ham United, and the chance to be reacquainted with Bobby Zamora. Unfortunately, Argentinian Carlos Tevez ran the show in a convincing 3-0 win.

Wednesday 7th January 1981

David Coleman commentated on the Albion from the Goldstone Ground for the first time, for BBC One's Sportsnight. Manchester United won the FA Cup third-round replay 2-0 in front of 26,915 fans. It was the second of three games against the Red Devils in seven days.

Thursday 7th January 1982

'Super' Basir Savage was born in London. Bas endeared himself to not just Albion fans, but football supporters across the land, with his unique 'moonwalk' goal celebration. It became so popular it was regularly featured on Soccer AM, won a magazine award and spawned a successful range of T-shirts. Savage wore the stripes for just over a year from January 2007.

Saturday 7th January 2012

Long before being sprinkled with Hollywood dust, 2,000+ Wrexham fans made the journey from North Wales for a FA Cup third-round tie at Falmer. Adrian Cieslewicz's 62nd-minute strike cancelled out Jake Forster-Caskey's opener. The 1-1 scoreline resulted in a replay at the Racecourse Ground. The game in Sussex will be remembered for the incredible atmosphere generated by the Welsh contingent.

Saturday 8th January 1921

For the first time as a Football League club, Brighton & Hove Albion entered the FA Cup. Nearly 17,000 fans were at the Goldstone Ground for the visit of First Division Oldham Athletic. They went home happy as Zach March (2), Jack Doran and George Coomber all made the scoresheet in a 4-1 victory.

Saturday 8th January 2005

Over 5,000 Albion fans made themselves heard at White Hart Lane in this third-round FA Cup tie. Richard Carpenter levelled the scores with an excellent second-half free-kick but was powerless to stop Robbie Keane's world-class finish near the end to send Tottenham Hotspur through. Final score: 2-1 to Spurs.

Saturday 8th January 2011

Referee Graham Scott spotted an off-the-ball incident between former Albion man Paul Kitson and Adam El-Abd and had no hesitation in showing the petulant Portsmouth striker the red card – just 13 minutes into this FA Cup tie! The Championship side showed no signs of their recent Premier League stay as Albion earned a thoroughly deserved passage to the next round with strikes from Chris Wood, Ashley Barnes and Fran Sandaza.

Saturday 9th January 1946

Four days earlier, Albion won 2-1 at Carrow Road in an FA Cup third-round, first-leg fixture. On this day, for the one and only time, Brighton hosted a second-leg match in the competition. Charlie Chase, Jock Davie (2) and Bert Stephens made it four to Norwich's one, to set up a tie with Aldershot.

Saturday 9th January 1965

Flintshire-born Barrie Rees made his Albion debut in the 3-1 Goldstone Ground win over Crewe Alexandra in the Fourth Division. Tragically, the young winger would only make a further 11 appearances in the club's colours.

Tuesday 10th January 1948

Fratton Park was the venue for this south-coast derby in the FA Cup third round. Pompey were doing well in the First Division while Albion languished at the bottom of the Third Division (South). The travelling supporters in the crowd of 37,646 were not expecting to witness progression in the competition, and they were right. The Sussex boys lost 4-1 to their Hampshire counterparts, who would go on to win the First Division title in the following two seasons.

Tuesday 10th January 1984

After a six-week loan spell, Northern Ireland international midfielder Danny Wilson signed permanently from Nottingham Forest in a £45,000 deal. He would go on to win the League Cup with Luton Town and lead Barnsley to their one – and, so far, only – season in the top division.

Saturday 11th January 1964

Edgeley Park, Stockport was the location for Wally Gould's debut in an Albion shirt. The Yorkshireman was a popular figure marauding down the Goldstone flanks and netted an impressive 46 times in 193 appearances. He was released in February 1968 and embarked on a successful career in South African football.

Saturday 12th January 1935

Arsenal – who would go on to win their third successive First Division title later in the season – were the visitors for a FA Cup third-round tie. The north London club were such a massive draw that spectators were genuinely put off by fears of a crush. The crowd was only 22,343, 10,000 fewer than the record gate set two years earlier against West Ham United. The Gunners won 2-0.

Saturday 12th January 1963

The biggest freeze of the 20th century was playing havoc with the fixture list. Director Harold Paris borrowed a tarmacadam melting machine from the Brighton Corporation to help thaw the Goldstone pitch. Crystal Palace were the visitors for what was one of only four games in the country to survive the Arctic weather. The pitch was a quagmire and a goal from Peter Donnelly was not enough to prevent a 2-1 defeat.

Sunday 12th January 1975

David Eugene Junior McDougald was born in Texas. Released by Tottenham Hotspur, the nippy forward joined Albion in 1994 and top scored in his two seasons on the south coast before moving to Rotherham United. A journeyman career in non-league beckoned and from 2001 to 2006 the American appeared in 31 episodes of Sky TV's Dream Team, a series featuring the fictional football club, Harchester United. Four episodes of the programme were written by *Build a Bonfire* and *We Want Falmer!* author Paul Hodson.

Wednesday 12th January 1983

After a 1-1 draw at the Goldstone Ground, Albion headed north for a FA Cup third-round replay at Newcastle United. Over 32,000 Geordies did their best to unsettle the opposition, but it didn't stop Peter Ward firing home a left-foot effort on 62 minutes – his 95th and final goal for the club. The home side had two 'goals' disallowed by referee Trelford Mills in the last four minutes. Albion went through.

Wednesday 13th January 1971

Flying winger Peter O'Sullivan made his Wales under-23 debut as substitute in a 1-0 defeat in Swansea.

Saturday 13th January 1973

Chelsea were the visitors to Hove for a third-round FA Cup tie. The occasion was marred as violence on the terraces, and on the pitch, compounded Albion's 2-0 loss. Left-back George Ley and Chelsea's Ron 'Chopper' Harris were sent off in front of 29,287 fans.

Saturday 13th January 2009

Excavated chalk from the Village Way South site was placed on the field north of the road, saving thousands of truck journeys.

Thursday 13th January 2011

Some of the chalk-graffiti-covered blue perimeter hoardings were replaced with green fencing at Falmer. The structural coving tidied up exposed steelwork as troughs for the undersoil heating were being prepared.

Saturday 14th January 1911

In Yorkshire, Leeds City were dispatched 3-1 in a FA Cup first-round tie. Bullet Jones (2) and Jimmy Smith – who scored 40 times in just 65 appearances – were the scorers. On arrival at Brighton Station in the early hours of Sunday morning, 2,000 ecstatic locals belted out Good Old Brighton by the Sea to their returning heroes. Eight years later Leeds City were expelled from the Second Division mid-season due to financial irregularities. Another club formed in the city soon after.

Saturday 14th January 1961

Albion beat Liverpool 3-1 in this Second Division contest at the Goldstone Ground. Recent signing from Chelsea, striker Tony Nicholas, centre-forward Dennis Windross, and defender Roy Jennings were the names on the scoresheet. Windross was understudy to Brian Clough at Middlesbrough before heading south.

Saturday 14th January 2023

On a day when Roberto De Zerbi said post-match that his Brighton side 'have a dream' of qualifying for Europe, his charges walloped Liverpool 3-0 at Falmer to take another step to making it a reality. On 47 minutes, Solly March converted Kaoru Mitoma's low cross after Alexis Mac Allister had intercepted a loose pass.

The Sussex-born winger then doubled Albion's advantage just six minutes later with an absolute peach of a left-footed strike from Evan Ferguson's through-ball. Second-half substitute Danny Welbeck flicked the ball over a defender before expertly finishing past Allison to put the icing on the Albion cake. 3-0 to the stripes. "I have a fantastic team of fantastic players," said De Zerbi. "It is an honour to work with them."

Wednesday 15th January 1992

Joël Ivo Veltman was born in the Netherlands. After winning the Eredivisie with Ajax three times, the Dutch international right-back/centre-back decided to sign for the Albion for a ridiculously cheap fee of £900,000 in 2020. An absolute bargain, the defender – who has his own song sung to the tune of Chase the Sun by Planet Funk – is a model of consistency and is popular with Albion fans across the world.

Saturday 15th January 2005

Written by Albion poet laureate Attila the Stockbroker and performed with his band Seagull Ska (made up of Albion fans), Tom Hark (We Want Falmer!) reached number 17 in the UK music charts. A remake of the Brighton-based Piranhas' hit, the song highlighted the club's struggle for a new stadium and remained in the Top 40 for three weeks.

Friday 15th January 2021

Viktor Gyökeres returned from his spell with Swansea City and immediately headed back out on loan to Coventry City for the rest of the season. The 22-year-old linked up once again with Albion team-mate Leo Østigård, who was also on loan with the Championship side. After moving permanently to the Sky Blues, the Swede transferred to Sporting Lisbon in the summer of 2023.

Saturday 16th January 1982

Albion skipper Steve Foster played for 85 minutes with a broken nose after a collision with David Cross in the 1-0 First Division home win over West Ham United.

Wednesday 16th January 1991

Newcastle United were the visitors to the Goldstone Ground on a wet and miserable evening. The 7,684 fans in attendance were treated to a four-goal show from Bryan Wade, in his first full home appearance, in the 4-2 victory.

The Bath-born forward's first came just before half-time, plucking a 70-yard hoof from defence out of the air with his right foot, outpacing a defender then firing into the bottom corner from just inside the Magpies box. The second was route one football again: a goal kick was flicked on to Wade who tore past the visiting defence before rounding John Burridge and firing into an empty net.

The hat-trick arrived with a looping header from a Crumplin cross, and he finished a quick counter-attack for his and the Albion's fourth. The Bath-born Wade turned out 22 times in the stripes, netting on nine occasions.

Wednesday 16th January 2013

Leonardo Ulloa signed for the Albion, on a four-and-a-half-year deal for an undisclosed fee, believed to be around £2 million, from Spanish side Almería.

The 6ft 2" Argentinian forward only stayed on the coast for 18 months but certainly made an impact among the Albion faithful, scoring 23 times in just 50 appearances. He left in an £8 million deal to Leicester City and famously won the Premier League in 2016, against all the odds.

Saturday 17th January 1971

Pat Saward's Buy-a-Player Fund was boosted in a match between an Albion side – which included Jimmy Tarbuck – and Eastbourne United. The comedian missed a penalty in the 3-2 United victory. The initiative eventually raised £50,000 which was used to purchase Bert Murray from Birmingham City.

Saturday 17th January 1981

Goalkeeper Perry Digweed made the first of his 201 appearances between the sticks for the Albion. The Chelsea-born custodian was signed from Fulham for £150,000 in 1981 by Alan Mullery and was Player of the Year in the 1990/91 campaign, which culminated in the Play-Off Final at Wembley.

Saturday 18th January 1958

Hove-born Adrian Thorne scored on his Albion debut against Southend United in this Third Division (South) fixture at the Goldstone. The local lad attended Brighton, Hove and Sussex Grammar School in Dyke Road before signing on his 17th birthday in August 1954.

Sunday 19th January 1890

George Coomber was born in West Hoathly, Sussex. On moving to London to complete a glass-blowing apprenticeship, the half-back turned out for Tufnell Park. George played for Watford and Spurs during the Great War and eventually started for the Albion in 1919 going on to score six times in 272 appearances.

Saturday 19th January 1980

Nearly 30,000 fans were at the Goldstone Ground for the First Division visit of Tottenham Hotspur. After two consecutive 2-0 away wins – at Mansfield Town, in the FA Cup, and Bolton Wanderers in the league – Albion couldn't make the hat-trick and went down by the same scoreline.

Friday 19th January 2018

The last of Albion's new signings for the 2017/18 season joined the club – 'striker' Jürgen Locadia arrived from PSV Eindhoven for a record fee of £15 million. Other new players for the campaign, who made the first team, were: Maty Ryan, Pascal Gross, Markus Suttner, Steven Alzate, Davy Pröpper, José Izquierdo, Ezequiel Schelotto, Tim Krul and Viktor Gyökeres. A notable outward loan for the season was Ben White's move to League Two side Newport County.

Monday 20th January 1908

It was Monday afternoon. The Albion travelled to Stamford Bridge to face two-time league champions Preston North End for a FA Cup first round, second replay. The 20,000 crowd was the largest, thus far, to watch the club. Dick Wombwell netted the decisive goal and the team were mobbed by ecstatic fans upon their return to Brighton Station.

Tuesday 20th January 1925

Geoff Pinchbeck was born in Cleethorpes. The centre-forward joined Albion from First Division Everton for £2,000 in 1949. Five goals and 14 starts later, Port Vale splashed out £3,500 for his services. A tidy profit in just three months!

Sunday 20th January 1974

Albion played Sunday football for the first time at the Goldstone Ground as part of an experiment during a period of national crisis: a state of emergency had been declared as industrial unrest brought the country to its knees. The biggest crowd of the season, 18,885, saw goals from Tony Towner and Ken Beamish in a 2-1 win over Rochdale. The fans didn't pay for entry – it was illegal to charge. Instead, they paid a subscription to become members of the Dolphins Club for the day. A turnstile was provided for those reluctant to pay anything.

Thursday 20th January 2000

Lewes Councillors warned they would force a public inquiry if the Albion pressed ahead with plans for a stadium at Falmer. The *Evening Argus* reported that at the previous evening's meeting at Lewes Town Hall, district councillors had unanimously rejected proposals as outlined in Brighton & Hove Council's Local Plan. They said the idea of a stadium at Falmer was 'unbelievable' and went against several of Brighton & Hove's own planning policy guidelines.

Friday 20th January 2023

Leandro Trossard completed his move to title challengers Arsenal. The Belgian winger departed after 121 appearances, 25 goals and 14 assists for the Albion. Technical director David Weir commented; "Leandro has made a big contribution to the first team's success in recent times. The move is a good one for all parties involved and we wish him well for the future."

Wednesday 21st January 1987

Twenty or so hardy fans helped clear the pitch and terraces of snow before the FA Cup third-round replay with Sheffield United. The 7,019 crowd saw Dale Jasper score for Albion in the 2-1 defeat.

Friday 22nd January 1999

Manager Brian Horton left Priestfield, Gillingham for First Division side Port Vale. In 43 games under the former club captain the record read: won 14, drawn 10 and lost 19. Horton's assistant, Jeff Wood, was put in temporary charge of the Albion.

Friday 22nd January 2021

In a surprise move, goalkeeper Maty Ryan joined Arsenal on loan until the end of the season after being Albion's first choice for almost three and a half seasons. He was overtaken by Rob Sánchez in mid-December.

Saturday 23rd January 1965

Robert Codner was born in Walthamstow, London. With 47 goals in 315 appearances, predominantly in the second tier, the midfielder was one of the most frustrating players in the club's history with moments of absolute brilliance, contrasted with, shall we say, less great ones!

Saturday 23rd January 1982

Future policeman Keith Cassells tore lacklustre Albion apart as Third Division Oxford United – roared on by over 3,000 fans in a sea of yellow in the north-east corner – stuffed their First Division counterparts 3-0 at the Goldstone in the FA Cup fourth round. The result provoked this *Evening Argus* response from an unhappy punter; "11 clockwork clowns for sale." The club's telephone number was quoted!

Saturday 23rd January 1993

Ryan Giggs scored the only goal of the game as the Red Devils beat Albion in the FA Cup fourth round in front of 33,610 Old Trafford spectators. It was the third time third-tier Albion had played the soon-to-be-Premier-League-champions-for-the-first-time-in-26-years Manchester United in four months.

Monday 23rd January 2006

Early Day Motion (EDM) 1151 condemned Lewes District Council's action and received its 50th signature in the House of Commons.

Saturday 23rd January 2010

Albion travelled to Aston Villa for an FA Cup fourth-round tie and, unsurprisingly, the away following was huge! Over 6,000 fans made the trip from Sussex to make up a near-40,000 crowd. Nathan Delfouneso fired the Premier League outfit ahead after just five minutes before Tommy Elphick equalised just before half-time when Elliott Bennett's corner fell invitingly for the young defender. England attacker Ashley Young (48th) and Fabian Delph (63rd) made it three for the Villans, but Nicky Forster gave the enormous travelling contingent reason for slight optimism with a great on-the-turn strike in the last minute. Albion were by no means disgraced by the final 3-2 scoreline.

Saturday 23rd January 2016

Albion moved up to third in the Championship, beating 10-man Huddersfield Town 2-1. Bobby Zamora, who had ended his side's six-game goal drought in the 1-0 win at Blackburn Rovers a week earlier, found the net for the second game in a row. The 35-year-old cleared a corner from inside his own six-yard box, sprinted forward, and was on hand to convert Anthony Knockaert's pass after a swift counter-attack.

Saturday 24th January 1931

For the fifth time in seven years, Albion played Watford in the FA Cup. The Hertfordshire side won 2-0 in front of 22,700 Vicarage Road fans.

Thursday 24th January 2002

Albion wilted in front of the Sky TV cameras at Griffin Park. On-loan Ben Burgess grabbed a hat-trick for Brentford in the 4-0 rout.

Thursday 24th January 2019

Alexis Mac Allister signed for £7 million from Argentinos Juniors, a club famous for being where Diego Maradona started his career. The Argentinian midfielder donned the blue and white stripes 112 times, scoring 20 goals, before being snapped up by the team he supported as a boy, Liverpool. A humble and shy man, Alexis conducted himself in an exemplary manner while representing the club and his inevitable departure was met with sadness among the Albion support, but also with a huge amount of love and respect for the joy he'd given us. Without doubt, an Albion legend who will forever have a place in our collective hearts. Mucha suerte y gracias, Alexis! *(See 24th December 1998)*.

Saturday 25th January 1930

Confidence buoyed by consecutive 1-0 away victories, 8,000 Albion fans travelled west to Fratton Park to boost the attendance to 37,522. It was the biggest crowd Brighton had played in front of since a trip to Sheffield Wednesday in 1914. First Division Pompey were no match for the rampaging Hugh Vallance whose goal decided the FA Cup fourth-round tie. A week later, the stripes won 8-2 at Merthyr Town.

Sunday 25th January 2015

Defending champions Arsenal reached the FA Cup fifth round, clinging on for a 3-2 victory against a spirited Albion side at Falmer. A month into his tenure, Chris Hughton started Chris O'Grady, on his 29th birthday, who notched his second goal for the club in the competition with a neat finish from the edge of the box in the 50th minute. The home side came on strong towards the end, with Baldock clipping in the second (75th) after a precise through-ball from Solly March.

Saturday 26th January 1991

Nearly 7,000 Sussex folk wiped their eyes in disbelief as Albion came back from 2-0 down at Anfield. Mike Small converted a penalty (72nd) past Bruce Grobbelaar after Paul McCarthy had been upended. Just two minutes later, Dean Wilkins flicked on for Clive Walker to shoot from the edge of the box.

The Liverpool keeper Grobbelaar could only parry it away and the ball arrived at John Crumplin's feet on the flank. The right back sent over a high cross to Small, who rose between home defenders to head it back across the area. John Byrne busted a gut to meet the perfect cross and dived, full stretch, to send a magnificent header into the net – in front of the travelling hordes – from the edge of the six-yard box. A tremendous goal.

The game will be forever remembered for 'Johnny Crumplin Football Genius' reverberating around the magnificent old stadium, as Albion's defender kept England international winger John Barnes firmly in his pocket for the whole game.

Thursday 26th January 2006

Lewes District Council's Scrutiny Committee rejected Ed Bassford's request to review the decision to challenge. Will a new stadium at Falmer ever get built?

Saturday 27th January 2007

An unremarkable League One scoreless draw resulted in an unwanted statistic; Albion had never won on 27th January in their 87-year league history. No more than one goal has been scored in seven draws and seven defeats up to the summer of 2011. The hex was broken at Middlesbrough in 2018 when Glenn Murray scored the only goal of the game.

Wednesday 28th January 1920

Frank Morrad was born in Middlesex. The non-attacking full-back worked as a part-time bookmaker and joined Albion after failing to hold down a first-team berth at Fulham. He made his debut against Aldershot in February 1948 and would appear intermittently over the next four seasons. After his retirement from football in 1954 – and a final season at Bedford Town – he ran a chain of betting shops in west London.

Saturday 28th January 1922

Huddersfield Town – who would go on to bag a hat-trick of successive league titles under the expert tutelage of Herbert Chapman in the mid-1920s – attracted the highest Goldstone Ground gate so far – 22,241. The FA Cup second-round tie ended goalless.

Saturday 28th January 1928

A gate of just 4,494 was registered at the Goldstone for the visit of Crystal Palace. The rivalry was not as keen in the 1920s and Albion's average crowd at the time was around the 7,500 mark. Despite the low attendance, the Hove side ran out 4-2 winners in the Third Division (South) fixture with future record appearance holder Tug Wilson grabbing a brace.

Saturday 28th January 1961

One of the most celebrated games in Albion history. Visitors Burnley were reigning Football League champions, and their fourth-round FA Cup visit attracted a 28,672 gate. The 3-3 draw included goals from Jack Bertolini, Bob McNicol and Dennis Windross. Right-back McNicol's strike was one of the greatest ever seen at the Goldstone; a 35-yard rocket after a run from his own half. It was his only goal for the club!

Saturday 28th January 1978

Albion's FA Cup fourth-round tie with Notts County was postponed due to a waterlogged pitch. Seven hundred fans from Nottinghamshire were stranded in Hove after their special train could not be stopped in time.

Wednesday 28th January 2009

Albion's 'housekeeping' planning application, relating to the stadium changes and chalk re-profiling, was recommended for approval by council officers. Chief executive Martin Perry said; "This is another very important step for the club, if the councillors take that recommendation and grant permission for our stadium changes application, it will mean we will be in a position to commence work on the main stadium construction as planned in April of this year. This report considers a revised application for a Community Stadium which comprises two distinct parts. The first part proposes revisions to the approved

Community Stadium while the second proposes re-contouring the land south of Village Way using the chalk spoil from the excavations for the stadium."

Saturday 29th January 1927

After scoring 41 goals in the previous 13 Goldstone encounters, the omens were good for the 7,472 fans in attendance for the visit of Bristol Rovers. A 2-0 half-time lead gave no indication of the second-half avalanche that was to follow as inside-left Jimmy Hopkins, with a hat-trick, Tommy Cook and centre-half Paul Mooney added to inside-right Sam Jennings' first-half brace to make it 7-0!

Saturday 29th January 1966

In the previous seven Goldstone Ground fixtures before this date, 27 Albion goals were scored and the Third Division visit of Mansfield Town continued the trend. Brian Tawse (2), centre-forward Jack Smith – 36 strikes in a total of 96 run-outs – Charlie Livesey and an own goal fired the Albion into a 5-2 interval lead. Despite a spirited fightback the Stags went down 6-4.

Saturday 29th January 1983

The last time Manchester City visited the Goldstone they lost 4-1 in a First Division fixture. Today was FA Cup fourth-round day and the Albion's only victory in the last nine outings was the 1-0 last-round replay win at Newcastle United. Lying one place off the bottom of the top-flight, Brighton fans were due a lift and it duly arrived when Jimmy Case opened the scoring before Michael Robinson netted twice against his former club.

Neil Smillie added one more to better last year's scoreline: 4-0 to the Albion. The programme highlighted Mike Bamber's meeting with Brighton Borough Council regarding proposals for a new stadium, just 28-and-a-half years before the first game at Falmer!

Saturday 29th January 1984

The live TV cameras – a rarity in those days – were present, along with nearly 20,000 fans, for the visit of champions Liverpool for a FA Cup fourth-round tie at the Goldstone Ground. Tony Grealish found Gerry Ryan with a lofted pass in the 57th minute and the Irishman dinked the ball home. Just a minute later a slide-rule pass found Terry Connor galloping through on goal. The striker took a touch before shooting – and celebrated as the ball left his foot – into the top corner from just outside the box. Another memorable Albion victory over Liverpool. The cameras perfectly captured the pandemonium behind the roofless north goal.

Tuesday 29th January 2008

Glenn Murray made his Albion debut at Northampton Town, replacing Nathan Elder, in a 1-0 League One defeat. The Cumbrian-born striker arrived on the south coast in a £300,000 deal from Rochdale, the highest fee paid by the club since Andy Ritchie's move from Manchester United for £500,000 in 1980. Scout Barry Lloyd suggested the club sign him, based on a pre-match warm-up the former Albion boss had seen.

Saturday 29th January 2011

Yet again, Albion showed why they were so dominant in League One with an excellent performance at Championship side Watford in this FA Cup fourth-round tie. On a freezing cold afternoon, Albion took the lead after 17 minutes when Gary Dicker dispossessed Will Buckley and fed the ball into Chris Wood on the edge of the area. The big Kiwi chested the ball into the path of Ashley Barnes and the Bath-born striker's powerful drive squirmed out of Rene Gilmartin's grasp and into the back of the net to make it 1-0 in front of nearly 4,000 travelling supporters.

Sunday 29th January 2022

Just 15 days after they were dispatched convincingly in a Premier League fixture, the FA Cup holders Liverpool returned to Sussex for this fourth-round tie. Japanese winger Kaoru Mitoma nicked a spectacular stoppage-time winner, taking a cross down and then gently flicking it inside the defender before volleying home with the outside of his right foot in the same movement.

Four bamboozled Reds defenders looked on in a mixture of admiration and confusion. What a player, what a goal. Albion had equalised in the first half from a deflected Tariq Lamptey effort as Lewis Dunk deftly diverted the ball in. The 2-1 win earned Albion a fifth-round trip to Stoke City.

Saturday 30th January 1937

Albion hosted Bristol Rovers in this Third Division (South) fixture. Alec Law – who scored 40 goals in 74 appearances – found the net along with Joe Wilson, Hugh Stephens and Bobby Farrell (2) to make it 5-2 to the home side. The comprehensive result left Albion top of the division, one point above Notts County and two ahead of Luton Town.

Wednesday 30th January 1991

After coming back from 2-0 down at champions Liverpool to draw 2-2 in the FA Cup fourth round, Albion entertained the best team in the land at the Goldstone Ground. England international midfielder Steve McMahon fired the Reds ahead before Mike Small ran through the static defence to slot home a first-half equaliser.

Cue extra-time and it was John Byrne who raced on to a misplaced pass to fire across Bruce Grobbelaar to send the North Stand into raptures. Unfortunately, a famous win was not forthcoming as Ian Rush – with a great finish into the top corner – and McMahon, again, with a tap in, gave the Merseysiders a 3-2 victory. Small had a backwards header disallowed!

Wednesday 31st January 1906

F Harding, WG Edwards and Dick Kitto made their one and only appearances for the Albion in the 0-0 United League home draw with Clapton Orient.

Wednesday 31st January 1934

After defeating Swindon Town 3-1 at the Goldstone in the FA Cup third round, Albion headed north to Bolton Wanderers – three-time winners in the previous decade – after a 1-1 draw. Things didn't go quite according to plan as the Trotters hit the Albion for six. Brighton's goal in the 6-1 drubbing was scored by a Bolton player!

Saturday 31st January 1942

Jock Davey bagged five goals in the 8-2 London War League victory over Chelsea at the Goldstone Ground.

Saturday 31st January 1953

Roy Jennings, club captain from 1960 to 1964, made the first of his 297 Albion appearances. The Swindon-born defender, who spent six years at full-back before converting to a more central berth, netted 22 times in his 12 years on the coast. He would go on to enjoy another five seasons with Crawley Town after leaving the Albion.

Monday 31st January 2022

The last of 14 players to sign for the Albion in the 2021/22 season put pen to paper. Deniz Undav arrived from Tony Bloom's other club, Royale Union Saint-Gilloise, for an undisclosed fee. The German striker had scored 37 goals in 56 appearances for the Belgian club before arriving on the south coast. Other notable signings included Enock Mwepu, Jeremy Sarmiento, Kjell Scherpen, Kaoru Mitoma and Marc Cucurella.

Tuesday 31st January 2023

Chairman Tony Bloom paid tribute to Shane Duffy, who joined Fulham on a permanent basis, having been on loan since the start of the season. "Shane has played such an important role during his time at the club. He was a key character in our promotion to the Premier League in his first season here. I'd like to thank him for everything and to wish him and his family all the best for the future from everyone associated with the club."

Dogma – February 2024:
A beautiful stained-glass-effect tribute from Gullski.

© *Dogma*

FEBRUARY

Wednesday 1st February 1908

Southern League Albion enjoyed a two-day stay in Birkdale before playing Liverpool at Anfield. A penalty from Jack Hall was cancelled out by a home-side equaliser 15 minutes from the end. The players disembarked their train at Preston Park to avoid the jubilant fans at Brighton Station!

Saturday 1st February 1913

Everton had tried to tempt Albion into switching this second-round FA Cup tie to Goodison Park. Around 11,000 rain-soaked Goldstone fans watched a goalless draw.

Wednesday 1st February 1967

Goals from Eric Whitington, Kit Napier and Charlie Livesey – the first by an Albion substitute – sealed a 3-1 FA Cup victory over Aldershot. The prospect of a fourth-round tie against First Division Chelsea attracted a crowd of 29,208 to the Goldstone, generating record gate receipts of £6,250.

Saturday 1st February 2003

Big Dave Beasant made his Albion debut between the sticks in the 1-0 Championship defeat at Walsall. The Wimbledon FA Cup winner celebrated his 44th birthday – thus becoming the club's oldest-ever player – and went on to make 16 appearances in the relegation campaign.

Tuesday 1st February 2011

Workmen in a cherry-picker carefully installed the streamlined coving on the exterior arch of the West Stand at Falmer. A few metres below, external panelling was being slotted into place. Just over 50 miles north, Albion were held to a goalless draw at Leyton Orient in a somewhat low-key display.

"It was awful to watch, and I don't usually like to apologise," explained boss Gus Poyet. "But, to every single Brighton fan I feel I must. I don't know if it was exciting for them because it wasn't for me. It was the worst game that we have been involved in this season. When you play these games and it's not working, it's very important that the team on the pitch realise that and get something from it."

Monday 1st February 2016

The last of the club's 18 new signings for the season, Jiří Skalák, joined from Czech club FK Mladá Boleslav. The others, in chronological order from when they signed, were: Tomer Hemed, Liam Rosenior, Joe Ward, Daniel Akindayini, Gaëtan Bong, Niki Mäenpää, Vahid Hambo, Jack Harper, Bobby Zamora, Uwe Hünemeier, Jamie Murphy, Connor Goldson, Elvis Manu, Richie Towell, Anthony Knockaert, Henrik Bjørdal and Jonah Ayunga. Heading out the door in the other direction during 2015/16 were Bradley Barry, George Cole, Shamir Fenelon, Paddy McCourt, Jimmy Muitt, Daniel Pappoe, Cameron Wiltshire, Craig Mackail-Smith and Jeffrey Monakana.

Saturday 2nd February 1924

One of Albion's most famous victories. Everton were the visitors in a second-round FA Cup tie. A record crowd of 27,450 saw Albion tear apart a team that included six internationals. A hat-trick from Tommy Cook, a penalty from Wally Little and a late goal from Andy Neil sealed an astonishing 5-2 win.

Wednesday 2nd February 2005

The public inquiry for the potential stadium at Falmer reconvened under a different inspector.

Tuesday 2nd February 2021

Brighton & Hove Albion became Women in Football's (WIF) first official Corporate Member. The WIF Corporate Membership programme drove gender diversity, making 'change from within' across the football industry – from clubs and governing bodies to media and sponsors.

Saturday 3rd February 1906

Big-spending Middlesbrough – who had purchased Alf Common in the first ever £1,000 signing the previous year – offered to stage this second-round FA Cup tie at Ayresome Park. Albion's management declined. Goldstone admission was doubled to 1 shilling (5p) and 7,462 came through the turnstiles. The match finished 1-1 with Jimmy Kennedy notching Albion's equaliser five minutes before the final whistle.

Saturday 3rd February 1962

Albion lost 3-1 at Anfield in this Second Division fixture. Liverpool goalscorers included Roger Hunt and Ian St John. Up front for the Reds was future Seagulls boss Jimmy Melia.

Saturday 3rd February 2007

Another innovative method of getting the Falmer message across; a series of ten different picture postcards addressed to new Secretary of State Ruth Kelly were handed to supporters at Withdean. Many supporters sent them on to fans of other clubs around the world to post to Ms Kelly.

Wednesday 3rd February 2021

Steven Alzate got a fortuitous but deserved winner for Albion as they stunned Liverpool at Anfield to move 10 points clear of the Premier League relegation zone with a 1-0 victory. Dan Burn should have put Graham Potter's men ahead in the first half, only to slice over the crossbar, but it was the defender's header across goal that set up the winner. Nathaniel Phillips could only get a toe to it and the ball deflected off Alzate and beyond the Liverpool goalkeeper to secure only Albion's third-ever win at the famous old ground.

Saturday 3rd February 2024

A magnificent day for supporters of Brighton & Hove Albion Football Club. Our friends from up the road came to town with the sprightly Roy Hodgson – 76 years young – at the helm. Albion started like a dream, with captain Lewis Dunk heading in Pascal Gross' inswinging corner, directly in front of the Palace fans, after just three minutes.

Half an hour later, Jack Hinshelwood headed in Tariq Lamptey's left-footed cross at the back post. Just 17 seconds after that, the German midfielder again played a pivotal part, expertly gliding past his man before beautifully teeing up Facundo Buonanotte to curl one in from close range: two teenagers on the scoresheet in two minutes.

Palace danger man Michael Olise returned from injury – as it transpired prematurely – and pulled up just a few minutes after coming on at half-time, much to the derision of the home fans. João Pedro made it 4-1 after 85 minutes, expertly guiding his effort home after a delightful layoff from substitute Danny Welbeck. It was Albion's biggest home win over the old enemy since the 5-0 shellacking in 1956. On a day when the club broke a Premier League record: the starting line-up was the youngest fielded in the competition with an average age of 23 years and 284 days.

De Zerbi said; "We have to remember they played without Eze, Olise and they lost Guéhi after 20 minutes. Playing without three important players is very tough. Especially if you find the Brighton we watched today – because we had the poison."

And remember, it's not the 'M23 Derby', and never will be. UTA!

Saturday 4th February 1911

New banks of terracing on the east and north sides of the Goldstone Ground were in use for the first time for the visit of fellow Southern League side Coventry City in the FA Cup. A new record attendance of 13,000 witnessed a 0-0 draw.

Friday 4th February 1949

Brian 'Nobby' Horton was born in Hednesford. The inspirational midfielder – renowned for his non-stop chatter during matches – headed south after six seasons with Port Vale and captained his side to promotion to the First Division in 1979. Nobby moved into management and has occupied the hotseat at Hull City, Oxford United, Manchester City, Huddersfield Town, Albion, Port Vale and Macclesfield Town.

Saturday 4th February 1950

Albion's reserves played in front of a 30,000 crowd at Highbury! The vast majority of those present were there to claim a ticket for Arsenal's forthcoming FA Cup fifth-round tie with Burnley. The Gunners won the Football Combination Cup game 2-1.

Thursday 4th February 2010

The foundations of the West Stand were being dug at Falmer. The first concrete slabs were in place while the main white arch waited patiently where the pitch would soon be.

Friday 4th February 2011

The sheeting to complete the corners of the stadium – to enclose the venue – was installed at Falmer.

Tuesday 5th February 1901

Tommy Cook was born in Cuckfield. The greatest goalscorer (so far) in the club's history, 123 in 209 starts, the centre-forward signed as an amateur in 1921 after leaving Southdown bus company. He topped the leading scorer charts in three seasons and led the England attack against Wales in 1925 as a Third Division player. An outstanding cricketer too, Tommy scored 20,198 runs for his county between 1922 and 1937. Tragically, the great man took his own life in 1950 after failing to fully recover from a plane crash in which he was the only survivor. A true Albion legend.

Saturday 5th February 1910

Albion's second-string entertained Norwich City – who played home games in a disused quarry, The Nest, at the time – at the Goldstone Ground. The Canaries centre-half, Henrie Reid, left the pitch unwell and tragically died of heart failure in the dressing room.

Saturday 5th February 1985

Manager Chris Cattlin revealed he had made a firm enquiry for St Mirren striker Frank McAvennie but the asking price was too high. "Brighton's money must be spent wisely and I will ensure that happens," explained the rock shop owner. Next season, the bleached-blond Scottish hitman netted 26 goals for West Ham United in the First Division as the east London club finished third in the top-flight – their highest-ever position.

Thursday 5th February 2004

Everyone concerned with the Albion received yet another well-aimed kick to their collective nether regions as planning inspector Charles Hoile declared the desired stadium at Falmer to be 'too small'. The Brighton & Hove Local Plan inquiry, conducted by Hoile, found "a provincial city's professional football club [was] not a national consideration and should not override planning policy which restricts development on the South Downs."

Four possible alternative sites were listed for a new stadium; Brighton Station, Withdean, Toad's Hole Valley and Sheepcote Valley. Council leader Ken Bodfish said Sheepcote, a former tip, should not be considered because it had poor road and public transport access.

Saturday 6th February 1982

Everton were the Goldstone visitors for a First Division fixture. Tony Grealish, Gerry Ryan and Steve Foster all registered to give Albion all three points – the first season of the new system (no longer two points) – in a 3-1 victory that moved the Seagulls into eighth place and UEFA Cup contention.

Thursday 6th February 2004

Renewal letters were posted to just over 5,000 season ticket holders as the club incentivised supporters with a three-year deal to generate some much-needed revenue. Around £2.5 million had been spent to bring Withdean up to Football League standard and more still was being spent on the planning application and public inquiry for Falmer. Dick Knight said; "This club, in the last six years, has spent over £5 million trying to resolve the disgraceful legacy we inherited of a football club without a home, in addition to enormous ongoing match costs." It cost Albion £40,000 per game at Withdean, which represented more than half of ticket revenue, compared to a Football League average of five to ten per cent.

Thursday 7th February 1929

One of Albion's all-time greats, Jimmy Langley, was born in Kilburn, London. The left-back signed from Leeds United in 1953. Immensely popular, Jimmy moved to Fulham for £12,000 in 1957 and earned full England honours a year later. The avid cigarette card collector was deeply superstitious and had to tap the left-hand post with each boot prior to kick-off in every game.

Saturday 7th February 1987

The natives were restless after the poor 3-0 home defeat to fellow Second Division strugglers Sunderland. Demonstrations inside the Goldstone Ground, and in Newtown Road after the game, called for chairman Bryan Bedson's head.

Saturday 7th February 2004

Mark McGhee, Dick Knight, the directors and all the players joined the 1,600-strong Albion support in a post-match 'We Want Falmer' protest after the 1-1 draw at Wycombe Wanderers.

Saturday 7th February 2015

Danny Holla's free-kick was glanced home by Lewis Dunk to put Albion ahead against Nottingham Forest. Substitute Beram Kayal's header set up a tense finish but it wasn't to be as the visitors ran out 3-2 winners. It was Dunk's last goal of the 2014/15 season. The Brighton-born defender eventually finished top of the goalscoring pile for the campaign with seven strikes.

Saturday 8th February 1997

A very special day in the history of Brighton & Hove Football Club. Albion fans had been protesting all season and internet forum North Stand Chat was the place for fans to discuss ideas and all things Albion. Plymouth Argyle supporter, Richard Vaughan, suggested fans from every club in the league should lend their support and call for Archer and Bellotti to leave by turning up for the Hartlepool United game. Danny Baker, who had been approached by Albion fan Warren Chrismas, backed the idea on national radio. Fans United was born. The rain and mist didn't dampen the remarkable scenes: fans from clubs around the world roared the Albion to a 5-0 victory. The result effectively saved the club – as the Albion stayed up with a better 'goals scored' – from relegation to the Conference and possible oblivion. A truly inspiring occasion.

Thursday 8th February 2007

Exactly ten years after the historic Fans United Day at the Goldstone, Early Day Motion 882 was tabled in the Commons in support of the stadium at Falmer.

Tuesday 8th February 2011

The special under-pitch layers at Falmer were almost complete. Images released today showed just how far sunk into the ground the stadium actually is. Wires hanged from various internal suspended ceilings awaiting their accompanying fixtures and fittings.

Saturday 9th February 1946

The FA Cup returned after six years of war. The competition was to be played in a two-leg format and First Division Derby County were the visitors in the fifth round. The crowd of 23,456 was the biggest for 12 years. Unfortunately, the eventual winners went home happy with a 4-1 first-leg win and would win the reverse fixture 6-0.

Sunday 9th February 1997

After the euphoria of Fans United the previous day, Albion fans were brought back to Earth with a bump after Goodbye Goldstone was shown on ITV. The 'live debate' was supposed to be an opportunity for a group of dedicated Albion fans to put much-needed questions to the unpopular (polite way of putting it) board.

David Bellotti (performing like a politician; polished and question-avoiding) and Bill Archer (who was on a live satellite link-up from Liverpool, wearing an eye-patch, looking like a Bond villain) were spouting their usual lies, particularly about a supposed planning application that Ivor Caplin had disproved before the broadcast. The programme was actually recorded, and then edited, pretty much in favour of the Albion board. Presenter Geoff Clarke promised the fans in attendance the chance to ask questions and it simply didn't happen. People got frustrated and irate and the supporters came across badly. As Paul Samrah said in the excellent *Build a Bonfire*; "I am afraid it was the low point of our campaign."

Saturday 10th February 1923

Albion's 2-1 Third Division (South) victory at Watford was not only the start of a four-game winning streak but also marked the debut of young Ulsterman Jimmy Hopkins. The inside-left had an exceptional turn of speed and arrived on the south coast after two seasons at recently relocated Arsenal. He scored 75 goals in 233 games.

Saturday 10th February 1973

A shocking run of 13 consecutive defeats thankfully came to an end at the Goldstone Ground. The 2-0 win over Luton Town came courtesy of a brace from Ken Beamish and saw the introduction of Brighton-born winger Tony Towner to the Hove faithful. The tricky flanker netted on 25 occasions in his 183 appearances over seven seasons and was sold to Millwall for £65,000 in 1978 when Gerry Ryan arrived at the club.

Tuesday 10th February 2004

A group of hardy Albion fans descended on Downing Street with 91 bouquets of flowers! En route to the evening game at Luton Town, the supporters made their special delivery – from every league club – to the Office of the Deputy Prime Minister in Whitehall. Fans of clubs all over the country emailed their support for the Albion to the DPM which caused his address to temporarily close due to the sheer weight of messages.

Saturday 11th February 1905

Due to an impending FA Cup replay, Fulham postponed their reserve fixture with Albion at Craven Cottage and instead sent their second XI to Hove for the Southern League First Division match on the same day. The Cottagers were fined £20 for postponing the reserve match, and £20 for fielding their second string. Fulham reserves won 4-1! The league game was never replayed.

Saturday 11th February 1967

Albion faced Notts County in front of 22,256 fans at the Goldstone in a reserve fixture! Tickets were on sale for the FA Cup visit of high-flying Chelsea the following weekend. Around 15,000 supporters actually stayed for the match.

Saturday 11th February 1978

Pop group Slade recorded a video for their single 'Give Us a Goal' before the 2-1 Second Division win over Burnley, in front of a packed North Stand.

Monday 11th February 2002

Despite the greasy surface and incessant rain, Albion turned on the style in a top-of-the-table Second Division clash with Reading. Bobby Zamora opened the scoring (58th) after a sublime back-heel from Paul Brooker. Steve Melton made it two with a brilliant volley 60 seconds later before Junior Lewis, on his full debut, slid in the third to make it 3-1. Melton left for Hull City in the November of this year, before a journeyman route to retirement that featured Boston United, Tamworth, King's Lynn, Lincoln United, Lincoln Moorlands Railway, Grantham Town and Workshop Town.

Wednesday 11th February 2009

Former Albion chief executive Ron Pavey sadly lost his battle against cancer, aged 74. Chairman Dick Knight said; "He was a pioneer and innovator even in his playing days, helping to found and organise the Sussex Sunday League in the early 1960s. At the Albion, for many years his clever thinking and hard-working influence were everywhere, helping to bring the club into the modern era and to forge new links with supporters. He never lost his love for the club. This true Sussex football hero will be sadly missed."

Friday 11th February 2011

A tractor skilfully spread out the first layer – Mansfield Sand's MM45 sand – of the new high-tech pitch at Falmer. Next would be the Fibrelastic rootzone pitch, specially designed to minimise potential player injury.

Saturday 12th February 1966

In manager Archie Macaulay's programme notes against Scunthorpe United, the Scot recorded his pleasure in "noting my request to supporters to refrain from throwing toilet rolls on to the pitch during play has been acted upon".

Saturday 12th February 1983

Michael Robinson made his 100th First Division appearance for Albion in the 0-0 draw with West Bromwich Albion. Left-back Graham Pearce listed bird watching, 'the feathered kind', as his hobby in the programme.

Saturday 12th February 2000

Robert Lester Zamora – Bobby to his legions of fans – marked his loan debut with Albion's only goal in a Withdean Stadium draw with Plymouth Argyle.

Wednesday 13th February 1907

An unusual incident influenced the result along the coast. Albion were playing Hastings & St Leonards United when Julius Gregory, the left-back, was injured. Hugh MacDonald, the Albion goalkeeper, somewhat bizarrely – as there were no substitutes – came out of goal to take Gregory's place. With no-one between the sticks, Albion unsurprisingly lost the game 6-1!

Saturday 13th February 1965

Long-serving *Evening Argus* reporter John Vinicombe recalled a memorable trip back from a 1-0 victory at Torquay in the 1978 season handbook; "Archie (the manager), well-pleased, ordered drinks all round with sumptuous dinner after which the coach set out for Brighton. One stop was followed by another, and another, and another. To say that staff and players of Brighton & Hove Albion were sloshed would be an understatement. We were all very nearly paralysed."

Saturday 13th February 2010

Michel Kuipers made his last appearance. The Dutchman arrived on the coast in June 2000 and played a huge part in the club's two championships and one promotion during his ten years. The popular goalkeeper joined Crawley Town in the summer of 2010 and, despite being sent off twice in his first month, helped the Red Devils win promotion to the Football League. The former Dutch marine featured 288 times for Albion.

Sunday 14th February 1971

Albion fans organised a walk along Brighton seafront in support of Pat Saward's Buy-a-Player Fund. The initiative raised around £1,500 which went towards the eventual purchase of Bert Murray, the 'People's Player', from Birmingham City.

Saturday 14th February 1987

Brighton-born Ian Chapman became Albion's youngest-ever player. The left-back replaced Chris Hutchings for the Second Division trip to Birmingham City. The tenacious defender, who packed a cracking shot, was surprisingly released by manager Jimmy Case and left for Gillingham in 1996, after 16 strikes in 331 appearances.

Saturday 14th February 1998

There was plenty of love on the terraces as Albion faced Doncaster Rovers at Gillingham's Priestfield Stadium. The game was billed as 'Fans United 2 – The Heart of Football' to help highlight the joint plight of Albion and the South Yorkshire outfit; they were rooted to the foot of the league after being ripped off by an unscrupulous chairman. Sound familiar? An absolutely shocking game of football ensued and no-one in the 6,339 crowd – over 4,000 up on the average – was surprised to see a

0-0 stalemate. On a positive note, the Mobile Club Shop made its debut in Redfern Street.

Saturday 14th February 2004

Albion fans took a detour en route to a match at Grimsby Town to deliver a giant Valentine's card to John Prescott's constituency office in east Hull.

Saturday 15th February 1986

Basement club Peterborough United hosted Second Division Albion in this FA Cup fifth-round tie. The visitors, who saw off Hull City and Newcastle United away in the previous two rounds, had only Graham Pearce left from the defeated 1983 Cup Final side. On a snowy day, Steve Jacobs fired the orange ball home to make it 2-2 and send the 5,000-plus Albion fans among the 15,812 crowd back to Sussex looking forward to a replay.

Saturday 15th February 1997

A 2-1 Third Division defeat at Carlisle United will only be remembered for one reason; Hereford hero Robbie Reinelt made his debut.

Saturday 15th February 2003

Most Albion fans in the Centenary Stand at Valley Parade couldn't see Bobby Zamora's winner – up the other end of the pitch – in this First Division fixture against Bradford City.

Saturday 16th February 1924

Jack Jenkins made his Wales debut in a 2-0 Home Championship defeat in Scotland. The full-back made his Football League bow after his 30th birthday and went on to represent the Albion for seven seasons, notching up 231 starts and four goals.

Saturday 16th February 1962

The Goldstone Ground saw its first postponement in the hardest winter for years. While other clubs saw fixture after fixture cancelled, Albion managed to keep playing at home until the game against Watford was called off, ironically, due to a waterlogged pitch following the first thaw since the snow arrived on Boxing Day.

Tuesday 17th February 1976

Peter Taylor decided on an ultra-defensive formation at Southend United in an attempt to end the dismal away form. The club's Third Division promotion challenge was suffering so the manager opted for four central defenders: Dennis Burnett, Andy Rollings, Graham Winstanley and Steve Piper. It failed spectacularly; Albion lost 4-0!

Saturday 17th February 2007

Twice European Champions Nottingham Forest were the Withdean visitors for this League One victory. Quickfire goals from Dean Hammond (72nd) and Nick Ward (73rd) gave the Albion a 2-1 victory. The result, in front of 7,749 fans, shot Albion up to 11th, ahead on goal difference of four clubs with the same points.

Tuesday 17th February 2009

The second leg of the Johnstone's Paint Trophy Southern Area Final saw Albion visit Kenilworth Road. Luton Town took the lead in the first minute following a shocking mix-up between Michel Kuipers and Adam Virgo. Nicky Forster notched his 200th career goal on 20 minutes. Penalties. Virgo and Elphick converted, as did Martin, Craddock and Asafa Hall for the Hatters. Then Jason Jarrett saw Price turn his spot-kick on to the post. Luton scored and it was down to Chris Birchall – who would leave Albion to line up alongside David Beckham at LA Galaxy – to salvage the tie. He didn't and the Wembley dream was over.

Friday 17th February 2023

It was reported that the committee of the Robert Eaton Memorial Fund (REMF) had decided to wind down all fundraising operations. Robert Eaton was an Albion fan who died in the Twin Towers attack in New York in 2001. The eponymous charity was founded, initially with a football match between fans of Brighton and Crystal Palace, to raise funds for football projects in the Hispanic communities of Queens, New York, namely Los Peladitos.

Over 22 years of fundraising provided kit and equipment for youth and children's sports clubs around the world, with £330,000 donated to beneficiaries across the UK, USA, Australia, New Zealand, South East Asia and Africa. Angela Ridge, Judith Lake and Barbara Stephenson, Robert's sisters, said; "It has been a source of immense pride and satisfaction that, out of something so horrific, this charity would be such a force for good for so long - all in our brother's name. We know it gave our parents great comfort with all the hard work being put in by so many volunteers."

Saturday 18th February 1967

First Division Chelsea arrived for a FA Cup fourth-round tie. A 35,000 sell-out Goldstone crowd witnessed a 1-1 draw, with Dave Turner netting for Albion. The London club's flamboyant boss Tommy Docherty had this to say in the programme; "They have a First Division set-up at the Goldstone Ground, and First Division ideas, as well as a first-class pitch. The day cannot be far away when they become one of our top clubs." Meanwhile, on page 13, Turner – at 22 the club's youngest-ever captain at the time – recalled how he "fell off the settee" when he heard the cup draw.

Saturday 18th February 1984

Southern Sound, now Southern FM, reported on their first Albion away game; the 3-1 FA Cup fifth-round defeat at Watford's Vicarage Road. Swansea City were dispatched in the third round, while league champions Liverpool returned home after strikes from Gerry Ryan and Terry Connor gave the Albion a thoroughly deserved 2-0 victory in round four.

Wednesday 18th February 1987

Flying winger Steve Penney scored his first goal for Northern Ireland in the 1-1 draw with Israel in Tel Aviv. On the same day, in Swansea, Dean Saunders represented his country for the fifth and final time as an Albion player, before his £60,000 transfer to Oxford United, in the 0-0 draw with the USSR.

Tuesday 18th February 2003

The public inquiry began at Hove Town Hall. Albion launched their case for a new stadium at Falmer by saying the club's survival depended on the plans going ahead. Speaking to *The Argus*, Jonathan Clay, representing the club, said the stadium was essential to the cultural and urban regeneration of Brighton & Hove. "It is the club's case that the provision of a modern, safe, comfortable and convenient stadium for a city of the size and regional importance of the city of Brighton

& Hove is a consideration of national significance." Mr Clay likened Brighton to Barcelona in terms of its regional importance and that it was 'simply extraordinary' that the team found itself in cramped, temporary accommodation at Withdean.

Saturday 18th February 2017

Oluwafikayomi Oluwadamilola 'Fikayo' Tomori made his on-loan debut in the 2-0 victory at Barnsley. The 19-year-old Chelsea centre-back slotted seamlessly into Albion's rearguard and, despite only featuring nine times, certainly made an impression at Falmer. As of June 2024, Tomori had established himself as a regular at AC Milan, winning Serie A in 2022.

Sunday 19th February 1961

Justin Fashanu was born in Hackney, London. After a stunning goal against Liverpool, the Norwich City striker moved to Nottingham Forest in 1981. A fall-out with Brian Clough precipitated a move to Notts County – after a nine-game loan spell at Southampton – before Chris Cattlin paid £115,000 for his services in 1985.

The troubled striker managed just two strikes in 20 Albion appearances and spent the next 12 years plying his trade at various clubs across Europe and North America. Tragically, Justin took his own life in May 1998. An eponymous organisation made fantastic strides to combat homophobia in sport and held its first meeting at Withdean Stadium in 2009.

Saturday 19th February 1972

It was goalless after 45 minutes at Gay Meadow. The floodgates opened in the second period as Albion ran out 5-3 winners with strikes from Peter O'Sullivan (2), Kit Napier, Willie Irvine and an own goal. The 1971/72 campaign produced the club's best away record in the league to that point: 12 wins and just five defeats, scoring 43 goals.

Tuesday 19th February 2008

The fifth fixture of the season against Cheltenham Town proved unattractive as Withdean Stadium recorded its lowest league attendance during its 12 years as Albion's home – just 4,395.

Saturday 19th February 2011

Albion's first appearance in the FA Cup fifth round since 1985 ended in a 3-0 defeat at Stoke City. Gus Poyet's men attempted to impose their passing style, while the Potters stuck to their tried and tested formula: use strength and height to create havoc in the opposition box. Unsurprisingly, a Rory Delap long throw broke the deadlock on 15 minutes when huge Norwegian John Carew beat Peter Brezovan to the ball to head home. Their other goals were from within the six-yard box too. Albion were out, but by no means disgraced.

Saturday 19th February 2012

A day to forget for Lewis Dunk, Brighton & Hove Albion and particularly Liam Bridcutt. Luis Suarez was on fire as Liverpool hammered the stripes 6-1 at Anfield in the FA Cup fifth round. In what was a first for the club, Albion contrived to net a hat-trick of own goals; Dunk with one and Bridcutt with a brace!

Saturday 20th February 1982

Albion fans looked on all misty-eyed as Peter Ward scored for Nottingham Forest in the 1-0 First Division defeat at the Goldstone Ground.

Sunday 20th February 1983

FA Cup victories over Newcastle United and Manchester City were rewarded with a fifth-round tie at league champions Liverpool! No team had won at Anfield for almost a year and Albion had been victorious on the road – at St. James' Park in the third round – only once all season. Amazingly, Gerry Ryan put the Seagulls ahead just after the half hour mark. Australian Craig Johnston equalised with an acrobatic strike with 20 minutes remaining, only for former Kop favourite Jimmy Case to blast home the winner from 20 yards just 60 seconds later. A magnificent triumph for Jimmy Melia's men.

Saturday 20th February 2016

Dale Stephens was on the scoresheet as Albion went down 4-1 at Cardiff City. The defeat was only the fifth all season in the league and turned out to be the last in 2015/16 – apart from the play-offs.

Monday 20th February 2017

'The Goldstone Days – 20 Years On' was on at the Theatre Royal Brighton. A thousand fans were in attendance – along with many former players and directors – for a riotous trip down memory (Goldstone) lane hosted by Garry Richardson, and occasionally interrupted by the wise-cracking Peter Brackley whose character supplied a steady stream of excellent one-liners on past Albion players. Landmark events were celebrated with humour and insight and Dick Knight spoke passionately about the rebuilding of the club. The two-hour spectacular also featured action clips, comedy sketches and interviews, live on stage or on film. A wonderful way to remember our dear old home.

Saturday 21st February 1914

Albion, cheered on by around 400 travelling fans, bowed out of the FA Cup at the third-round stage, losing 3-0 to The Wednesday in Sheffield. The Owls – who were once known as the Blades before relocating to the north of the city in Hillsborough – were so impressed by the performance of Albion's centre-half David Parkes that they offered a fee of £1,500, plus forward George Beech, for the promising 21-year-old. Parkes subsequently moved to Yorkshire the following month for what was a record sum for a Brighton player at the time.

Saturday 21st February 1953

Eric Gill made the first of 247 consecutive appearances for the Albion between the sticks and got off to a great start, keeping a clean sheet at Reading's Elm Park.

Sunday 21st February 1982

The first-team squad and coaching staff flew off to Torremolinos in Spain for a short break and a spot of golf.

Saturday 21st February 2009

In a classic case of 'never go back', manager Micky Adams was sacked as Albion boss with the club staring relegation in the face in 21st position. The former Leeds United, Southampton and Coventry City full-back later acknowledged that it had been a mistake to return to the Albion, a sentiment echoed by the majority of the Withdean faithful. His first-tenure achievements, however, will never be forgotten.

Saturday 21st February 2015

A rare chink of light in an otherwise disappointing campaign – Íñigo Calderón and Joao Teixeira both scored twice as Albion dispatched Birmingham in a seven-goal thriller.

Saturday 22nd February 1902

The Albion played their first-ever game at the Goldstone Ground, Newtown Road, Hove as a Sussex Senior Cup semi-final was taking place at the County Ground, the club's home. The opponents for the historic friendly were Southampton Wanderers, who were soundly beaten 7-1. The club moved permanently to the Goldstone Ground for the 1902/03 season and became the sole occupants in 1904.

Saturday 22nd February 1969

Alex Dawson – a big, powerful centre-forward who was once a Busby Babe at Manchester United – scored four times at Hartlepool in a 5-2 Albion Third Division win; the fourth successive victory.

Saturday 23rd February 1963

A nine-goal bonanza surprised the 5,934 in attendance for this Third Division game at Elm Park. Reading were 2-1 up at the break but Albion fought back with a second goal from Alan Jackson, plus Roy Jennings (2) and Steve Burtenshaw; for a final score of 5-4.

Tuesday 23rd February 1982

Steve Foster shone on his debut in the centre of England's defence in the 4-0 Wembley demolition of Northern Ireland in a Home International; the first Albion player to wear the Three Lions since Tommy Cook in 1925. Albion team-mate, left-back Sammy Nelson, lined up for the opposition.

Tuesday 23rd February 2010

Albion's first trip to The Valley since January 1985. Charlton Athletic were sitting in fourth place while their guests were languishing in 18th, just three points above the drop zone. Glenn Murray was missing through illness, so Forster started on his own up front. But, it was flying right-back Iñigo Calderón who broke the deadlock after 26 minutes, carrying the ball from inside Albion's half to the edge of the area before driving a powerful low shot into the far corner. With 12 minutes remaining Elliott Bennett sent the 2,322 away fans – in a crowd of 17,508 – behind the goal into raptures, smashing an unstoppable shot past the Addicks stopper to make it 2-0. Deep into injury time, the south-east Londoners grabbed a consolation.

Saturday 24th February 1976

A historical day in Hove. A bumper crowd of 33,300 – over 19,000 up on the visit of Halifax Town three days earlier – were at the Goldstone for the Third Division clash with arch-rivals Crystal Palace. Northern Ireland international Sammy Morgan's brace earned a 2-0 victory for Peter Taylor's men, but the day will be remembered for the first, en masse, chant of 'Seagulls' as a reply to the Croydon outfit's nickname 'Eagles'.

Saturday 24th February 1990

Sergei Gotsmanov made his debut in the 2-1 Second Division defeat at Sunderland. The midfielder scored four times in 16 appearances before being transferred to Southampton for £150,000 six months later. The Belarusian had represented the USSR 31 times, and even scored against England at Wembley, before his move to the Albion from Dinamo Minsk.

Tuesday 24th February 2015

Íñigo Calderón netted his third goal in two matches, against Leeds United, in a 2-0 win. For the first and only time in his career, the Spaniard scored with his face! The popular Basque followed up a drive by Beram Kayal which came back off the keeper and smacked into Calderón's right cheek and into the net.

Saturday 24th February 2024

On his 400th Albion appearance, Lewis Dunk headed in a last-minute equaliser – his 31st Albion goal – from a pinpoint Pascal Gross cross, to claim a share of the spoils against Everton. A few minutes earlier Albion's Billy Gilmour was sent off for a studs-up challenge on Amadou Onana. Dunk has made a habit of popping up with big moments – usually headers – for his hometown club since promotion to the top-flight. "Lewis is a legend of Brighton – he is an example every day," said Roberto De Zerbi. "I think he could play at a different level but we are lucky because he is our captain, our player. He is the soul of the team."

Saturday 25th February 1911

Don Welsh was born in Manchester. After playing for Valletta in Malta while in the Navy, the half-back joined Torquay United. Charlton Athletic paid £3,250 for his services and the left-sided player won the FA Cup in 1947. Just three months later, Welsh took over the hotseat at the Albion from Tommy Cook – as the club applied for re-election for the one and only time – before leaving for Liverpool in March 1951. The Reds were relegated too – from the top division – and to rub salt into the wounds, they swapped places with Everton.

Wednesday 25th February 1998

He had no hair, but we didn't care. Steve Gritt took over from Jimmy Case in December 1996 when the club was at its lowest ebb; ten points adrift in professional football's basement, home crowds below 4,000, and antipathy spreading like wildfire across the unkempt Goldstone terraces. A hate figure on his arrival, the former Charlton man somehow galvanised the squad, and the fans, who got behind their team to create a cauldron of noise at home games.

His scream on the final whistle at Hereford just about encapsulated his time in charge. Unfortunately, a shocking start to Albion's tenure at Gillingham cost him his job on this day. Whatever the future holds, Steve Gritt is assured of a very warm welcome when he visits the American Express Community Stadium.

Wednesday 26th February 1958

Major Carlo Campbell died, aged 70, at the Sussex County Hospital. A fighter pilot in World War I, the Albion chairman – held in high esteem across the country – had been advised to slow down by his doctors. His deputy, Alec Whitcher, told the *Brighton & Hove Herald*; "The major's death is a grievous blow to us all."

Thursday 26th February 1998

Albion midfield legend Brian Horton began his 11-month tenure as Albion boss. A good start – a 3-2 home (Gillingham) win over Chester City – gave false hope and only one further win was registered on the way to a 23rd-place finish. The following campaign showed improvement, but Horton moved to Port Vale in January 1999. His final record: played 43; 14 wins, 10 draws, 19 defeats.

Saturday 26th February 2000

Albion went goal crazy at the Deva Stadium! Bobby Zamora grabbed a quick-fire brace in the first 20 minutes. The floodgates opened in the second half as Keith McPherson, Paul Brooker, Zamora (pen), Darren Freeman and future double-winning captain Paul Rogers added their names to the scoresheet: 7-1 to the Albion!

Friday 27th February 1903

The *Evening Argus* proudly proclaimed that "the Brighton & Hove Albion management have been successful in inducing Woolwich Arsenal to visit Brighton the club should be congratulated on their enterprise".

Saturday 27th February 1974

'The People's Player', Bert Murray, made his debut in the 2-1 Third Division victory over Wrexham. The utility player was on the verge of signing for Fulham when manager Pat Saward stepped in to sign the Chelsea League Cup winner. The following season Bert was instrumental in the exciting promotion charge, scoring 12 times, and was voted Player of the Season.

Saturday 27th February 1982

The club tried to entice fans to splash out on the new executive boxes that were to be installed as part of the new North Stand at the Goldstone.

Wednesday 27th February 1991

A group of hardy souls departed Newtown Road for Newcastle's St. James' Park. The coach made a pit stop at Toddington services for fans to enjoy light refreshments and a kickabout. A youngster crawled underneath the vehicle to retrieve the ball. On continuing the long journey north, the police instructed the vehicle to pull over at the next services and ordered the bemused fans to disembark.

The car park area was cleared – with a Brighton & Hove Buses coach surrounded by acres of vehicle-less concrete – and it was nearly three hours before everyone could move on. Was there a bomb? Did someone see the youth getting the ball and assume he was planting a device? It transpired that Chelsea fans on their way to Sheffield Wednesday thought it would be funny to phone the police saying that someone had put a bomb on the coach. The occupants arrived with ten minutes to spare, got soaked to the skin on an uncovered terrace, and had to endure a painfully dull 0-0 draw. The attendance was just 12,692.

Saturday 27th February 1993

Kurt Nogan's hot streak was about to start. Unfortunately, only 2,033 people witnessed the striker's brace at Wigan Athletic's Springfield Park. The former Luton man scored 15 times in the last 18 games of the season to become the first player since Garry Nelson five years earlier to net more than 20 league goals in a campaign.

Saturday 28th February 1903

Frank Scott scored five in an 8-0 mauling at Southall in a Southern League Division Two fixture. The Lincolnshire-born centre forward netted 34 times in 50 Albion appearances from 1902 to 1904. A fine goal ratio.

Saturday 28th February 1925

Once immortalised in a fanzine title, Tommy Cook represented England for the one and only time in the 2-1 Home Championship victory over Wales in Swansea.

Saturday 28th February 1953

A crowd of 10,000 fans turned up at the Goldstone for a reserve fixture. There were no cup tickets available, or any other initiative, for the Football Combination Cup visit of Tottenham Hotspur.

Saturday 28th February 1998

An Albion mainstay during the glory years of the late 1970s, Brian Horton returned for his first game in charge against Chester City at 'home' in Gillingham. A strike from Andy Ansah, and a brace by Kerry Mayo, handed the new boss a 3-2 victory.

Saturday 28th February 2004

Local lad Adam Virgo scored his first Albion goal in the Second Division 1-1 draw at Stockport County's Edgeley Park.

Saturday 28th February 2009

In only his sixth appearance since a £150,000 move from Stockport County the previous month, Jim McNulty suffered a horrific injury in the 4-0 home defeat to Crewe Alexandra. The left-back was accidentally kneed in the back which ended in his right kidney being removed in an operation at the Nuffield Hospital in Woodingdean. Albion physio Malcolm Stuart later revealed; "He underwent surgery, and the idea was to try to save the kidney if we could, but the damage was too great."

Saturday 29th February 1908

Dundonians Dave Dougal (outside-right) and Tom Rodger (inside-left) both made their Southern League debuts in the 1-0 Hove defeat to Crystal Palace. Dougal managed one goal in 14 Albion run-outs, while his countryman equalled his scoring tally but made one more appearance.

Saturday 29th February 1936

Albion have won every competitive game on this date! Alec Law grabbed both goals in the 2-1 Third Division (South) victory at Gillingham.

Scars & Stripes – March 1999:
What was to become an area of outstanding beauty.

© *Scars & Stripes*

MARCH

Thursday 1st March 1951

Schoolboy high-jump and 800 metres champion Gerry Fell was born in Nottinghamshire. Signed by Peter Taylor in 1974, the unusually tall winger possessed electric pace and a powerful shot, and went on to net 20 times in 91 Albion appearances before departing for Southend United in 1977 as part of the deal that brought Paul Clark to the club.

Saturday 1st March 1958

Dave Hollins, brother of future Chelsea manager John, wore Albion's goalkeeping jersey for the first time in the Third Division (South) 2-2 draw at Coventry City. The Welshman – who was in goal for the record 9-0 defeat at Middlesbrough in August – moved to Newcastle United for £11,000 in 1961. His friendship with fellow goalkeeper Eric Gill is immortalised in Spencer Vignes' excellent book, *Eric & Dave*.

Friday 1st March 2002

A government 'design watchdog' strongly backed plans for a stadium at Falmer. *The Argus* reported how the Commission for Architecture and the Built Environment (CABE) said it was impressed by the way the structure would blend in with its surroundings. The club had submitted two planning applications for a 22,000-seat stadium at Village Way North or Village Way South. Both sites are in areas of outstanding natural beauty – which now includes a six-lane motorway, a busy railway line and two universities – and on the edge of the proposed South Downs National Park.

Tuesday 1st March 2011

Albion kicked off what was to be a record-breaking month with a 1-0 victory at Huish Park. On 25 minutes Glenn Murray teed up Elliott Bennett for a low 20-yard drive that flew past keeper Stephen Henderson and into the Yeovil net. It was the first of eight consecutive league wins.

Saturday 2nd March 1912

Jimmy Smith scored three in the 7-1 Southern League Division One demolition of Watford at the Goldstone Ground. The diminutive forward established a new record of 25 league goals in his first full season and managed 40 strikes overall in just 65 games. Eight months later he was sold for £735 (plus Bobby Simpson) to Bradford Park Avenue. He was tragically killed in action on the Western Front in 1918.

Saturday 2nd March 1957

Goalkeeper Eric Gill had made 247 consecutive appearances – 231 league and 16 in the FA Cup – and was due to break the record of Tottenham Hotspur's Ted Ditchburn at Coventry City. Unfortunately, the £400 signing from Charlton Athletic felt unwell and was sent home from Brighton Station. Billy Lane's men wore an unusual change strip of black shirts with white sleeves. The 2-1 win at Highfield Road left Albion sandwiched in sixth spot in Third Division (South) between Walsall and Queens Park Rangers, all on 37 points. Colchester United were top, Torquay United second, while Norwich City were rock bottom.

Friday 2nd March 2007

Interested parties received notice of a decision on or by 9th July – either way – on whether a stadium would be built at Falmer.

Saturday 2nd March 2013

Leonardo Ulloa became the first player to score a hat-trick at Falmer in the 4-1 win over Huddersfield Town. 'Spanish Dave' got his name on the scoresheet too, converting from the spot in the 81st minute.

Saturday 3rd March 1990

Barry Lloyd mooted the future success of the Albion's 'Football in the Community' initiative; "Here in Sussex our community covers many hundreds of square miles. We can confidently look forward to the time when we have one of the most successful schemes in the country."

Wednesday 3rd March 2010

Albion centre-back Adam El-Abd had split loyalties as England took on Egypt at Wembley in a World Cup warm-up. The Brighton-born defender explained; "My dad's Egyptian and my mum's English so I'm completely split down the middle. Obviously, given the choice, I will always choose England – but hopefully my dad doesn't read this as he'd go crazy if he heard me say that!" The Egyptian Footbal Association requested DVDs of the defender when he was 21. "They have said they won't consider players in League One, which is fair enough, but who knows what the future holds." For the record, Peter Crouch (2) and Shaun Wright-Phillips scored as England won 3-1 and Adam would go on to represent his dad's country seven times.

Friday 4th March 1921

Wilfred McCoy was born in Birmingham. Known by his nickname 'Tim' (after the famous cowboy) the big centre-half's career was interrupted by the war and he eventually made his peacetime debut, in 1951, 11 years after his first wartime appearance at Portsmouth.

Saturday 4th March 1972

The team coach failed to arrive at Albion's Manchester hotel. Four taxis ferried Pat Saward and his team to Halifax and they arrived at The Shay just in time. That's where the bad luck ended. Willie Irvine, Bert Murray, Kit Napier and John Templeman (2) smashed home the goals in a resounding 5-0 victory.

Wednesday 4th March 1998

The *Evening Argus* revealed a shortlist of permanent sites for Albion's new stadium (in no particular order); Falmer, Waterhall, Greyhound Stadium, Shoreham Harbour.

Sunday 4th March 2007

Albion received the 'Football League Community Club of the Year' award from *FourFourTwo* magazine. Joint managing director of Albion in the Community, Steve Ford, commented; "To be judged by our peers to be the best community scheme in the Football League, out of 72 clubs, was absolutely fantastic."

Thursday 4th March 2010

A magnificent arch was in place above the East Stand, supported by two huge, temporary towers, until it is ready to link up with its West Stand counterpart. From the sky, the obstructing university buildings have now been demolished.

Friday 4th March 2011

Charlie Oatway's autobiography *Tackling Life: The True Story of a Footballing Bad Lad Made Good* hit the shelves of Sussex bookstores. The Albion first-team coach, who had only learnt the two 'Rs' in 2004, detailed his struggle with dyslexia, the law and his later redemption with the Albion, and wrote the book as a thank you to the club and their study skills programme that helped him achieve his football qualifications. The former midfielder said; "The idea behind having a study centre at a professional football club is simple. People who didn't do well at school and think that learning is for other people are less likely to be scared off by going along to somewhere like a football club than going along to a college." Proceeds from sales went to the club's award-winning Albion in the Community scheme.

Saturday 5th March 1927

The receipts from the 9,447 in attendance for a 3-2 Third Division (South) win over Gillingham went to Tommy Cook. Before the 1930s, long-serving players due a benefit were often rewarded with gate money from a league game rather than a testimonial. Albion's record league goalscorer netted just over £437. The lowest admission price between the wars was one shilling (5p).

Saturday 5th March 1977

The 1-1 Third Division draw with Tranmere Rovers was marred by the injury sustained by Peter Grummitt in a collision with visiting forward Ronnie Moore, which ended his professional career.

Tuesday 5th March 2002

Albion kept up the pressure on Second Division leaders Reading with a 4-0 thumping of Wycombe Wanderers at Withdean. Bobby Zamora (2), Paul Brooker and Paul Watson with a 25-yard free-kick were the scorers.

Saturday 5th March 2011

The type of game supporters relish – but managers hate! Carlisle United went ahead after just three minutes before Glenn Murray was put through to level. Ashley Barnes smashed home a powerful angled shot (53rd) but Ben Marshall equalised on the hour. The Somerset-born striker then netted with the outside of his foot (63rd) to make it 3-2 before Harry Arter netted for the Cumbrians from close range in injury time. In the third minute of added-on time Albion forced a throw, deep in the opposition half. The ball eventually fell – from a considerable height – to Liam Bridcutt on the edge of the area. The former Chelsea starlet unleashed an amazing first-time left-foot volley past the United stopper to cue pandemonium among the 7,466 Withdean faithful.

Saturday 6th March 1982

Albion travelled to Anfield to face a mighty Liverpool side that included Ian Rush, Kenny Dalglish and Mark Lawrenson. Jimmy Case found himself wide on the right and sent over an inviting centre which Michael Robinson nodded across for Andy Ritchie to fire goalwards. Bruce Grobbelaar palmed the ball on to Alan Hansen's legs and over the line. The 1-0 win sent the Albion into eighth place in the First Division.

Saturday 6th March 1985

In the programme against Blackburn Rovers, Glen Wilson waxed lyrical about his time with the Albion: "To me, Brighton is the most wonderful club in the country. It's a great club, it always has been. We've got very good supporters and I think the club has always tried to remain close to the people who come along and support them. Every day I come to work here, is like a day going to Wembley. That's how attached I've become to the club."

Saturday 6th March 2004

National Falmer Day. Albion were without a game, so supporters travelled to matches the length and breadth of the country to spread the word about the proposed new stadium plans. In a day that epitomised the spirit and ingenuity of Albion fans, the message was made loud and clear at grounds in Bognor, Bournemouth, Blackpool and Berwick Rangers – plus many hundreds more. A wonderful effort by all concerned.

Friday 6th March 2009

After a fortnight under the caretaker stewardship of Bob Booker and Dean White, Russell Slade rode into Withdean with one objective – keep Albion in League One. The bald former Yeovil Town boss strode purposefully on to the Leyton Orient turf the following day to acknowledge the excellent Albion support and take his place in the dugout to bark orders at his disjointed team that included five loanees; Mikkel Andersen, Matthew Heath, Gary Borrowdale, Al Bangura and Lloyd Owusu. Not the best start – a 2-1 defeat.

Saturday 7th March 1981

Just under 15,000 Goldstone fans were present for 19-year-old Tony Vessey's one and only Albion run-out. The central defender was spotted playing Sunday League football in Derby. On leaving the south coast, Vessey had a brief spell in Sweden at Vasalund before playing for Worthing and Crawley Town, where he made over 400 appearances.

Saturday 7th March 1998

On this day in 1998, Albion drew 0-0 with Hartlepool United at 'home' (Gillingham) in front of a crowd of 2,811.

Saturday 7th March 2020

Albion's last game before English football closed down due to COVID-19 – an uninspiring 0-0 draw against Wolverhampton Wanderers at Molineux.

Thursday 7th March 2024

After finishing top of their group, Albion travelled to Rome for their first-ever fixture in the knockout phase of the Europa League. The pre-match build-up was marred by the news that two Albion fans, Jack Stephenson and Andrew Le Goubin, had been attacked and stabbed by a group of six men in black clothes and balaclavas in the city centre. Jack needed ten stitches in his leg from three incisions and spent 13 hours in hospital.

To the match and the Giallorossi took an early lead through Paulo Dybala but the Sussex side gradually grew into the game, hitting the post through Simon Adingra's deflected cross. Roma made it two when Lewis Dunk's poor touch was punished by Romelu Lukaku just before half-time. Albion continued to search for a way back into the game but were hit by a sucker punch when Mancini slid in a third, quickly followed by Cristante's header. Albion's 3,500 fans among the 64,000 inside the Olympic Stadium did their club proud, helping to create an incredible atmosphere that will live long in the memory. But it wasn't to be. Roberto De Zerbi reflected on the 4-0 reverse; "We played our game. We gave our best. Maybe our best now is this performance."

Saturday 8th March 1986

First Division Southampton were the Goldstone visitors. It was only the Albion's second FA Cup sixth-round tie, and the 25,069 fans present were hoping for an upset against a side that included four England internationals. Saints overwhelmed their hosts to win 2-0.

Saturday 8th March 1997

In an incident-packed campaign most of the action was taking place off the pitch. Not this time, though, as Leyton Orient visited the Goldstone Ground. A real belter of a contest exploded into life as Craig Maskell scored twice in the first seven minutes. Unbelievably, Orient were then 3-2 up by the hour mark.

Ian Baird equalised only for Scott McGleish – still reviled by Albion fans to this day – to fire the Londoners into the lead again. He celebrated wildly in front of the North Stand, much to the chagrin of the home crowd. Then all hell broke loose: O's defender Mark Warren was sent off and veteran Ray Wilkins was lunged at – and fortunately missed – by a pitch encroacher. Scottish winger Paul McDonald then levelled from the spot with five minutes remaining to make it 4-4. What a game! As of April 2024, McGleish is still playing, aged 50, for Hertfordshire-based Leverstock Green in the Spartan South Midlands League Premier Division.

Saturday 9th March 2002

An entertaining encounter at the Madejski Stadium saw the automatic promotion contenders play out a 0-0 draw. Albion wide man Gary Hart fired in an angled drive in the final minute, in front of an ecstatic travelling army of over 3,000 fans. Referee Mike Dean disallowed it.

Saturday 9th March 2013

Ashley Barnes was handed a seven-game ban for deliberately tripping referee Nigel Miller in a Championship contest at Bolton Wanderers. The striker was shown a straight red card in stoppage time as the home side ran out 1-0 winners. The 23-year-old was handed an immediate four-match ban because it was his second dismissal of the campaign. It was extended by another three games at a disciplinary meeting at The FA.

Sunday 9th March 2019

Anthony Knockaert's yellow card after 28 seconds was the quickest in the Premier League for a decade. Glenn Murray – who replaced Florin Andone who injured his thigh during the warm-up – gave Albion the lead at Crystal Palace, with his 100th league goal for the Albion, pouncing on a mistake before superbly volleying into the far corner from 18 yards in the first half. With 12 minutes remaining the French winger atoned for his first-minute caution with a sublime curling left-foot effort from just outside the box that nestled in the top corner. The south Londoners dominated almost every statistic – with more territory, possession, shots and crosses than Albion – but Roy Hodgson's men lost 2-1. It was Chris Hughton's last victory of the season.

Saturday 10th March 1928

Ernie 'Tug' Wilson enjoyed the first of two benefit matches. The record appearance holder – 566 games – netted just over £326 from the Third Division (South) game against Gillingham at the Goldstone Ground. The 7,860 spectators did not see any goals.

Saturday 10th March 1951

A 2-2 draw at Bournemouth & Boscombe Athletic saw the beginning of a decade in charge for Billy Lane. The former striker – who scored 177 times in 317 league outings for seven clubs – joined as Don Welsh's assistant from Guildford City in 1950 and on becoming boss re-introduced the blue and white stripes. Lane, who changed his surname from Lohn because of potential German connotations, oversaw the club's first league promotion in 1958. Today's result left Albion in 18th place in Third Division (South). Nottingham Forest were sitting pretty at the top of the table while our friends from Croydon were three points adrift at the bottom.

Sunday 10th March 1974

Power cuts brought the country to its knees. Albion – trying to increase gate revenue – hosted only their second-ever Sunday match; a Third Division 2-1 win over Hereford United. It worked as 17,061 fans attended compared to the season's average of 10,848.

Monday 11th March 1974

In Epping, Essex a hero is born... Robbie Reinelt arrived on the planet. The journeyman striker cost Albion £15,000 from Colchester United in February 1997. After an inauspicious start – two goals in 11 games – and Reinelt found himself on the bench for the end-of-season nail-biter at Hereford.

Saturday 11th March 1995

Albion enjoyed a third successive league win at the Goldstone Ground. John Byrne, Paul McCarthy, George Parris and Junior McDougald found the target in the 4-0 Third Division victory.

Wednesday 11th March 1998

Councillor Neil Commin branded the Falmer site 'totally unsuitable'. He said; "Our planning policies for this area are to protect the Downland and the Falmer conservation area and to limit further traffic growth. This proposal clearly goes against all these objectives."

Saturday 12th March 1960

Bill Curry scored one of his three hat-tricks for the season in the 5-1 Second Division win over Bristol City at the Goldstone Ground.

Saturday 12th March 1983

The Goldstone Ground was full to its 28,000 capacity for the visit of Norwich City in the FA Cup sixth round. It was the furthest the Albion had ever progressed in the competition and the excitement in the twin towns was almost at fever pitch!

Jimmy Case had netted in the previous three rounds, and it was the Scouser who fired the Albion to a semi-final date with Sheffield Wednesday at Highbury. Andy Ritchie flicked on for the midfielder to muscle past the Canaries defence to slot past future England keeper Chris Woods in front of an ecstatic North Stand. Wembley beware, the Seagulls were almost there!

Tuesday 12th March 1997

Good news from London. At the offices of the Centre for Dispute Resolution, director Greg Stanley explained to the press that a deal had been struck between him and chairman Bill Archer, and the consortium led by Dick Knight. It was almost another six months before the deal was finally done. A year later, Albion submitted a planning application to use Withdean Stadium.

Friday 12th March 2010

The West Stand skeleton was rapidly rising to display its three tiers and five storeys – it'll be stunning when it is finished. Meanwhile, across the pitch, the smooth grey cladding was beginning to cover the A27-facing back of the East Stand.

Monday 13th March 1978

The Brighton Trades & Labour Club in Lewes Road, Brighton hosted the first-ever Seagull Lottery draw. The 50,000, 20-pence tickets quickly sold out each week and there was even a waiting list! The draw was made in pubs and clubs across the county and proved popular until 1991.

Saturday 14th March 1925

Inside-right Sam Jennings' debut. Charlie Webb paid a club-record fee of £650 to West Ham United and the Nottinghamshire-born hitman didn't disappoint, scoring 63 goals in just 115 starts.

Saturday 14th March 1987

Dean Saunders – who would eventually go on to be transferred for over £10 million in total – was sold for a paltry £60,000 to Oxford United. His replacement, Richard Tiltman, scored his one and only ever Albion goal in the 3-1 defeat at Barnsley on this day. Sussex-born Tiltman represented the stripes just 13 times before moving to Crawley Town. His tour of non-league clubs in his home county ended at Worthing, via Perth Italia, based in Australia, in the late 1990s.

Saturday 14th March 2009

Russell Slade enjoyed his first win – on his Theatre of Trees debut – as Albion boss against Yeovil Town, the club that had sacked him after four straight victories just a month earlier. A comprehensive 5-0 thrashing of the Glovers, with a brace apiece for Dean Cox and Nicky Forster and a goal from Glenn Murray, left Albion in the relegation places with 11 games left.

Thursday 14th March 2024

Albion's historic European adventure was over. Roberto De Zerbi's side fought hard but couldn't overturn a four-goal deficit from the week before in Rome. Danny Welbeck's fantastic curling effort eight minutes before the break gave the home fans hope. Simon Adingra had a point-blank close-range header blocked by the Roma keeper, who also saved from Igor. Jan Paul van Hecke was also just off target with two headed attempts. The final scoreline of 1-0 maybe didn't reflect Albion's dominance.

Albion won all five Europa League matches when scoring the opening goal but their first venture into Europe ultimately ended in disappointment. But it was an incredible experience and will live long in the memory of the fans who made the four trips to the continent.

Monday 15th March 1909

Charlie Webb became the first Albion player to represent his country. The inside-left featured for the Republic of Ireland in the 5-0 defeat against Scotland in Glasgow.

Saturday 15th March 1980

After playing Manchester United for the first time – a Goldstone Ground 0-0 stalemate (the sixth draw in a row) – Peter Ward and his wife were among a panel of fashion competition judges at Butlin's Ocean Hotel in Saltdean, alongside pop sensations Dollar.

Thursday 16th March 1905

An extraordinary meeting of Albion shareholders was called at the Presbyterian Lecture Hall in North Road, Brighton. The directors in attendance agreed to purchase 750 shares to fund the players' summer wages. It was announced that John Jackson was to be replaced by respected Middlesex Football Association administrator Frank Scott-Walford, due to his poor bookkeeping which he'd neglected for four months, leaving the club's finances in a mess.

Tuesday 16th March 1999

The *Evening Argus* reported how John Woodruff, landlord of The Swan in Falmer, refused to serve regulars who wouldn't sign his petition opposing the new stadium that could possibly be built across the six-lane motorway – and busy railway line – from his pub. Four people who had been visiting the hostelry every week for the past eight years were refused a drink after saying they wanted the club to have a permanent home in the village. Hope someone bought them a pint elsewhere.

Tuesday 16th March 2004

Chris Iwelumo scored a 25-yard screamer on his Albion debut in the 2-0 Division Two win at Chesterfield. Guy Butters also netted to leave the promotion-chasers in fourth, with nine games remaining.

Tuesday 16th March 2010

With the construction of Falmer at full speed, the club opened a presentation suite to show supporters footage of what the completed stadium would look like, and its high-tech facilities. From now, fans could view the works from a viewing platform in the south-east corner.

Wednesday 16th March 2011

The exterior banking that surrounds the West and South stands was secured using steel mesh and netting. Trees were then planted along the perimeter, as well as the corner where the North Stand meets the West.

Friday 17th March 1967

Brian Dear – who once scored five goals in 20 minutes for West Ham United – made the first of only seven appearances on loan from the Upton Park outfit. The club's first player signed in such a deal, the Plaistow-born inside-forward scored five times during his Goldstone stay but a £20,000 price tag was deemed too expensive. England's most capped player, Peter Shilton, regarded Dear to be the toughest opponent of his career.

Saturday 17th March 1973

Ken Beamish's strike earned Albion a draw against Sheffield Wednesday at Hillsborough. It was the first point for Pat Saward's team away from the Goldstone for nearly five months. Ten years later, to the day, genial Liverpudlian Jimmy Melia was appointed Albion manager.

Sunday 17th March 2013

Albion crushed Crystal Palace 3-0 in the Championship, with goals from Ulloa (2) and a stupendous direct free-kick from Spanish Dave (Lopez). It was the home side's first victory over the old enemy since 1988.

Tuesday 18th March 1986

Blackburn Rovers entertained Albion at Ewood Park. A gate of just 3,616 watched the visitors tear apart the home side. Terry Connor, Danny Wilson (2) and Dean Saunders scored in a 4-1 win which moved Chris Cattlin's men up to sixth place in Division Two.

Saturday 18th March 1995

Nicky Rust's run of five consecutive Third Division clean sheets came to an end in the 1-0 loss at York City.

Saturday 19th March 1932

Ernest 'Ernie' King made his debut in the 3-0 defeat at Fulham in the Third Division (South). The full-back, a sliding tackle expert, made 217 appearances without scoring.

Saturday 19th March 1983

Steve Gatting scored at Manchester United. The 1-1 First Division draw in front of 36,700 Old Trafford fans proved to be former United starlet Andy Ritchie's final game before being swapped for Leeds United's Terry Connor in a deal rated at £500,000.

Saturday 19th March 1988

Gary Chivers – who almost became a Malta international – joined Albion in a £40,000 deal from Watford. The popular defender began his career with Chelsea and, after making 252 appearances and scoring 16 times, moved to AFC Bournemouth in 1993. He enjoyed a long spell as a matchday club ambassador in the club's hospitality areas in the West Stand.

Sunday 19th March 2023

Fourth-tier Grimsby Town had knocked out five teams from divisions above them to reach their first FA Cup quarter-final for 84 years. The Mariners travelled to Sussex in their thousands and, resplendent in their fetching pink away kit, set about trying to make history. Deniz Undav fired Albion in front after six minutes.

Evan Ferguson added a superb second five minutes into the second period, stretching to bring down Alexis Mac Allister's clipped pass with his left foot, before stroking the ball into the bottom corner. The Irishman made it three on 70 minutes, Solly March grabbed a fourth with a diving header before Kaoru Mitoma's deflected 90th-minute shot snuck in to complete the scoring. The Grimsby fans did their club proud as Albion reached a third FA Cup semi-final in their history.

Friday 20th March 1970

A great day in the history of Brighton & Hove Albion – Tony Bloom was born! With the Albion coursing through his veins, he took over as chairman from Dick Knight in May 2009. The mathematics graduate left Manchester University, worked for Victor Chandler, created and sold a betting website, and amassed a personal fortune from property and finance. When the economic crisis increasingly looked like it would curtail stadium construction in 2009, Tony stepped in to underwrite the £93 million cost in unsecured, interest-free loans – an incredible gesture that essentially placed Albion on a firm financial footing for decades to come.

When asked about comparisons to Roman Abramovich, the professional poker player had this to say in *The Times*; "There are huge differences between us, and one of the most significant is that I have been a passionate Brighton fan for over 30 years. He [Abramovich] wanted to buy a Premier League and he chose Chelsea, and good luck to him for doing that. My Grandad Harry was vice-chairman of Brighton for nine years in the 1970s, my uncle Ray has been involved with the club for 20 years, and I saw my first match at the Goldstone Ground in 1978." Fast-forward to the 2020s and look what's happened!

Wednesday 20th March 1991

Garry Nelson replaced the injured Mike Small and grabbed a brace in the 2-0 Goldstone win over West Bromwich Albion. The win, in front of 6,676 fans, moved the Albion up two places to fifth. Above Brighton in the Division Two (Championship) table were Middlesbrough, Sheffield Wednesday, West Ham United and top-of-the-table, Oldham Athletic.

Saturday 20th March 1999

Phil King, Lee Doherty, Duncan McArthur and Keith McPherson all made their Albion debuts in the 0-0 Third Division draw at Hartlepool. Only McPherson made any impact, going on to make 37 appearances. The others each featured on three occasions.

Wednesday 20th March 2002

Despite submitting more than 7,000 drawings and 130,000 pages of text, Albion were asked for more details regarding the stadium planning application. If anyone ever suggests securing the Falmer site was easy, show them this fact!

Tuesday 20th March 2012

Albion beat Derby County 2-0 at home. Former Valencia star Vicente was inspirational, setting up both goals – for Íñigo Calderón and Ashley Barnes – in just his fourth start for the club. The victory, in the 38th Championship fixture of the season, sent the stripes up to fourth, and a play-off spot. It was the last win of the campaign.

Sunday 21st March 1965

Paul Rogers was born in Portsmouth. 'Dodge', as he is affectionately known by Albion fans, was a late starter. He joined Sheffield United from Sutton United as a 26-year-old in 1992 and represented Wigan Athletic and Notts County before settling in Sussex. Guaranteed a place in the history books, the former midfielder is best remembered for being club captain during the back-to-back championship triumphs of 2001 and 2002. He enjoyed a long career in Albion's commercial department before setting up his own business.

Saturday 21st March 1987

An Albion legend made his debut at Ipswich Town. John Crumplin began his Albion career as a winger and a succession of below-par showings resulted in barracking by some sections of the crowd. A move to right-back revitalised the Bath-born player and, with renewed confidence, he became the darling of the North Stand with some wholehearted performances. *Gull's Eye* released a 'Johnny Crumplin Football Genius' T-shirt – initially meant to be ironic – that became a collector's item.

Saturday 22nd March 1958

Crystal Palace cruised into a two-goal lead in front of 19,517 fans at the Goldstone Ground. Denis Foreman grabbed one back on the hour before Dave Sexton equalised with ten minutes remaining. Manager Billy Lane headed down the tunnel just as the final seconds were ticking down. Big centre-forward Peter Harburn nicked the winner with just five seconds on the clock to cue a wild pitch invasion from the North Stand by celebrating fans.

Monday 22nd March 1982

Manager Mike Bailey and chairman Mike Bamber hosted an 'Albion Forum', sponsored by Whitbread, at the Foyer Hall in The Brighton Centre.

Monday 22nd March 2010

The construction of the bridge over the A27 was nearing completion. More girders arrived on site, East Stand cladding was almost complete, and terracing was being added to the triple-decker West Stand.

Tuesday 22nd March 2011

Work to sow the pitch began at Falmer. Photographs – taken facing the stadium site from opposite the village pond – gave absolutely no indication of the super-modern and beautifully designed football arena just a few hundred yards away.

Monday 22nd March 2021

Former Albion player Frank Worthington died at the age of 72. The flamboyant forward played for more than 20 clubs including Huddersfield Town, Leicester City and Bolton Wanderers during a long career that stretched from 1966 to 1991. One of English football's great mavericks, Frank plotted up on the south coast from Southampton, aged 35, in 1984. He scored eight goals in 35 appearances in his solitary season and was offered another one-year contract but opted to join Tranmere Rovers as player-manager instead. A self-confessed playboy, Worthington undertook a medical at Liverpool in 1972 ahead of a proposed transfer to Anfield. On hearing of his high blood pressure, manager Bill Shankly sent him to Majorca for a week for health reasons but after encounters with five separate women, including a former Miss Great Britain, he returned with even higher blood pressure and the transfer fell through.

Friday 23rd March 1973

Ian Goodwin scored the only goal in the Goldstone friendly win over Spartak Moscow. The Russians – who included five internationals in their line-up – played the Albion as a warm-up for their Cup Winners' Cup quarter-final against AC Milan.

Tuesday 23rd March 2004

Early Day Motion (EDM) – a motion, expressed as a single sentence, tabled by Members of Parliament for debate 'on an early day' (namely an unspecified date in the future) – 889 was tabled. Its 145 signatures was the biggest number of MPs to support a sports-based EDM.

Wednesday 23rd March 2011

The club website announced that Albion fan Neil English had become the 10,000th season ticket holder at the American Express Community Stadium. Managing director Ken Brown confirmed the club had now sold over 14,000 tickets, including approximately 2,600 corporate seats in the 1901 Club. He said; "We have been advising fans that the only way they can guarantee a seat next season is by purchasing a season ticket. Some fans may be waiting to see which division we will be playing in – but that may be too late."

Saturday 23rd March 2013

In the early hours of Saturday morning, at a packed specially designed marquee in Jubilee Square, Brighton – and after nearly seven days of blood, sweat and tears – Albion in the Community's (AITC) Dan Lawson broke the world record for the longest distance run on a treadmill in a week. The 40-year-old, who was joined in the final hours by Tony Bloom, Paul Barber and crews from BBC and ITV local news, ran 518 miles to beat the previous record of 517.63 miles set in 2012 by Sharon Gayter, a lecturer at Teesside University. During his mammoth run to raise funds for AITC, 'The Running Dan' burned off nearly 60,000 calories and ran for up to 15 hours a day. Tony Bloom said; "What Dan has achieved is remarkable. Everyone at Brighton & Hove Albion and AITC is immensely proud of him."

Thursday 24th March 1881

William Jones was born in Staffordshire. 'Bullet' enjoyed two spells with the Albion – 1909–1912 and 1913–1920 – finding the target 69 times in 179 matches. The 5ft 5in striker was incredibly popular in Hove and on hanging up his boots undertook a variety of roles around the Goldstone Ground.

Saturday 24th March 1973

Tricia Burtenshaw was crowned Miss Albion at the Supporters' Club dance at the Arlington Hotel in Brighton.

Wednesday 24th March 2010

Lee Hendrie revealed to the club website that Albion's attractive style of football was the main factor behind his move to the south coast. The diminutive midfielder, who won an England cap in 1998, arrived from Derby County stating; "There are lots of teams in League One that like to play the ball long, but I want to get the ball down and play football, so that's my main reason for coming here. I spoke to Gus Poyet, and he has his ideas, and wants to play good football. I know it's a big club, wanting to go places, and they've started to get things right recently." The former Aston Villa man made eight appearances.

Wednesday 25th March 1903

W Ward had a better goals-to-game ratio than his namesake Peter, albeit in just three matches! On his debut the outside-right grabbed a brace in the 9-1 thumping of Hitchin Town and in his final appearance notched a hat-trick in the South East League fixture versus Bedford Queen's Engineering Works.

Saturday 25th March 1905

Albion enjoyed a 3-1 Goldstone Ground win over West Ham United in the Southern League Division One. On picking himself up after putting his side 2-1 ahead, Bertie Lyon was kicked by the Hammers' England goalkeeper Matt Kingsley. The crowd spilled on to the pitch and swarmed around the West Ham players. Ugly scenes ensued and when order was restored Kingsley was sent off and Lyon was carried to the dressing room to receive treatment.

Friday 25th March 1910

In the first of four games in just five days, Albion disposed of Exeter City in a 2-1 Southern League Division One win. The *Brighton & Hove Herald* reported that; "The gate amounted to £338 and over 4,000 bicycles were housed during the game. Longstaff opened the scoring. Needless to say, the great crowd cheered; the noise must have been heard miles away." The result saw Albion cement their position at the top.

Saturday 25th March 1972

Pat Saward dropped skipper John Napier, in favour of Ian Goodwin, for the visit of Third Division leaders Aston Villa. Albion triumphed 2-1 with goals in either half from Willie Irvine and Kit Napier, in front of 28,833 Goldstone fans. Irvine's superb strike was eventually voted runner-up in Match of the Day's Goal of the Season competition.

Saturday 25th March 1989

"Football was very different in Saudi Arabia. In one match the keeper was lobbed by an attacker and his whole team dropped to their knees to pray. The ball bounced over the crossbar. They danced around in delight – personally I blame it on the Astroturf," recalled Albion midfielder Geoff Cooper, who was signed for £4,000 from Bognor Regis Town, making nine Albion appearances between 1987 and 1989.

Saturday 25th March 2023

Dogma unveiled their Pride of the South Coast mural. Depicting Lewis Dunk, Tariq Lamptey, Pascal Gross, Robert Sánchez and Solly March and situated at the bottom of Farm Road, Hove (visible to westbound traffic on Western Road), the piece of art was designed by the fanzine's Iain Budgen and painted by SinnaOne. One of just a handful of football murals in the UK that have originated (and been paid for) by an independent fan group instead of a club or organisation, it marked the realisation of one of *Dogma*'s founding objectives: bringing the club, and fan culture, to the heart of the city via street art projects and events.

Saturday 26th March 1910

The crowd were in hysterics as the referee got caught up in the action and received a swift kick to the knee. Mr Muir had to be on his toes at the beginning of the second half as Albion netted three times in four minutes against New Brompton in a 5-1 Goldstone victory. It was the second of three games in four days!

Wednesday 27th March 1912

Brighton & Hove Albion Supporters' Club was formed – one of the earliest in the country – by Harry Edwards.

Saturday 27th March 1965

Promising right-half Barrie Rees was tragically killed in a car crash on the A5 en route to his parents' house in Rhyl. The Welshman had arrived less than three months earlier from Everton and had already made a big impression among the Goldstone faithful.

League champions in 1963, the Toffees were looking to trim their extensive squad the following campaign. Albion had Rees watched several times and moved quickly to secure his services for £8,000. Everton manager Harry Catterick told reporters; "We felt that Rees would stand a better chance of regular league football if we let him go to Brighton. Our position is that we have many fine youngsters coming through from our youth policy and we did not wish to stand in Rees' way." In his 12 appearances as a wing-half, it was clear Albion had signed a player with potential to develop into a mainstay of the team, and a possible full Wales international.

He shone in the Fourth Division and in his memoir *Mad Man: From the Gutter to the Stars, the Ad Man who Saved Brighton*, Dick Knight wrote that Barrie was 'one of Brighton's classiest-ever players'. Barrie turned 21 a month after his move south and would drive his Austin Mini (purchased from club-mate Bobby Baxter) on the long journey back to visit family when opportunities arose. On this day, he drove north through the early hours to celebrate his uncle's large win on the football pools. Tragically, he pulled out into the path of an oncoming lorry on the A5, near Nuneaton. Barrie's girlfriend, Barbara, gave birth to their child, a son, seven months later. So much promise, so young. A sad day in the history of the Albion.

Saturday 27th March 1976

A memorable day in Brighton & Hove Albion folklore. Manager Peter Taylor decided to bring on a slightly built 20-year-old forward to replace leading scorer Fred Binney at league leaders Hereford United. With his first touch, in his first Albion appearance, Peter Ward netted after 50 seconds. A legend was born...

Saturday 28th March 1998

Anti-Albion Save Withdean Environment Action Team (SWEAT) distributed a six-page leaflet around the Westdene and Withdean areas of Brighton advising residents to object to plans for Albion to use the ground for home matches.

Saturday 29th March 1980

Gary Williams gave the Albion a second 1-0 league victory over Nottingham Forest; the only club to achieve the double over the European Cup holders during the season. Before the match, world middleweight champion Alan Minter was presented with a tracksuit – in the club's new all-blue colours for the following campaign – embroidered with his name, by chairman Mike Bamber.

Saturday 29th March 1997

Despised chairman Bill Archer was in attendance as Albion went down 2-1 at Chester City. When asked by a fan when there might be an announcement on the mediation talks his reply was; "What's it got to do with you?"

Tuesday 29th March 2011

Albion, unbeaten in six games as they chased the incredible milestone of winning every game in March, faced Dagenham & Redbridge. Standing in their way was a very bobbly pitch and the moonwalking and multicolour-haired former Brighton striker Bas Savage. The Essex outfit's winger, Danny Green, looked the most likely threat, marauding down the right flank. In an even contest, the visitors finally broke the deadlock with their only real chance on the hour. A scissor-kick cross from Craig Noone was met at the far post by Glenn Murray whose close-range volley crashed off the underside of the bar and into the net for his 20th of the season.

The victory took Albion's lead at the top back to 13 points, with just eight games remaining. The goal should have stuck in the throat of Southampton boss Nigel Adkins – who suggested earlier in the campaign that Gus Poyet's men would have to 'keep up' with Saints to achieve promotion – who was looking on from the main stand. The result made it a post-war record of eight successive victories and equalled the Football League record of eight wins in one calendar month. A fantastic achievement by all concerned; 24 points, 13 goals scored and just four conceded.

Friday 30th March 1962

One of only three Albion players to progress through the club's ranks to full England international honours, the others are Tommy Cook and Lewis Dunk, Gary Stevens was born in Hillingdon, Middlesex. The versatile defender/midfielder was released by Ipswich Town in 1978 and arrived at the Goldstone as an apprentice.

A reserve team place cemented, manager Alan Mullery decided to throw the youngster into the First Division melting pot to replace the injured Mark Lawrenson against, ironically, Ipswich Town. The 17-year-old didn't disappoint and was a mainstay for the next three seasons, winning Player of the Season in 1983 and scoring in the never-to-be-forgotten FA Cup Final in the same year.

Saturday 30th March 1968

Only 5,813 were at the Goldstone Ground to see Kit Napier's strike in the 1-0 Division Three win over Southport. The poor crowd was blamed on the BBC's live coverage of the Grand National.

Wednesday 30th March 1983

Having scored nine league goals for the bottom team in the First Division, Michael Robinson was called up by the Republic of Ireland for the last time as an Albion player and played in the 1-0 European Championship qualifying win in Malta.

Saturday 31st March 1934

Oliver 'Buster' Brown made his debut in the 3-0 Third Division (South) victory at Gillingham. The powerful forward would go on to score 45 goals in just 66 appearances.

Saturday 31st March 1956

This top-of-the-table showdown against Leyton Orient was the second Albion game in as many days. The majority of the 25,550 fans crammed into Brisbane Road went home disappointed. A single second-half goal from Malcolm Stephens secured a priceless victory for Billy Lane's side who were two points behind the Os but had played two games more.

Friday 31st March 1972

A Torquay United defender admitted a handball to the referee which allowed Albion back into this Third Division Goldstone fixture. Just under 28,000 fans witnessed a 3-1 victory. Imagine that happening in this day and age?!

Scars & Stripes – April 1998:
A liar performing well in front of the TV cameras.

© *Scars & Stripes*

APRIL

Saturday 1st April 1989

Albion were 2-1 up against Manchester City at the Goldstone Ground. The Maine Road outfit were incensed as chief 'ball-boy' Keith Cuss appeared to head a ball further out of play as the promotion-challenging visitors chased an equaliser. The home side held on for a vital three points in the battle against relegation from the Second Division.

Tuesday 1st April 1997

Barnet were the basement visitors for the last-ever floodlit game at the Goldstone Ground. Ian Baird chested in the only goal, in front of the North Stand, to win the game for the bottom-placed Seagulls. Steve Gritt's rejuvenated side were now just two points behind both Hartlepool United and Hereford United with five games to play.

Monday 1st April 2002

Visitors Bristol City conceded the first goal, a glancing Junior Lewis header from a Paul Watson free kick, but equalised through Tommy Doherty. The end-to-end contest was nearly over – Albion needed three points to go top of Division Two, while the Robins were chasing a play-off spot – as Gary Hart floated over a measured ball. Substitute Lee Steele flung himself goalward and connected to make it 2-1. The final whistle blew and Albion were league leaders.

Thursday 1st April 2010

Southampton were the visitors at Withdean. The south-coast derby with South Coast Club – so christened by *The Sun* after they banned photographers from St Mary's – had added spice with former boss Dean Wilkins in the dugout and Albion youth product Dean Hammond in the Saints midfield. In the 12th minute, Andrew Crofts laid the ball back to the edge of the area, and Elliott Bennett arrived to plant the ball emphatically past Kelvin Davis.

Hammond got the slightest of touches on Jon Otsemobor's free-kick four minutes before the interval. The Hastings-born schemer ensured a career's worth of vitriol from the Albion support after celebrating wildly in front of the South Stand. On-loan Ashley Barnes converted LuaLua's cross (66th) to make it 2-1 but Lee Barnard salvaged a point one minute from time. Meanwhile, a few miles up the road at Falmer, the North Stand's skeleton framework was taking shape nicely.

Saturday 2nd April 1983

Albion enjoyed their fifth successive win on this date. Despite beating Tottenham Hotspur 2-1 in front of 20,359 fans at the Goldstone, the Seagulls were still bottom of the First Division.

Tuesday 2nd April 1985

Trevor Aylott fired past Graham Moseley to give Crystal Palace a 1-0 win at Selhurst Park. Then tragedy struck. Opposing defender Henry Hughton – brother of Chris – scythed down Republic of Ireland striker Gerry Ryan in a shocking challenge which could also be described as common assault. The Irishman's leg was broken in two places, ending his playing career. Spurred on by their team-mate's injury, the Albion fought back, and Danny Wilson equalised within ten minutes. A few weeks later, legendary Albion reporter John Vinicombe highlighted how the winger bore no grudges, describing; "the immense dignity and true manliness that Ryan displayed in refusing to condemn or indeed utter any harsh word against the player responsible. Where others have sued and raged, slandered, cursed and threatened, Ryan said nothing."

Thursday 2nd April 2021

Albion's deputy chairman and chief executive Paul Barber, technical director Dan Ashworth and head coach Graham Potter each took a significant voluntary pay cut for the next three months to help protect jobs at the club as the realisation of COVID-19 restrictions began to bite. In a staff communiqué, Barber explained; "To help Tony to ensure none of our core staff suffer a wage reduction during this uncertain period for our business, Graham Potter, Dan Ashworth and I have voluntarily taken a pay reduction for the months of April, May and June. We consider ourselves to be very fortunate to be working for the best of clubs at the most difficult of times, so it is entirely appropriate that we play a very small part in reducing the financial burden on Tony."

Saturday 2nd April 2022

Brighton & Hove Albion's Cerebral Palsy team beat Derby County Community Trust CP 4-0 at the University of Northampton.

Tuesday 2nd April 2024

Albion released their accounts for the historic 2022/23 season. The revenue matched the performances on the pitch as profits after tax rose from £24.1 million in the previous financial year to £122.8 million. The turnover for the period was the highest ever – up by 17.2% to £204.5 million, compared to £174.5 million in 2021/22. Paul Barber said; "For the first time since Tony made his first interest-free loan to the club back in 2007, we have been able to make a substantial re-payment to him reducing the loan balance from £406.5 million to £373.3 million."

Wednesday 3rd April 1974

A gate of 9,851 witnessed Barry Bridges, Ronnie Welch, Billy McEwan and Ronnie Howell hit the target in the Third Division 4-1 thrashing of Cambridge United. It was the best home win during Brian Clough's tenure.

Saturday 3rd April 1982

Three coachloads of supporters from France arrived at the Goldstone Ground to watch a First Division fixture with Southampton. Many of the 150 travellers in the South Stand left their homes at 3am to catch the ferry from Dieppe. Albion support in the area across the Channel had grown to such an extent that another two trips were organised. A shop window in Grand Rue was decked out in blue and white, and action photos from recent matches.

Neil McNab's first-half penalty earned a 1-1 draw in front of 20,977 fans. However, it was another two points dropped in the quest for a UEFA Cup spot and Mike Bailey's side remained in 11th place.

Sunday 3rd April 2011

In what promised to be a manic month of work at Falmer, the first blue seats were bolted on to the West Stand Upper tier terracing, nearest the away end.

Saturday 4th April 1908

A 2-0 Southern League win over Millwall was the first under Jack Robson's stewardship. Frank Scott-Walford's departure to Leeds City had opened the manager's door for the former goalkeeper who would build Albion's first successful team by signing players such as Charlie Webb, Billy Booth and Bullet Jones.

The Southern League title, Southern Charity Cup and Charity Shield successes alerted Manchester United who acquired his services in 1914.

Monday 4th April 1910

Albion lifted their first trophy of a momentous season with a 1-0 win over Brentford. The Southern Professional Charity Cup Final was played at Stamford Bridge and it took extra-time to separate the two sides. Bullet Jones scored the decisive goal before the 3,000 spectators saw skipper Joe Leeming presented with the trophy.

Saturday 4th April 2009

On a sunny day, over 2,000 Albion fans made the trip to MK Dons. A thoroughly depressing performance – a 2-0 reverse – meant the stripes were now six points adrift in the relegation mire of League One with just seven games remaining. Only a miracle could save us now.

Saturday 5th April 1952

One of the most experienced men ever to represent the Albion was born in Liverpool. Dennis Mortimer played over 200 times for Coventry City before attracting the attention of Aston Villa. Success followed with a 3-2 League Cup Final win over Everton in 1977, the league title in 1981 and the European Cup win against Bayern Munich in 1982, when the midfielder wore the captain's armband. Dennis joined the Seagulls in August 1985 and was a virtual-ever-present the following campaign. He left for Birmingham City a year later.

Saturday 5th April 1980

Old foes Albion and Crystal Palace met for the first time in the top-flight at Selhurst Park. Peter Ward gave Albion the lead in front of a 31,466 partisan crowd but the home side equalised after the break.

Friday 6th April 1990

Sergei Gotsmanov scored a wonderful goal in the 2-0 Goldstone win over Hull City. "Skipping round tackles and holding your arms aloft BEFORE slotting the ball into the net is the stuff of which dreams are made," raved manager Barry Lloyd.

Tuesday 6th April 1999

Albion's ninth defeat in ten games – the other was a draw – resulted in the sack for manager Jeff Wood. The 3-1 'home' defeat to Cambridge United was contested in front of a paltry 2,621 fans at Gillingham.

Saturday 6th April 2002

Albion were on the verge of the First Division (second tier) after a 1-0 win at Peterborough United. Leading scorer Bobby Zamora volleyed home (63rd) in front of nearly 4,000 vociferous Albion fans in the Moyes End for his 32nd goal of the season. Gary Hart's leg break after just eight minutes put a severe dampener on the celebrations.

Saturday 6th April 2019

Albion's first FA Cup semi-final since 1983. Gabriel Jesus' stooping header after only four minutes, converted from Kevin de Bruyne's right-wing cross, was Manchester City's only goal in an uninspiring contest. Brighton's players were given a standing ovation at the final whistle for the endeavour shown to keep them in contention right until the end. Albion didn't lack application; they just didn't have the pace or goal threat their build-up work possibly deserved. The starting line-up was Ryan, Montoya, Duffy, Dunk, Bernardo, Pröpper, Stephens, Bissouma (Locadia 82), Knockaert, Murray (Andone 66), Jahanbakhsh (Izquierdo 70).

Saturday 7th April 1984

A very young-looking Jonathan Pearce, the new sports producer on Southern Sound, wrote his first column for the matchday programme against Grimsby Town.

Wednesday 7th April 1993

Forward Kurt Nogan started a goalscoring run of seven in five consecutive games with a strike in the 3-1 Goldstone Second Division (third tier) win over Mansfield Town. The gate was just 4,731.

Sunday 7th April 2002

Reading drew 2-2 at Tranmere Rovers to hand Albion a second successive promotion, without kicking a ball!

Friday 7th April 2006

Planning permission for Albion's new home at Falmer was sensationally quashed after John Prescott admitted making a blunder in his letter of approval! The Deputy Prime Minister made a fundamental factual error when he said 'Yes' last October, and reconsidered the application. In his approval correspondence, Prescott made a number of references to the arena being inside the development boundary of Brighton & Hove, as designated by the Local Plan. But, as Lewes District Council pointed out, only a small part of the stadium site at Village Way was inside the boundary.

Friday 7th April 2017

On-loan left-back Sébastien Pocognoli scored a tremendous direct free-kick in front of the delirious travelling Sussex hoards at Queens Park Rangers. The Belgian's strike helped Albion to a 2-1 victory in the capital to keep Chris Hughton's men well and truly in the hunt for automatic promotion. After a successful spell on the coast Pocognoli went home and played for Standard Liège before finishing his career at Tony Bloom's other club Royale Union Saint-Gilloise, where he was manager (as of 2024).

Friday 8th April 1955

Peter Harburn enjoyed his Albion debut in the 1-1 draw at Priestfield. The big and powerful centre-forward joined the Brentford ground staff in 1946, then the Royal Navy as a boy seaman a year later. In 1949/50 he represented Uxbridge in the Corinthian League and the following year played for both Portsmouth and Albion's reserve teams, before finally signing up for the stripes full-time in 1955.

Saturday 8th April 1978

With Albion needing the two points for their chase, Alan Mullery took a gamble at Ewood Park with a 4-2-4 formation. Both sides were in the promotion hunt but a defeat would almost certainly have meant Second Division football the following season. Eric Potts scored the decisive goal.

Tuesday 8th April 1980

Two strikes from Peter Ward, and an own goal, secured a 3-0 win over Wolverhampton Wanderers at the Goldstone Ground. It was the first league meeting between the clubs in Sussex and earned a double for Alan Mullery's side. It happened the next four seasons the clubs faced each other.

Wednesday 8th April 1998

Another bad day for the Albion. Brighton & Hove Council revealed they had received 850 letters of objection regarding the club's use of Withdean – and just 129 in favour.

Tuesday 8th April 2014

In typically understated fashion, Albion fanzine *The Seagull Love Review* announced its retirement on page seven of issue 58; 'TSLR Towers was in the process of being repossessed. Seriously though, we can't be bothered with doing a fanzine next season, so we'd just like to thank you for reading this inane column for six years. You'll still find us online, and in various pubs near Albion matches.' A great production incorporating traditional fanzine values, TSLR oversaw huge progression in the club's history, both on and off the pitch.

Sunday 9th April 1876

Alf Sharp, the first professional footballer signed by a Brighton club, was born in the town. The inside-forward played for Brighton United before joining the Albion in 1901 and making just one appearance, against Shepherd's Bush.

Friday 9th April 1971

A Good Friday crowd of 22,687 – nearly 13,000 more than the season's average – were crammed into the Goldstone for the visit of Aston Villa. It was the famous club's first campaign in the third tier, but the Midlands side had no answer to Kit Napier's second-half strike. The victory left the Villans in third, while Albion propped up the table, one place above Gillingham.

Saturday 9th April 2011

Evoking memories of the much-loved Goldstone Ground, the first seats were installed in the brand-new North Stand at Falmer. The terrace of the same name at Albion's home of 95 years saw much drama and intrigue during its lifetime; the euphoria of promotions, derby wins, championships and amazing goals were tempered with the memories of the old lady's untimely demise and the pain and heartache supporters suffered during the hated former regime's disastrous reign. Onwards and upwards to Falmer, but the Goldstone's legacy will never be forgotten.

Monday 10th April 1961

The Goldstone Ground switched on its distinctive 'drenchlighting' floodlights, which cost £13,523, for the first time in a friendly against six-times champions of Denmark, Boldklubben Frem. After two bankruptcies (1993 and 2010) and demotion to the Danish non-league, the club have bounced back from the brink and now ply their trade in the second division of Danish football (as of 2024).

Saturday 10th April 1965

Ex-England striker Bobby Smith and defender Norman Gall grabbed the goals in the 2-1 Goldstone victory over Tranmere Rovers. The 24,017 attendance was the third-highest crowd in the country after First Division Everton and Newcastle United. To put the feat into perspective – Albion's game was in the Fourth Division!

Saturday 10th April 1982

Terry Neill's Arsenal were the visitors in front of 21,019 fans at the Goldstone Ground. Andy Ritchie and Michael Robinson both struck in the second half to send the Albion up to tenth in the First Division with a 2-1 victory.

Sunday 10th April 2011

The stunning interiors of Falmer Stadium were gradually coming to life. The dressing rooms had taken delivery of their pine-panelled sunken baths, the cooking equipment for the various concourses had arrived, while the stunning curved ceiling detail in the main function areas glided above the activity below.

Tuesday 11th April 1904

After a meeting at the Royal Pavilion, Brighton & Hove Albion Football Club became a limited company. George Broadbridge, the club's first chairman, was joined on the board by directors Reg Alderton, Charles Bunker, Tom Cooter, Frederick Stevens, Albert Grinyer (licensee of the Albion Inn) and Ben Parker.

Saturday 11th April 1953

Steve Burtenshaw made his Albion debut in the 5-1 victory at Exeter City. The wing-half came from a famous local footballing family and joined the Goldstone ground staff after leaving Portslade Secondary School in 1951. Granted a testimonial in 1963, after 16 years' service, Steve held a variety of coaching roles, including posts at Arsenal, Queens Park Rangers and Sheffield Wednesday. He scored three times in 252 appearances for the club.

Saturday 11th April 1998

Bring Home the Albion issued 'You are Killing the Albion' leaflets to fans across Sussex, urging them to write in support to their respective councillors. The battle to save the club from extinction was now well and truly underway.

Monday 12th April 1971

It was a very happy Easter for the Albion. A 3-2 Third Division win over Bradford City at Valley Parade, in front of 4,109 fans, was the club's third over the long weekend; the only side in England who managed to earn six out of six points. Pat Saward was rewarded with the first Manager of the Month award for an Albion boss.

Saturday 12th April 1986

Chairman Brian Bedson wrote an open letter to Albion fans regarding information reported in the *Evening Argus* suggesting that the club did not want promotion to the First Division. "The club amassed a deficit of over £1.3 million on the trading of players during the ten-year period prior to me joining the board in 1983. All too often this club has been bailed out by selling its assets in the past. The sale of Lawrenson, Robinson and Stevens were all examples." In the same programme, manager Chris Cattlin revealed how Colin Clarke had been recommended. "He had been given two free transfers and suffered a broken leg in the recent past. I spoke to ten Fourth Division managers and their assessment was mixed, so I declined to sign him." Clarke went on to score over 100 league goals for AFC Bournemouth, Portsmouth, Southampton and Queens Park Rangers – the latter two in the top-flight – and become Northern Ireland's second-highest scorer.

Monday 12th April 1999

Albion began its campaign for a 'Yes Yes' vote in the referendum over Falmer at Hove Town Hall: 'Yes' to a stadium, and 'Yes' to a stadium at Falmer. A website was launched, posters were placed around the city, and every household was leafleted – twice. Wearing a green 'Yes Yes' T-shirt, new manager Micky Adams walked on to the stage to a standing ovation.

Tuesday 12th April 2011

Casper Ankergren conceded a Withdean goal after just 21 seconds against Dagenham & Redbridge. Not the most auspicious of starts as Albion sought the three points required to guarantee promotion to the Championship. Craig Noone was creating havoc down the left with two rasping shots, one of which hit the bar, before Iñigo Calderón converted from close range. Before the Withdean faithful could regain their composure, leading marksman Glenn Murray made it two. Albion were a tad lacklustre as the second period began and the relegation-battlers rattled off their second (48th) and third (53rd) goals in quick succession.

News filtered through that Southampton were losing at Rochdale. Liam Bridcutt fired in a cannonball 25-yarder (56th) and then substitute Ashley Barnes nodded home from a corner with his first touch in the 63rd minute. Phew! Four goals in 15 minutes. Despite the jitters, Gus Poyet's men held on to secure a fourth promotion in 12 Withdean seasons – a remarkable achievement. The League One table read: Albion, played 41, 90 points; South Coast Club, played 40, 74 points. That is a gap of 16 points. Yes, Mr Adkins, we are keeping up! If you missed this in 2011, have a look at Nigel Adkins comments about the Albion around the time.

Monday 13th April 1914

Joe Leeming was granted a benefit game and stepped down from the first team to play in the reserves against Southampton on Easter Monday, when a good turnout could be expected. Around 3,500 supporters attended the 3-2 win at the Goldstone, netting the full-back £118, which was £11,271.01 in 2024 terms.

Friday 13th April 1979

Albion had their second-highest gate of the campaign, 30,859, for the Second Division visit of Charlton Athletic. After just 11 minutes, following a partially cleared free-kick, Paul Clark smashed the ball home from 25 yards. Midway through the second half, Welshman Peter O'Sullivan tore down the left flank on a trademark run and centred for Malcolm Poskett. The striker failed to make a connection but panicked the defender into scoring an own goal. The win put Albion top, two points from Sunderland with Crystal Palace and Stoke City a further point away. It was the first victory on this date since the club had joined the Football League in 1920. As of April 2024, there had been three more.

Tuesday 13th April 1999

Just 2,207 hardy souls were present at Priestfield for Micky Adams' first 'home' game in charge – a 1-0 win over Shrewsbury Town.

Saturday 13th April 2002

The penultimate fixture of the season – the World Cup necessitated an early conclusion – was at home to Swindon Town. A forgettable game will be consigned to a small section of the history books. What will be remembered, though, were the events after the final whistle. Brentford's draw at Queens Park Rangers, and Reading's share of four goals at Peterborough United, meant it was Albion's title. Club captain Paul Rogers lifted the league championship for a second successive season.

Saturday 14th April 2001

A healthy contingent from Sussex was present at Home Park to see Albion take on Plymouth Argyle. Three points would be enough for an automatic promotion spot from the Third Division – despite the fact there were six games remaining – as long as Hartlepool lost, and Rochdale failed to win. Paul Brooker netted from a corner after three minutes and Bobby Zamora struck 13 minutes later to send the visitors in 2-0 up at half-time. Rochdale drew at Macclesfield Town while Hull City took the lead at Victoria Park, and kept it until the final whistle; Albion were up but could they carry on and win the title?

Sunday 14th April 1991

Martín Montoya Torralbo was born in Gavà, Spain. The right-back represented Barcelona and Valencia before arriving on the south coast for £6.3 million in August 2018. After 56 appearances in two seasons, the defender moved to Real Betis. As of summer 2024, he can be found plying his trade with Aris, who are based in Greece, not Essex.

Saturday 14th April 2012

Albion were comprehensively beaten 6-0 at West Ham. A Vaz Tê hat-trick helped to condemn Gus Poyet's men to a third straight defeat to sit eighth in the Championship table.

Wednesday 15th April 1970

An inconsistent run now meant promotion could be achieved if Orient lost their five games in hand, and Albion beat Mansfield Town at the Goldstone Ground. A 2-1 defeat left the Seagulls on 55 points in fifth. The east London club went up as eventual Third Division champions.

Saturday 15th April 1978

Tottenham Hotspur made their first league visit to the Goldstone Ground. It was the London club's only season away from the top-flight in 28 years and 32,647 fans saw a 3-1 win secured with goals from Paul Clark, Graham Winstanley and Eric Potts. As a consequence of the violence by Spurs fans, a perimeter fence was erected the following season.

Friday 15th April 1988

In the matchday programme, Albion midfielder Adrian Owers looked into the future by predicting the end of the back pass to the goalkeeper. It became law four years later. In 2009, he represented England in FIFA's Senior World Cup.

Saturday 15th April 2023

In what proved to be a warm-up to his Goal of the Season strike a few weeks later, Julio Enciso scored an absolute beauty at Stamford Bridge as Albion came back from a goal down to beat Frank Lampard's Chelsea 2-1. The Paraguayan teenager collected possession 35 yards out, took a couple of strides forward and thwacked a right-footed piledriver winner that arrowed into the top left-hand corner. Few goalkeepers would have had a chance of saving it, even with extra arms. Substitute Danny Welbeck had levelled Conor Gallagher's deflected strike. Albion remained seventh in the Premier League table. Chelsea were 11th.

Wednesday 16th April 1969

Centre-half John Napier won the club's inaugural Player of the Season award. Alex Dawson and John Templeman were runners-up, with Dave Turner fourth. The following players have collected the coveted award twice: Norman Gall (1971, 1974), Steve Foster (1980, 1993), Danny Cullip (2000, 2003), Bobby Zamora (2001, 2002), Liam Bridcutt (2012, 2013), Lewis Dunk (2020, 2021). But one player has won it thrice – Pascal Gross in 2018, 2023 and 2024.

Saturday 16th April 1983

Hundreds of coaches departed the Greyhound Stadium and snaked their way to north London for the FA Cup semi-final. Albion had avoided Manchester United and Arsenal and were drawn against Sheffield Wednesday at Highbury. Jimmy Case continued his goalscoring run – this time in the away colours of yellow – by smashing a bending 35-yard free-kick against the underside of the bar, and in, to give the Albion a 14th-minute lead in front of 54,627 fans.

On a beautiful sunny day, Yugoslav international midfielder Ante Mirocevic scrambled home a very scrappy equaliser (57th) before Michael Robinson swivelled and shot (78th) to fire the Seagulls to Wembley for the first time in their 82-year history! A day no Albion fan will ever forget.

Wednesday 16th April 1986

It was popular manager Chris Cattlin's last game as Albion manager as the North Stand held up banners pleading for the former left-back to stay. The rock shop boss was quoted as saying that he 'managed the club because he wanted to, not because he needed to.'

Monday 16th April 1990

Not quite as successful as his brother Marco, Ricardo Gabbiadini played for just 14 minutes in an Albion shirt. The forward replaced Kevin Bremner in the 3-0 Second Division defeat at Portsmouth.

Tuesday 16th April 1991

History was made at Portsmouth's Fratton Park. The first Romanian to play in the Football League, Stefan Iovan, made his Albion debut. The defender played in two European Cup finals with Steaua Bucharest – beating Barcelona on penalties in 1986 and losing 4-0 to AC Milan in 1989 – and won 34 caps for his country.

Wednesday 16th April 1994

'Johnny Crumplin, Football Genius!' reverberated around the Racecourse Ground in Wrexham. The right-back scored direct from a corner, falling over as he struck the ball, in the 3-1 win. Class is permanent.

Friday 16th April 2011

A poignant day in the construction of Albion's new home as a 'working days until handover 28' sign appeared under the South Stand. The West Stand Upper seating was completed, the pitch perimeter Astroturf was in place, while – if you looked carefully – the first green shoots of the playing surface were heading skyward. A gap where the white seagull will fly appeared among the blue seats of the North Stand. A 'Well Done Gus and Team' banner was proudly displayed from the East Stand.

Saturday 16th April 2011

Could Albion wrap up the title at Walsall? Over 2,000 fans made the journey to the Banks's Stadium to see if Gus Poyet's men could secure a third divisional championship in ten years. In the fifth minute, Adam El-Abd flicked on Elliott Bennett's free-kick at the near post and Iñigo Calderón knocked the loose ball home for his eighth of the season, equalling Paul Watson's seasonal record – in 2000/01, also a title-winning campaign – as the club's highest-scoring full-back. 1-0 Albion.

The Saddlers soon equalised (11th) but Glenn Murray reinvigorated the party just after half-time (47th), glancing in a header from a Bennett corner. With the away end rocking, Bennett fittingly crowned the title with a thunderous strike from just outside the box in the last minute. On the final whistle, Albion fans invaded the pitch, and the players and management came out to join them when the playing surface was cleared. The fans could relax in the four remaining games, but the manager wanted 100 points.

Saturday 16th April 2022

You wait around for ages for a win then two turn up in a week. Albion headed to north London for the second successive Saturday to face a Tottenham Hotspur side sitting in fourth place and fighting for a Champions League berth. The Sussex men, fresh from dispatching Arsenal 2-1 at the Emirates seven days earlier, left it very late as Leandro Trossard beat Lloris with a fine finish with the outside of his right foot to seal the three points in the 90th minute. The result lifted Graham Potter's men to tenth in the Premier League table.

Saturday 17th April 1982

The end-of-season slump started here. A Michael Robinson effort at Notts County didn't make a dent in the Magpies' tally of four. Just a couple of months earlier Mike Bailey's side had been in contention for a UEFA Cup place. Six defeats in the last seven games ended the European dream. Final score at Meadow Lane: Magpies 4, Seagulls 1.

Monday 17th April 2006

It was the third-to-last game of the season and Sheffield Wednesday were the visitors to Withdean Stadium. Albion had to win to have any chance of remaining in the Championship; the Owls were one place, and seven points, above. Gary Hart turned the ball into his own net after just eight minutes and Burton O'Brien rounded Wayne Henderson to fire into an empty net with 20 minutes remaining. Dean Hammond received his marching orders towards the final whistle to end two battling years just one division away from the Premiership.

Saturday 17th April 2017

Championship leaders Brighton & Hove Albion were promoted to the Premier League for the very first time after beating relegation-threatened Wigan Athletic at Falmer. Albion had to wait for Huddersfield Town to lose at Derby County in the 5pm kick-off before the return to the top-flight after 34 years could be confirmed. Glenn Murray fired Albion ahead from the edge of the box (37th) and Solly March made it two (65th) before one-time Albion target Nick Powell's header made for a nervy final five minutes. Chris Hughton's men had bounced back from the near-miss of 2015/16, winning 28 of their 43 matches, bettering last season's total of 89 points – with three games remaining. Albion's promotion party came almost 20 years to the day since they were less than 30 minutes from dropping out of the Football League in the do-or-die last game of the 1996/97 season at Hereford United.

Promotion to the Premier League was worth an estimated £170 million to the club and Albion manager Chris Hughton told BBC Radio 5 Live his players were up for the challenge of promotion straight away, despite the heartbreak of the previous campaign; "It had something to do with how the season ended last season, but I think it was more the fact that the players enjoyed being up that end of the table, competing, getting into the play-offs. I think it was a conscious decision that they wanted that again, and the signs were there early in the season. We recruited well, in the summer, but it was real steely determination from the players that got us promoted."

Sam Baldock, Oliver Norwood and David Stockdale were among the happy players who crowd-surfed their way through a train to Brighton, from Falmer, for the promotion party. On arrival at the station, players were carried shoulder-high down Queens Road as the city rejoiced. What a night!

Wednesday 18th April 1951

Albion historians were reaching for their scrapbooks as the team smashed the best-ever victory in the Football League (equalled in 1965) with a 9-1 annihilation of Newport County at the Goldstone. Both clubs were lying in mid-table as the home side went in at the break two up. Then the floodgates opened. Johnny McNichol scored four, while Ken Bennett (2) and Doug Keene also featured on the scoresheet. Des Tennant and Jack Mansell both scored penalties.

Saturday 18th April 1981

Albion completed the league double over Crystal Palace at Selhurst Park. John Gregory (2) and Gordon Smith netted in the resounding 3-0 victory.

Saturday 19th April 1980

The penultimate home game of the season resulted in a 2-1 win over Middlesbrough but events off the pitch grabbed the headlines. A few hours after the last of the 20,427 fans had made their way home, the South Stand ignited in flames. The wooden seating and supporting structure was destroyed, leaving just the roof. The stand re-opened as an all-seater the following season.

Friday 19th April 1991

Steve Cook was born in Hastings. The defender made his first-team debut during the amazing League Cup third-round victory over Manchester City on 24th September 2008. The 17-year-old replaced right-back Andy Whing in the 85th minute as Albion stunned the recently rich City in a penalty shoot-out (5-3) after a 2-2 draw in normal time. Loan spells at Eastleigh, Eastbourne Borough, Mansfield Town and AFC Bournemouth followed, which resulted in a permanent move along the coast. Cook joined the Dean Court side at just the right time as the club began their ascent to the top-flight. Three seasons in League One were followed by two in the division higher, then five consecutive campaigns in the Premier League, including a few games alongside former Albion player Tommy Elphick. Cook left the Cherries in 2022, moving to Nottingham Forest and helping them to promotion to the top division for the first time in 23 years.

Saturday 19th April 2003

Leicester City required three points from this First Division fixture at the Walkers Bowl. Old friend of the Albion, Micky Adams, was in charge of the home side who duly picked up the required result to leapfrog Pompey at the top and earn a place in the Premiership. At the final whistle, the former Seagulls boss came straight over to applaud the 3,000-plus travelling army from Sussex.

Tuesday 19th April 2016

Anthony Knockaert inspired his side to a 4-0 victory over Queens Park Rangers. The Frenchman curled Albion ahead with a superb free-kick before Jiri Skalak thundered home from 30 yards. Connor Goldson headed home a third before Knockaert completed the rout in the 84th minute. The result drew Albion level on points with second-placed Burnley on 84 points, with Middlesbrough two points clear at the top. Manager Chris Hughton said; "I hope it goes to the last game because it will mean we would have won our next two matches. No one knows what is going to happen. It is certainly more enjoyable than being at the other end of the table."

Saturday 20th April 1985

Irishman Adrian Walsh – keepie-uppie world record holder with 12,104 – demonstrated his juggling skills before the Goldstone 17,279 fans who witnessed the 1-1 draw with Leeds United.

Monday 20th April 1987

A 14-game run without a win came to an end at the Goldstone Ground against old adversaries Crystal Palace. Danny Wilson and Darren Hughes were the heroes as the Albion beat the Londoners 2-0. Unfortunately, the victory left the Seagulls six points adrift at the bottom of Division Two while the Selhurst residents were sitting in seventh place.

Wednesday 20th April 2011

Over 3,500 youngsters descended on Withdean for the Young Seagulls Open Day. The gates opened at 9am for the annual event where the club's youngest fans got the chance to meet players and coaching staff and watch Gus Poyet put his title-winning squad through their paces with an open training session. The huge success of Young Seagulls, Team Stripes – for 13–16 year-olds – and the return of Gully has attracted many young supporters to the Albion. Chairman Tony Bloom realised the importance of getting the 'lost generation' back and the innovative free membership grew exponentially.

Saturday 20th April 2013

Ashley Barnes scored twice on his return from a seven-game ban as Albion hammered Blackpool 6-1. The convincing victory saw Gus Poyet's men move to within one win of securing a place in the Championship play-offs. The other goals came from Will Buckley, Matthew Upson, Andrea Orlandi and David López in front of a crowd of 28,499. As of January 2024, López was still playing, turning out for UD Caravaca in the Spanish non-league – at the age of 41!

Tuesday 20th April 2021

Albion released a statement regarding the ill-judged, and frankly ridiculous, proposal of a European Super League. Here's an excerpt:

"Brighton & Hove Albion are totally opposed to plans for a breakaway European Super League as it would destroy the dreams of clubs at every level of the domestic game. These plans are the latest in an alarming and growing list of clandestine attempts from a small group of clubs whose actions would be wiping out close to 150 years of football's tradition, competition and sporting progress through merit. The ups and downs of football – promotion, relegation, winning titles and cups, challenging for, or missing out on, a European place – are all part and parcel of the drama, jeopardy, joy and heartbreak that makes our game the most watched and most loved in the world. Ultimately, we are committed to a thriving domestic league and pyramid with the ultimate reward of European competition for achievements and success on the field. We remain open to a transparent, calm and rational dialogue with all clubs to achieve this."

Saturday 21st April 1979

Albion drew 1-1 in Bedfordshire. The result left Albion second – and a point – behind Stoke City with just two games remaining. In the Luton programme, future Albion full-back Sammy Nelson was mentioned after the Northern Irishman bared his 'buttocks' at the Coventry City fans at Highfield Road after baiting from the terraces.

On the same day, Hove liberal candidate Dr James Walsh suggested closing Shoreham Airport to build a new home for Albion. "I think it's vital the club moves from its present restricting facilities at the Goldstone Ground. Several alternatives have been mentioned, including Withdean Stadium and Corals. One large area cries out for development and that's Shoreham Airport. In short it could become the regional sports and leisure centre of the south, on a par with Crystal Palace." (!)

Tuesday 21st April 2009

Just three weeks earlier, the drop to the Football League's basement had seemed inevitable, but after a 2-1 victory at Bristol Rovers, there was light at the end of the tunnel. As he had been in the four wins out of the last five outings, Gary Hart was in imperious form, setting up Lloyd Owusu and Calvin Andrew either side of the break as Albion came from behind to make the last two games very interesting indeed.

Saturday 22nd April 1957

Jeff Darey's first of 11 appearances in an Albion shirt – despite spending four seasons at the Goldstone Ground. The striker arrived from Chelsea as a part-time professional but struggled to make an impression as Peter Harburn and Adrian Thorne continued to bang in the goals.

Saturday 22nd April 1989

A week after the tragic events at Hillsborough, Albion played Swindon Town at the Goldstone. The game kicked off at 3.06 pm. The minute's silence was impeccably observed and £5,665 was collected for the appeal fund.

Saturday 23rd April 1910

After sitting top of the league since early February, Albion won their first championship by beating Swindon Town, their closest rivals, at the Goldstone in front of 11,000 spectators. Bullet Jones netted twice, with local boy Bert Longstaff grabbing the other, to collect the trophy with a game to spare. The *Evening Argus* reported; "Every preparation was made for the accommodation of a big crowd. Extra seating was provided on the west side, and it was needed. All the ring seats and the open stand rapidly became packed, and still the turnstiles clicked in a way that suggested a harvest of silver for the Albion's exchequer."

Monday 23rd April 1962

Albion were relegated with a game spare, going down 3-0 to Norwich City at Carrow Road in front of a crowd of 16,162. The Seagulls drew at home, and lost away, to eventual Second Division champions Liverpool. Crystal Palace finished 15th in the Third Division.

Monday 23rd April 1979

John Vinicombe reported in the *Evening Argus*; "The new Brighton bypass will play a vital part in deciding the site of the proposed £7 million home for Brighton & Hove Albion. It must be no fewer than 55 acres with space for 7,000 cars. The stadium would contain 25,000 seats and room for 10,000 standing. The purpose would be to attract all the family and to include facilities for other sports. The site could be possibly shared by a giant supermarket."

Thursday 23rd April 2009

The exterior blue hoardings – complete with viewing windows – were erected around the stadium site to secure the area. Over the forthcoming months, messages of support – and the odd dig at Palace – were scrawled in chalk along its length. On completion of the building works, the boards headed north to surround Wolves' Molineux redevelopment, where they were repainted gold.

Saturday 23rd April 2022

The filming of Brighton: Stand or Fall began at Withdean Stadium. The documentary/film will – eventually – cover the time since Albion left the Goldstone Ground using clips, fan interviews and comment from writers and journalists.

Sunday 23rd April 2023

Albion's third FA Cup semi-final in their history, and on the same day as the London Marathon. In what was a markedly closer contest than the one with their city rival City at the same stage of the competition four years earlier, Manchester United gave the Albion a good game. Rob Sánchez had a relatively quiet afternoon as Albion just couldn't convert their many chances past David De Gea in the United goal, who made three world-class saves in normal time. Two hours of pulsating football and it was time for the dreaded penalties. Sussex boy Solly March ultimately missed his spot kick and Albion were out, 7-6.

Saturday 24th April 1909

Albion required just one point from their Goldstone date with Norwich City to avoid relegation from Southern League Division One. Scottish inside-forward Jimmy Robertson calmed the nerves of the 5,000 fans present by netting Albion's goal in the 1-1 draw.

Tuesday 24th April 1973

Without tasting victory on the road since a 2-0 win at Huddersfield Town on 14th October, it was no surprise that Albion were relegated from Division Two after this 2-0 defeat at QPR's Loftus Road. Palace were relegated from the top-flight – despite beating Manchester United 5-0 – meaning the old foes missed each other again. Huddersfield accompanied Albion to the Third Division while QPR and Burnley headed to the First Division.

Tuesday 24th April 2007

Lewes District Council must be made up of people with incredibly long legs, or professional athletes. LDC claimed supporters could walk from the Clock Tower to Sheepcote Valley in 25 minutes. A healthy – but of average height – contingent of Albion fans put the theory to the test and, despite a swift pace, covered the three-plus miles in just under an hour. Seagulls Party supporters began distributing 11,000 election leaflets in four Lewes District Council wards.

Thursday 25th April 1910

The Mayor's Parlour in Hove Town Hall was the venue for a Brighton & Hove Albion dinner to celebrate promotion. The morning-dress occasion was believed to be the first football dinner in the towns for over 25 years. The cost was five shillings and with each ticket a lady could be admitted to the balconies at 8.30 pm.

Saturday 25th April 1959

The last game of the season was the first match of a remarkable run. Jack Bertolini would go on to enjoy a run of 193 consecutive matches. The right-half, born of Italian ancestry in Scotland, joined Albion in 1958, instead of Huddersfield Town, after his wife took a liking to the south coast. He made a total of 279 starts and scored 14 goals.

Saturday 25th April 1981

Albion were only out of the First Division drop zone courtesy of a better goal difference than Coventry City. A win at Sunderland's Roker Park was vital as the Seagulls aimed for a third successive season in the top-flight. Michael Robinson scored his 22nd goal of the campaign in the first half only for Alan Brown to equalise. With the clock ticking down, Gordon Smith crossed for left-back Gary Williams to smash home a last-minute winner.

Saturday 25th April 1998

The last home game of the first season at Gillingham ended 2-2 against Hull City. Former England striker Mark Hateley made a fleeting substitute appearance for the visitors, much to the annoyance of the police dogs on the touchline. Albion won only three 'home' games all season and today's draw was the tenth in a disappointing campaign. Off the pitch, pre-printed letters to Brighton & Hove Council were distributed among the 3,888 fans at Priestfield, along with postcards appealing for help from the Bring Home the Albion campaign.

Wednesday 25th April 2007

Clubs around the country rallied behind the Albion and hosted a letter of support for the stadium on their respective websites.

Monday 26th April 1965

Unbeaten at home all season, Albion hosted Darlington needing just a point for promotion from the Fourth Division. The omens were in the home side's favour: five straight Goldstone victories, 15 goals scored and just three conceded. The forward line was led by former England international Bobby Smith – who scored once – and was ably assisted by namesake Jack, with one strike, and popular winger Wally Gould, who grabbed another. The final score of 3-1, in front of a huge Hove crowd of 31,423, saw the Albion lift the championship with 63 points (two for a win) after scoring 102 league goals. The attendance on that day wouldn't look out of place at Falmer, but this was the fourth tier of English football!

Saturday 26th April 1997

The curtain came down on 95 years of football at the Goldstone Ground. Thanks to despised chairman Bill Archer's cold and calculated greed, the famous old stadium – loved by thousands across the globe – hosted a match (in the fourth tier) for the very last time, after being sold to property developers. Doncaster Rovers were the opponents in conditions rather apt for the occasion; grey, overcast and rainy. A tear-inducing two-minute Last Post was played by a lone bugler, Liz Fleet, before the teams emerged. In the directors' box for the first time were chairman-elect Dick Knight, with his colleagues Bob Pinnock and Martin Perry.

A scrappy, nervy affair was brought to life in the 16th minute when Albion forward Ian Baird and Rovers defender Darren Moore were both sent off for fighting. With few chances for either side, the occasion was getting to the home players with so much at stake – Albion needed three points for any chance to continue their 77-year spell in the Football League. On 68 minutes, winger Stuart Storer side-footed a volley into the roof of the net after Mark Morris had headed against the Doncaster Rovers bar to spark wild scenes as fans danced on to the pitch from the South Stand, as the goalscorer did a 'Klinsmann' right in front of them.

The souvenir hunters invaded the pitch on the final whistle – Albion had got the precious three points they required. One game left for the season: Hereford away.

Monday 27th April 1903

The club's first play-off game was a 'test match' against Watford at the Canning Town Memorial Ground, home of West Ham United. A place in the Southern League's First Division was up for grabs. Albion had finished joint champions of Division Two while Watford were at the foot of Division One. Only 200 spectators witnessed a 5-3 victory. A larger crowd greeted the team back at Brighton Station and escorted them to the club's headquarters, the Seven Stars in Ship Street.

Saturday 27th April 1957

It was 3-3 at half-time in this Third Division (South) fixture. A second-half deluge from the Albion attack shocked Reading. Roy Jennings, Dennis Foreman (2), Jeff Darey, Frankie Howard, and a hat-trick from Albert Mundy cemented an 8-3 hammering.

Saturday 27th April 1996

The natives were getting restless at the Goldstone – for a very good reason. The 'no profit' clause had been removed from the club's constitution, meaning the club's home for over 90 years could be sold to Chartwell to line the pockets of chairman Bill Archer. No announcement had been made as to where Albion would play their home games the following campaign and, added to the club's relegation to the basement for the first time since 1965, the atmosphere among the 9,852 in attendance was one of abject fury.

The game lasted just 16 minutes. Thousands of loyal Albion fans invaded the pitch and snapped both crossbars, forcing the referee to abandon the fixture. Exacerbated at their club's plight, supporters from across the county had organised the protest to gain national media attention – it worked. Two days later, the club announced a deal with Chartwell to lease back the Goldstone Ground for one, last, season.

Wednesday 28th April 1954

Albion needed to win at Crystal Palace for any chance of promotion to Division Two for the first time. Jimmy Leadbitter equalised on the hour to make it 1-1. Jack Arlidge's 'Postbag' column in the *Evening Argus* was full of debate over Albion's recent dip in form. A mixture of bitter disappointment and admiration for their spirited fight was characterised by Nobby Clarke of Freshfield Road, Brighton; "What does it matter which division we are in? I say again, well done and good luck for next season. To blazes with the 'Dismal Jimmies'."

Saturday 28th April 1962

Young Sussex-born goalkeeper Brian Powney made his Albion debut in the last game of the season at Derby County. The Seaford custodian holds the record number of appearances between the sticks – 386 – and shared testimonials with fellow long-serving stalwart Norman Gall in 1971 and 1972. Chris Ramsey, right-back for Albion in the FA Cup Final, was born in Birmingham on this date.

Tuesday 28th April 1981

Jacob Cohen's fourth appearance – while at the Albion – for Israel in the 3-1 defeat to Scotland in Glasgow. Signed from Maccabi Tel Aviv, the left-back made just six appearances for the first team during his brief sojourn on the south coast.

Saturday 28th April 2001

Bobby Zamora netted a hat-trick in the 4-1 Withdean demolition of Macclesfield Town to reach a final tally of 28 league goals for the season – the highest figure for a player during the 12-year tenure at the athletics track.

Tuesday 28th April 2020

Michael Robinson died in Madrid from a malignant melanoma, aged just 61. Born in Leicester but raised in Blackpool, the burly striker joined Albion from Manchester City in 1980 after beginning his career with Preston North End in 1975. He netted 43 times in 133 appearances and played for three different managers on the coast – a fantastic return in what was a predominantly struggling side. During his three seasons in Hove, he endeared himself to the Goldstone faithful with his infectious enthusiasm for the game, and lung-bursting runs. He'll be fondly remembered for his huge contribution to Albion's charge to the FA Cup Final in 1983, scoring twice in the fourth-round home victory over Manchester City, and notching the second in the semi-final win over Sheffield Wednesday at Highbury. For those unaware, FA Cup last-four ties used to be contested at neutral stadiums, not Wembley.

In the final versus Manchester United, Robinson ran himself ragged and in the very last minute of extra-time, found himself bearing down on Gary Bailey's goal. But, being the unselfish player he was, he squared it to Gordon Smith. A trophy-laden – First Division, League Cup, European Cup – but solitary campaign at Liverpool followed before two years with Queens Park Rangers and a couple of seasons at Osasuna, where he retired, at 30, from a knee injury. After a brief involvement with an air-freight business, Michael became an award-winning sports broadcaster on Spanish television, hosting the popular El Día Después and Informe Robinson shows for many years, and summarising on international rugby fixtures. A man of many talents, he voiced the Ugly Sister in the Spanish version of Shrek 2. The old North Stand used to serenade their hero; 'We'll take good care of you, Robinson, Robinson.' Much-loved on both sides of the English Channel. Rest in peace, Michael.

Sunday 28th April 2024

Albion's last home victory – and Roberto De Zerbi's – of the season: 1-0 over Champions-League-chasing Aston Villa. From March onwards, the Italian had been linked with 'big club' managerial vacancies across

Europe, suggesting that he'd not made an agreement with the board. After this victory, he said; "I think I would like to stay in Brighton because I love my players. I love this city. I love my club, my fans. I said in the meeting with the fans, if I'm happy but I want to keep my passion always."

Saturday 29th April 1978

Albion entertained Blackpool in this vital end-of-season encounter. If the Seagulls beat their fellow seasiders – and Southampton beat Tottenham Hotspur at The Dell, both of whom were in the hunt to go up – promotion to the top-flight would be achieved for the first time in the club's 77-year history. Peter Ward and Brian Horton scored to earn a 2-1 win but the other two somehow 'contrived' to play out a goalless draw. Saints and Spurs were up. Post-match, Alan Mullery addressed the despondent fans from the West Stand and confidently predicted that supporters wouldn't have too long to wait for the big step up.

Sunday 29th April 2012

The end of the inaugural season at the American Express Community Stadium concluded the day before with a draw at Barnsley. The players who made the most appearances (in parentheses), in each position, were as follows: Peter Brezovan (24), Íñigo Calderón (37), Lewis Dunk (36), Gordon Greer (47), Marcos Painter (18), Craig Noone (21), Alan Navarro (29), Liam Bridcutt (43), Will Buckley (22), Ashley Barnes (41) and Craig Mackail-Smith (44). Barnes top scored with 14 in all competitions, Mackail-Smith managed 10, while Matt Sparrow picked up two red cards in 21 games.

Saturday 29th April 2023

In what can only be described as a ridiculous game of football, Albion destroyed Wolverhampton Wanderers at Falmer. Roberto De Zerbi responded to his team's jaded performance at the City Ground three days earlier by making five changes, leaving out Kaoru Mitoma, Alexis Mac Allister and Moisés Caicedo and handing rare starts to Deniz Undav and Billy Gilmour. To say the Italian's selection paid off was a bit of an understatement! Undav broke the deadlock with his first Premier League goal, Pascal Gross made it two then doubled his tally midway through the first half with a magnificent strike, controlling Enciso's square ball before sending a swerving strike into the corner. Danny Welbeck's close-range header from Pervis Estupiñán's cross made it four without reply before half-time, and the former England forward grabbed his second early in the second period after intercepting

Nathan Collins' misplaced pass. Undav completed the scoring with another great finish, dispossessing Matheus Nunes on the edge of the area and lifting a perfectly weighted chip over the keeper. Brighton & Hove Albion 6, Wolves 0. The scoreline was kind to the opposition as Albion dominated in a fashion not seen by supporters before. And this was without Caicedo and Mac Allister, who both entered the fray on 65 minutes! Thirty shots, with eight on target. It felt like more, such was Albion's dominance.

Saturday 30th April 1907

Jack Hall became the first Albion player to exceed 30 goals in a season with his brace in the 3-3 United League draw with Crystal Palace. The centre-forward was also the first player to hit the net more than 50 times for the club.

Saturday 30th April 1938

A great day in Brighton & Hove Albion's history – Harry Richard Knight was born in Shoreham-by-Sea. A lifelong fan of the club, Dick was present in the highest-ever Goldstone Ground attendance (see Saturday 27th December 1958). Away from the sport, he made a name for himself in the advertising industry, first as a copywriter then as an agency owner and chairman at TWBA Holmes Knight Ritchie – in London and New York City. His successful career was winding down in the mid-1990s. Albion were in a mess; Goldstone sold (with no home to go to), bottom of the fourth division, and run by complete chancers with no affinity to the club. Liam Brady cared about his old club – and their legions of fans – and set about trying to help. In 1997, he drafted in his good friend Dick, who then galvanised an army of Albion fans who worked together with the eventual new board, headed by the former ad man.

From 1997 to 2009, Dick steered the good ship Albion through some incredibly troubled waters but his sheer enthusiasm for the club, and unbreakable determination, kept us afloat – plus four promotions – and oversaw permission for the new stadium at Falmer. He handed over the baton to Tony Bloom at the end of his tenure. Despite all the upheaval and distress in the club's recent history, we're fortunate to have had two such formidable men in charge of the Albion.

Club historian Tim Carder summed up Dick's involvement perfectly; "He was the only hope we had. There was no viable alternative. He gave us supporters someone to rally behind and 99 per cent of Albion fans were firmly behind him." Amen. Thank you, Dick.

Saturday 30th April 1958

After spending their entire Football League existence in the Third Division (South), Albion stood on the threshold of promotion to the second tier for the first time. Sitting in third place with a game remaining, the top two sides – Plymouth Argyle and Brentford, who were in pole position on goal difference – had no games left. An Albion defeat would send the Bees up. Adrian Thorne fired in five against Watford in front of 31,038 Goldstone fans to clinch the home side's first Football League title in a 6-0 win.

Saturday 30th April 1988

The matchday programme finished runner-up in the Third Division awards, and 17th overall in the Football League.

Saturday 30th April 2011

The curtain came down on 12 years at Withdean Stadium. The 316th competitive fixture at the athletics track saw Gordon Greer lift the League One trophy after a 3-2 defeat to automatic promotion-chasing Huddersfield Town. Ashley Barnes and Matt Sparrow registered the departing club's goals after Lee Clark's men had respectfully formed a guard of honour for the rightfully crowned champions. A touch of class sadly lacking when a club from along the south coast visited just a week earlier, seven days after the title was won at Walsall.

Some Withdean statistics: (in the league) games played 275; W 128, D 66, L 81, F 414, A 306. Leading goalscorer was Bobby Zamora (57), followed by Glenn Murray (30), Nicky Forster (29) and Gary Hart (24), who had also made the most appearances (184). The commemorative 100-page programme to mark the occasion sold 5,000 copies prior to kick-off. We all know Withdean's limitations, but the sometimes-picturesque ground did the Albion proud over 12 years.

Four promotions – three as champions – is an astonishing achievement for a club competing with the shackles of woeful facilities, a small capacity, rain and miscellaneous costs not associated with proper football arenas. No tears were shed but I'm sure most Albion fans can find a small place in their hearts for the Theatre of Trees.

Gull's Eye – May 1995:
An unerring look into the future.

© *Gull's Eye*

MAY

Saturday 1st May 1948

Swansea Town's Vetch Field was the venue for the last game of the season. Albion needed a win to avoid re-election to the Third Division (South). Sadly, it was not to be as the two teams played out a goalless draw. Just five points separated the bottom ten sides.

Saturday 1st May 2004

Albion hosted Notts County at Withdean. An own goal from 18-year-old debutant defender Kelvin Wilson earned the Seagulls three points, and more importantly, a play-off berth.

Friday 2nd May 1958

Second Division clubs were happy to welcome newly promoted Albion. Bristol Rovers manager Bert Tann said; "Brighton will be attractive opposition for us, and we look forward to renewing our rivalry with them on the field." Cardiff City assistant manager Bill Jones commented; "We know and like Brighton in this part of the world. Allan Brown, Sunderland boss, remarked; "There'll be a big welcome here for them, take it from me."

Saturday 2nd May 1981

Albion had won their last three games for a chance of remaining in the First Division. A victory against Leeds United at the Goldstone would guarantee top-flight football for a third season. On the half-hour mark, United keeper John Lukic took too many steps and an indirect free-kick was awarded just inside the box.

In a move involving John Gregory and Brian Horton, the ball fell to Steve Foster who dashed through to give his side the lead. Record signing Andy Ritchie made it two with ten minutes remaining and the Albion were safe!

Saturday 2nd May 1992

With the Second Division championship secured, Ipswich Town fans flocked to Portman Road. It was a slightly different story for the 2,000 plus Albion fans – many in fancy dress – in attendance. A victory – and other results going in their favour – was the Seagulls' only hope. Despite a Raphael Meade strike, a 3-1 defeat meant Third Division football in 1992/93.

Saturday 2nd May 1998

Over 2,000 Albion fans were at Sincil Bank – including many dressed as Mexicans – to witness Lincoln City's title win after a 2-1 victory. The Bring Home the Albion campaign handed out over 4,000 pre-stamped letters for supporters to send to Brighton & Hove Council.

Saturday 2nd May 2008

Nicky Forster reacted quickest to Gary Dicker's strike to fire the Albion into the lead on 73 minutes from close range against Stockport County, the club Dicker was on loan from. At Elland Road, Northampton Town fell further behind to leave the stripes out of the relegation zone. The Cobblers then conceded a third and Albion – under Russell Slade – had stayed up. An amazing achievement by the Wokingham-born miracle worker.

Wednesday 2nd May 2018

Two players from Brighton & Hove Albion Amputee FC were called up to a national development side. Danny Hemsley and Matt Nash were named in the 12-man squad and were an integral part of the BHAAFC squad, which was in only its second season of competitive football after being launched by Albion in the Community in 2016.

AITC's disability manager, Paul Brackley, said; "Everyone at AITC is absolutely delighted for Danny and Matt. They have both performed well throughout our national league campaign and thoroughly deserve this recognition."

Saturday 3rd May 1958

Just weeks after the Munich air disaster, Manchester United lost to two Nat Lofthouse goals in the FA Cup Final against Bolton Wanderers. Wearing red that day were Freddie Goodwin and Alex Dawson. The former signed the latter for Albion ten years later.

Wednesday 3rd May 1972

Just four days earlier, Rochdale's Spotland had been the venue for a 2-1 Albion victory. A bumper crowd of 34,766 packed into the Goldstone Ground for the return fixture to see if the Seagulls could get the point they required for promotion to the Second Division. John Templeman – who arrived in Hove after the disbandment of the Portsmouth reserve side in 1966 – scored his side's only goal to earn the priceless point.

Tuesday 3rd May 1977

It was the last home game of the season. Sheffield Wednesday attracted 30,756 Goldstone spectators: the 15th 20,000+ attendance of the season. Albion won 3-2 with strikes from goal machine Peter Ward, a Brian Horton spot-kick and one from Steve Piper, who was an ever-present for the campaign. Albion achieved promotion to the Second Division with two games spare, both of which ended in defeat to hand the title to Mansfield Town.

Saturday 3rd May 1997

Undoubtedly the most important and downright nerve-wracking game in the history of Brighton & Hove Albion Football Club: Albion faced Hereford United at Edgar Street. It was the last game of the season and both clubs could have potentially gone down to the Conference – the Bulls had to win to stay up while Steve Gritt's men needed just a point to survive in the Football League. The home side had been seven points ahead of their guests with ten games left. With no venue for home games secured for the following campaign, fans across the world realised this could be Albion's last game – ever. The 3,500+ away supporters felt a sense of foreboding after 20 minutes when local lad Kerry Mayo turned a Tony Agana cross past his own goalkeeper, Mark Ormerod. The first half was dire as both sets of players struggled to deal with their collective nerves.

A dreadfully sombre half-time saw the teams re-enter the fray to a tumultuous roar of encouragement from the away end. Gritt played his trump card in the 55th minute; the injured Paul McDonald was taken off and replaced by striker Robbie Reinelt. Within eight minutes the £15,000 purchase from Colchester United had written his name into Albion folklore. Craig Maskell controlled a poor defensive clearance on his knee before smashing a left-foot volley against the right-hand post from 20 yards. Reinelt – alert to the opportunity – won a short sprint with two defenders to drill home into the bottom right-hand corner. Cue absolute pandemonium on the terraces and scenes of celebration – the like of which will probably never be seen again!

There was still 30 minutes remaining and the players were almost as nervous as the fans, many of whom could not face the action and turned their backs, such was the tension. In the final few moments, Craig Maskell was put clean through but fired his right-footed shot wide. The ball went straight up the other end to find Adrian Foster bearing down on Mark Ormerod, who kept his nerve as the opposition forward shot straight at him. Albion were safe! Phew! Riot police lined the centre of the pitch, but no-one invaded. Everyone was simply too elated, and drained, to move from the terrace. For the players, fans and officials of both clubs, the match will stay in the memory for a very, very long time indeed. A game that should never be repeated – but never forgotten too.

Tuesday 3rd May 2001

Withdean Stadium was full of fans waving brown envelopes in reference to Chesterfield's off-the-field problems and rogue chairman Darren Brown's misdemeanours. The majority of the 6,847 in attendance were hoping to see the Albion lift their first championship trophy in 36 years. In an emotional, and historical, evening at their temporary home, it was fitting that dependable defender Danny Cullip should rise to thump home a header to secure the title.

Thursday 3rd May 2007

The Seagulls Party fared well at local elections: Steve Williams (Lewes Priory) polled 431 votes; Mark Jackson (Newhaven Denton and Meeching) 523; Roz South (Lewes Bridge) 262 and Edward Bassford (Ouse Valley and Ringmer) 467.

Saturday 3rd May 2008

Swansea City lifted the League One trophy after a 1-0 victory at Withdean Stadium. The result, in front of 7,283 fans, meant Albion finished the season in seventh position, one place and seven points outside a play-off berth. The game also marked the end of Skint's nine-year shirt sponsorship – the longest in the club's history. The record company, home of Fatboy Slim, became synonymous with the club and the players wore commemorative shirts to celebrate the end of the deal. Chairman Dick Knight commented; "The Skint name has been on the Albion shirt for longer than any other sponsorship in the Football League and has become an iconic symbol of the club. The message 'Team Mates 1999-2008' on the commemorative shirt says just how we feel about what great sponsors they have been."

Tommy Elphick pipped Nicky Forster to the Player of the Season; the 20-year-old central defender received 40% of the Albion supporters' vote. The Brighton-born player said; "To win this award, chosen by the fans, means a great deal and I would like to thank all those people who have voted for me. At the start of the campaign I was just hoping to establish myself in the side, get a few games under my belt and enjoy the season."

Saturday 3rd May 2014

From a delightful cross by Craig Mackail-Smith, Leo Ulloa nodded Albion into the play-offs with a last-gasp winner at Nottingham Forest. The narrow 2-1 victory earned the stripes a two-legged semi-final with Derby County for a place in the Premier League.

Friday 4th May 1979

The players relaxed with a round of golf at Gosforth Park before the biggest game in the club's 78-year history – at Newcastle United.

Saturday 4th May 1982

The programme – for the 2-0 victory over Wolverhampton Wanderers – documented that the club had six players away on international duty the previous week: Steve Foster (England), Mickey Thomas (Wales), Nelson (Northern Ireland), plus Robinson, Tony Grealish and Gerry Ryan with the Republic of Ireland.

Sunday 4th May 2003

Could Albion stay in the First Division? Grimsby Town were already relegated and the Seagulls needed to win – and hope Stoke City beat Reading at the Britannia – to retain their second-tier status. Michael Keane's spot-kick (23rd) at Blundell Park was equalised from 12 yards by Bobby Zamora on the stroke of half-time. Captain Danny Cullip fired his side into the lead two minutes into the second period and then news filtered through that former Albion loanee Ade Akinbiyi had scored for Stoke. It finished 2-2. Second division (third tier) football next season.

Friday 4th May 2007

Seagulls Party candidates took a very creditable 21.5% of the vote in the four contested Lewes District Council wards.

Saturday 4th May 2013

Albion's 2-0 victory over Wolverhampton Wanderers condemned the visitors to relegation to League One and cemented the home side's place in the Championship play-off spots. On a lovely sunny day, the biggest crowd of the campaign – 30,003 – were treated to a stadium-first after the match; DJs in the North Stand for 'Soul – A Play-Off Party!' Alan Wares and I played a selection of ska, soul, reggae, Stax and Northern Soul classics, on vinyl, to a packed concourse. Wolves fans joined the knees-up and The Liquidator was duly played for our guests. One of the evening's highlights was a rousing chorus of 'with a roof right over our heads' during 'Is This Love' by Bob Marley.

Friday 4th May 2018

Albion secured Premier League survival in their inaugural campaign with a 1-0 home victory over Manchester United. Pascal Gross' header from José Izquierdo's cross was cleared by Marcos Rojo – from just behind the line. Goal-line technology awarded the only goal of the game.

Saturday 5th May 1979

Over 10,000 Albion fans made the long journey to Newcastle to see if their team could join the top table of English football for the first time. Bizarrely, as Sunderland were also in the hunt for promotion, a healthy contingent of Mackems, who couldn't make it to Wrexham, were cheering on their bitter rivals at St. James' Park! It didn't make any difference as Brian Horton's diving header from a Gary Williams cross put the visitors ahead. Peter Ward made it two and Gerry Ryan claimed a third before half-time. The First Division was just 45 minutes away! Manager Alan Mullery was clearly over-excited as he tore a strip off his players during the interval, but they held on – despite the Magpies pulling one back – to claim their well-deserved place among the elite. The manager christened the 'Seagull Special' train the 'Paralytic Special' as it snaked its way back to Sussex jam-packed with players, staff and fans celebrating the greatest day in the club's history, so far. On TV that evening was Dad's Army, The Val Doonican Show, The Rockford Files, Celebrity Squares and Match of the Day.

Wednesday 5th May 1999

'Operation Morning Surprise', part of the new stadium referendum, saw 4,000 green 'Yes Yes' balloons tied to lampposts across the area to remind voters to do the right thing in the forthcoming election.

Friday 5th May 2006

Responsibility for planning moved from John Prescott to Ruth Kelly in a government reshuffle.

Thursday 6th May 1999

The referendum resulted in an 83% vote in favour of the council assisting the Albion to find a permanent home in the Brighton & Hove area, and a 68% vote in favour of Falmer.

Wednesday 6th May 2009

Albion in the Community's work in adult education was praised during Prime Minister's Questions by Gordon Brown. "I understand Brighton has delivered nearly 4,000 Skills for Life achievements and that is helping young people. Football clubs that are at the centre of their communities are good for every community."

Saturday 7th May 1988

Six straight wins – plus a draw at Chester City – in their last seven fixtures had moved Albion from sixth to an automatic promotion position in second. The nerves of the 19,800 Goldstone Ground crowd were eased in the 14th minute when Scottish striker Kevin Bremner stooped to head home in front of a packed North Stand. Strike-partner Garry Nelson grabbed his 32nd goal of the campaign almost straight from the second half kick-off to fire Albion two up. A consolation goal wasn't enough and Albion were promoted back to the second tier of English football.

Saturday 7th May 1983

With minds perhaps focused on the FA Cup Final in two weeks' time, the Albion were relegated at home to Manchester City – who gained revenge for the 4-0 FA Cup drubbing back in January – in the penultimate game of the season. Despite the payback for the fourth-round loss, the Sky Blues also dropped down to the Second Division, alongside Swansea City.

Saturday 7th May 2011

With promotion and the championship wrapped up, Albion travelled to Nottingham for the final game of an amazing season. Records broken for 2010/2011 included: most points – 95; most away points – 40; most wins in a calendar month – eight out of eight in March; most home and away 'doubles' – nine; and a player scoring most goals while on loan from another club – ten, Chris Wood.

Ashley Barnes netted his 20th goal of the campaign picking up the ball in space just outside the edge of the Notts County area before despatching a curling right-footed drive into the net. The home side's future was uncertain as, despite scores elsewhere going their way, they had to score to be sure of League One football next term. County's plight was ably assisted by Albion captain Gordon Greer, who diverted a right-wing cross past his own goalkeeper in the 36th minute. The scores stayed the same and the Magpies were safe. A good-natured pitch invasion by the home fans later and another season was over. Next time Albion played a home league game it would be at Falmer!

Sunday 7th May 2017

Albion drew 1-1 at Aston Villa in the final game of a tumultuous season that saw promotion to the Premier League for the first time. Of the 73 goals scored during the campaign Glenn Murray netted 22, with Anthony Knockaert (15), Sam Baldock (11) and Tomer Hemed (11) all chipping in over ten each. Albion picked up the most Championship points at home with 54, winning 17 of their 23 games. A three-month unbeaten run in October, November and December resulted in 11 wins out of 15. Let's not forget the defence, who conceded the fewest goals in the division with 36, including 21 clean sheets.

Saturday 7th May 2022

Nearly 39 years later, Albion finally put the ghost of the 1983 FA Cup Final defeat to rest with the absolute thrashing of Manchester United at Falmer. Despite home victories over the Red Devils previously, many fans were still hoping for proper retribution one day. Ecuador international Moisés Caicedo fired Albion into the lead with his first Premier League goal with a low 25-yard strike in only his sixth game. The visitors fell apart in the second half, conceding three goals in quick succession. Marc Cucurella (49th) drove the second into the roof of the net from Leandro Trossard's pull-back and the little Belgian then set up Pascal Gross to calmly steer in a third (57th).

Trossard scored Brighton's fourth when he bundled the ball over the line from close range, with the goal eventually given after a VAR review checked for a handball. It was United's fifth successive away loss which confirmed that they would not qualify for next season's Champions League. Albion were so dominant the away side got off lightly conceding just four. A dejected Cristiano Ronaldo, who played the full 90 minutes, looked unhappy at the final whistle. A wonderful result and a wonderful day. Brighton & Hove Albion 4, Manchester United 0.

Wednesday 8th May 1963

A 1-0 defeat at Bournemouth & Boscombe Athletic condemned Albion to their second successive relegation. Champions Northampton Town – on their rise to a solitary season in the top-flight – beat Albion 3-0 at the three-sided County Ground, and 5-0 at the Goldstone.

Tuesday 8th May 1979

Chairman Mike Bamber called for a referendum in Brighton & Hove about building a multi-sports complex at Toads Hole Valley. The club eventually moved into a new stadium 32 years later!

Sunday 8th May 2005

Ipswich Town were the visitors to Withdean Stadium for this final fixture of the campaign. Albion required just a point to retain their Championship status. Player of the Season Adam Virgo missed a clearance after just four minutes to let Finnish striker Shefki Kuqi through to score. The versatile Brightonian made amends five minutes later by smashing home the rebound from Gary Hart's header on the half-volley to earn the Seagulls a vital point.

Saturday 8th May 2003

The first edition of Albion Roar broadcast on the Radio Reverb website. In the 55-minute show, Jonny Harman and Richie Parker discussed all things Albion, spoke to departing players Bobby Zamora and Paul Brooker, and interviewed some new arrivals; Leon Knight, Wayne Henderson and Carl Wilson-Denis. Since the inaugural show, Roar has gone from strength to strength with guests ranging from Albion officials, ex players and local councillors to fans, authors and Premier League referees.

Thursday 8th May 2008

Albion fans were in shock as loyal club servant Dean Wilkins was relieved of his duties and replaced by Micky Adams. His 21-month tenure had seen steady improvement – a seventh-place finish in his first full season – and the Nicky Forster/Glenn Murray strike partnership was beginning to bear fruit. Wilkins' final statistics read: played 102, won 39, drew 24, lost 39 – a 38.2% win ratio. It was great to see so many Sussex-born players representing the club during his tenure.

Friday 8th May 2009

After completion of the roadworks the previous month, the diggers were busy excavating the three storeys' worth of earth to accommodate the stadium at Falmer.

Saturday 8th May 2010

Replacing Chris Holroyd on 76 minutes, Jake Forster-Caskey became the youngest peacetime Albion player at only 16 years and 13 days, beating Simon Fox's record by 225 days. The midfielder has a football pedigree; father Darren played for Tottenham Hotspur and made his name at Reading, while step-dad Nicky scored over 50 goals for the Albion.

Sunday 8th May 2011

Fans lined the seafront route as Albion staff and players snaked their way along the seafront in open-top buses. Charlie Oatway introduced his colleagues from the mezzanine walkway above the Volks nightclub. Chairman Tony Bloom took the microphone to rapturous applause, and the cheering got even louder as he announced Albion will kick-off at the American Express Community Stadium on 30th July with a prestigious friendly against Tottenham Hotspur. Exciting times ahead.

Saturday 9th May 1987

Terry Connor – Player of the Year – Darren Hughes, Danny Wilson and Kieran O'Regan made their last Albion appearances as 3,000 Leeds United fans ran amok after their 1-0 Goldstone victory.

On a lighter note, Tony Millard recalled a dinner conversation with comedian and Liverpool fan Stan Boardman; "Stan was a lifeguard at Black Rock and applied for a trial at the Goldstone and was turned down. He was offended as he'd played a couple of times for Liverpool's junior side. Said Stan; 'I hated Brighton and did so even more when they twice knocked the Reds out of the FA Cup'." To this day, it's unclear how Brighton fans feel about him.

Thursday 9th May 1996

Following the abandonment of the original game by a necessary pitch invasion – the club's plight was finally in the national domain – Albion hosted York City this Thursday morning. A gate of just 2,106 was watched over by a heavy police presence as the Minstermen won 3-1 and escaped relegation to the Third Division. John Byrne, Dean Wilkins and Ian Chapman made their last appearances in the stripes, as did Stuart Myall and Junior McDougald.

Thursday 10th May 1979

The *Evening Argus* reported that "champagne could be flowing at 30,000ft over America tomorrow night as the Seagulls celebrate being Second Division champions". Unfortunately, Crystal Palace beat Burnley the following day in front of 51,801 Selhurst Park fans – their highest-ever attendance – to claim the title.

Tuesday 10th May 1988

On the day Perfect by Fairground Attraction was number one in the United Kingdom, Adam Lallana was born in St Albans, Hertfordshire. His paternal grandfather was Spanish. Southampton paid AFC Bournemouth £3,000 compensation – with further payments of £5,000 and £10,000 when he signed scholarship and professional contracts respectively – for a 12-year-old Lallana in 2000. The midfielder enjoyed eight seasons at St Mary's, helping them rise from League One to the Premier League in consecutive campaigns, before Liverpool shelled out £25 million for him in 2014. A Premier League, Champions League, UEFA Super Cup and FIFA Club World Cup winner's medal followed. The 32-year-old former England international arrived at Falmer on a free transfer in 2020 and represented the club on almost 100 occasions.

Saturday 11th May 1968

Paul Bence's senior career with Albion lasted just 13 minutes. The Littlehampton-born defender came on as substitute in the final game of the season at Walsall, a 2-1 victory.

Saturday 11th May 1985

With a line-up including the flamboyant Frank Worthington, Albion took on Sheffield United at the Goldstone Ground hoping for three points, and for other results to go their way. Unfortunately, despite a 1-0 win over the Blades, Manchester City thrashed Charlton Athletic 5-1 and the Seagulls finished the season in sixth place, just behind Blackburn Rovers and Portsmouth. The play-offs were introduced in 1987.

Saturday 11th May 1991

A solitary victory in six games meant Albion must beat Ipswich Town in Hove to stay in contention for a trip to Wembley. Mike Small fired the home side in front before Player of the Year Perry Digweed sprang into action to save a penalty from Chris Kiwomya, who would level the scores with ten minutes remaining. John Byrne was fouled just outside the box and as the seconds ticked down, Dean Wilkins and Robert Codner debated who should take the direct free-kick. The former usurped the latter and curled the ball into the top corner past the despairing dive of one-England-cap-winning-goalkeeper Phil Parkes, to spark wild scenes on the terraces. Albion were in the play-offs, with a negative goal difference!

Wednesday 11th May 2011

The new pitch at Falmer received its first cut. The seats were all in and the stadium looked magnificent. All the work remaining was internal as the various hospitality areas and concourses were fitted out with facilities and equipment to rival any other stadium in the country.

Wednesday 12th May 1926

High up on the list of Albion's all-time goalscorers, Albert Mundy was born in Gosport, Hampshire. The forward topped the charts three times after moving along the coast from Portsmouth in 1953. During his five-year spell, Albert netted an impressive 90 times in just 178 starts.

Saturday 12th May 1984

Albion's only league game on this date, up to this point, was at Newcastle United for Kevin Keegan's last appearance. Although Gerry Ryan scored, the visitors were unable to deflate the 36,415 Geordie hero-worshippers who celebrated a 3-1 win and promotion to the top-flight. Albion finished their first season back in Division Two in ninth spot, 20 points away from a promotion place.

Sunday 12th May 2019

Glenn Murray scored Albion's only goal in a 4-1 home defeat to Manchester City. Pep Guardiola's men were presented with the Premier League trophy after the match. Albion's playing record for 2018/19 read: played 38, won 9, drew 9, lost 20, scored 35, conceded 60, goal difference minus 25, points 36. A final position of 17th, one place and two points above relegated Cardiff City.

Thursday 13th May 1909

Familiar to dedicated Albion fans, Gillingham was the birthplace of Bert Stephens. The prolific outside-left would surely have become Albion's all-time top scorer if it had not been for the outbreak of World War II. Bert had hit the target 87 times before the hostilities and would net 174 times in 366 appearances over a 13-year period.

Monday 13th May 2002

Plans for Falmer suffered another setback. Martin Small, planning officer for the Sussex Downs Conservation Board, said in *The Argus*: "We have a planning committee meeting today. We are taking a report which recommends we continue our objections to Falmer Stadium. National planning guidance on major city developments in areas of outstanding beauty [six-lane motorway and railway line] says development should only take place if it is in the national interest and there are no alternative sites. Using the Falmer site for a football stadium is not in the national interest and we are not convinced there are no alternative sites."

Sunday 13th May 2007

Soon-to-be Prime Minister Gordon Brown was quizzed by Falmer-For-All's Paul Samrah at The Dome. His questions regarding Albion's much-needed stadium were greeted by the biggest cheer of the afternoon.

Sunday 13th May 2018

Albion's final match of their first season back in the top division finished in a 4-0 reverse at Liverpool. Glenn Murray was Albion's leading Premier League goalscorer with 12, while Pascal Gross weighed in with 7, José Izquierdo 5, Anthony Knockaert 3; and Tomer Hemed, Leonardo Ulloa, Jürgen Locadia, Lewis Dunk and Solly March - all with one apiece. Maty Ryan kept eight clean sheets while Dunk and Shane Duffy came in joint top in the disciplinary charts, with five bookings each. Davy Pröpper was the only player who saw red all season and only Dunk and Ryan were ever-present in the league. Albion's playing record for 2017/18 read: played 38, won 9, drew 13, lost 16, scored 34, conceded 54, goal difference minus 20, points 40. A final position of 15th, one place above Huddersfield Town.

Saturday 14th May 1977

Peter Ward scored his last league goal of the season to complete a tally of 32, and 36 overall in all competitions. A record likely never to be beaten.

Saturday 14th May 1983

The prolific Chris Rodon arrived in Sussex after scoring 99 times for Pontardawe Athletic over three seasons in the Welsh league. Already relegated, the Welshman came on with 15 minutes remaining of the Albion's final First Division encounter, a 2-1 defeat at Norwich City.

Friday 14th May 1998

BHA (Bring Home the Albion) campaign spokesman Adrian Newnham handed in a 32,355-signature document in support of the Albion's bid to use Withdean Stadium as a temporary home to Lord Bassam, leader of Brighton & Hove Council, outside Brighton Town Hall – in 16 binders.

Sunday 14th May 2023

Arsenal's fading title hopes were ultimately crushed by a rampant Albion in north London. Recently departed Leandro Trossard hit the bar while both Martin Ødegaard and Bukayo Saka went close before Julio Enciso's close-range header put Brighton ahead and sub Deniz Undav doubled the lead after lobbing Aaron Ramsdale in the 86th minute. Ecuadorian left-back Pervis Estupiñán compounded the home side's misery in the 96th minute to make it 3-0 to the visitors.

Friday 15th May 1970

Albion played CD Carabanchel as part of Madrid's San Isidro Fiesta, the fourth game of a post-season holiday tour of Spain. A penalty from Alan Duffy, plus goals from Paul Flood and Kit Napier, gave Albion a 3-1 victory.

Saturday 15th May 1982

A 2-1 defeat against relegated Leeds United at Elland Road was Albion's only league game on this date. The loss resulted in a final First Division standing of 13th.

Sunday 16th May 1998

A SWEAT rally at Withdean Stadium was attended by around 300 local residents and a petition of 6,000 names – a fifth of those who signed in favour – was presented to Lord Bassam.

Thursday 16th May 2002

A total of 61,452 people said 'yes' in Albion's bid to build a community stadium at Falmer, with the most overwhelming encouragement coming from residents in Moulsecoomb and Bevendean. Support came from every area of the UK and many countries, including China, Colombia and the Ivory Coast. Paul Samrah, chairman of the Falmer for All campaign, said the size of the petition had exceeded all expectations. "The millennium city of Brighton & Hove deserves a stadium befitting its status. The people have said yes. We've done our bit." Eric Huxham, chair of Falmer

Parish Council, said; "We were never going to be able to compete with the club for numbers, but our own little petition has between 8,000 and 9,000 names on it. We have no objections to a stadium for Brighton & Hove, but this is the wrong place."

Sunday 16th May 2004

It was the first leg of the Second Division play-off semi-final against Swindon Town at the County Ground. With 17 minutes remaining, Chris Iwelumo won the ball inside the penalty area and passed back to substitute Gary Hart. The utility man spotted Richard Carpenter, in space, who then smashed home in front of the travelling support to give his side the advantage going into the second leg.

Tuesday 17th May 1966

Police reinforcements were called to the Goldstone to stop youths behind the goal throwing orange-peel and whistling during the reserve game against Notts County.

Tuesday 18th May 1954

Albion legend Jimmy Case was born in Liverpool. Pat Saward tried to sign the midfielder as early as 1971, from South Liverpool. After winning four league titles, one UEFA Cup, one League Cup and three European Cups, Jimmy arrived on the south coast for £350,000 in August 1981. After starring in the FA Cup run of 1983, and an outstanding 1983/84 season, Case was deemed surplus to requirements and sold to Southampton for £30,000 in March 1985. The Liverpudlian made over 200 First Division appearances for Saints before amazingly returning to the Goldstone as a 39-year-old in 1993.

Saturday 18th May 1963

After the worst winter in living memory, the season finally concluded as already relegated Albion drew 0-0 at Wrexham. Archie Macaulay's men would begin the 1963/64 season in Division Four, the first time the club had competed in the basement.

Monday 18th May 2009

Tony Bloom took over as chairman of Brighton & Hove Albion Football Club on the day it was announced full funding for the club's new home at Falmer had been finalised. The cost of the stadium project was £93 million, the majority of which would be funded by the new poker-playing chairman. Tony's predecessor Dick Knight – who saved the Albion in 1997 and kept the club alive when many had given up hope – stayed on as Honorary Life President. Dick said of his 12-year tenure; "Being chairman of the Albion has been the most rewarding period of my life. To be able to give something back to the club I've supported since I was a boy has been a privilege. Thanks to Tony's support, the club is now financially secure, the stadium is on its way, and the club now has the opportunity to reach its true potential."

Tony commented; "I would like to pay tribute to Dick. Nobody should be in any doubt that he saved the club from almost certain extinction at a time when no-one else was willing to come forward, and under his leadership we have had some very memorable times including our successful nine-year battle to secure the go-ahead for Falmer. I want to fulfil the dreams of so many of our great fans just as my grandfather Harry Bloom did in the glory days of the 1970s with Brian Clough, Peter Taylor and Alan Mullery." The new chairman made his fortune by selling the online gambling firm Premierbet in 2002 and his incredible generosity and belief in the club's potential has ensured a permanent place in Albion folklore, alongside the departing Mr Knight.

Tuesday 18th May 2021

After over a year of restrictions, there was light at the end of the COVID-19 tunnel as 7,495 Albion fans were allowed to watch their team take on newly-crowned champions Manchester City at Falmer. The Sky Blues blew a two-goal advantage as Leandro Trossard gave the home side hope with a cool close-range finish on 50 minutes. Adam Webster levelled, rising highest in the box to head home Pascal Gross' delivery and then, with 14 minutes left, Dan Burn sent the home fans into raptures with the winner, following up his own blocked shot to steer the rebound into the corner of the net. Brighton & Hove Albion 3, Manchester City 2.

"Eleven against 11 against Brighton is tough, 11 against 10 is difficult so we have to improve for the (Champions League) final," said Pep Guardiola.

Saturday 18th May 2024

Albion announced they'd reached a mutual agreement with Roberto De Zerbi to terminate his contract at the end of the 2023/24 season. The former attacking midfielder finished his playing career with Trento, in 2013, and took his first managerial role at Darfo Boario soon after. After an unremarkable five years at Foggia, Palermo and Benevento,

De Zerbi rocked up at Sassuolo (2018) and secured a top-ten finish in Serie A for only the second time in the club's 99-year history. His attacking philosophy cemented the Neroverdi's position in Italy's top division and it wasn't long before one of European football's big boys came knocking. Ukrainian giants Shakhtar Donetsk duly called and, in similar circumstances to his Albion departure, De Zerbi announced he was to leave Sassuolo at the conclusion of the 2020/21 campaign. His tenure in Donetsk got off to a flyer, winning the Ukrainian Super Cup against Dynamo Kyiv, just a few months later. Unfortunately, Russia's invasion of Ukraine meant Roberto had to leave. His side were top of the Ukrainian Premier League. As Jimmy Greaves once said, football is a funny old game and, of course, he is correct. Graham Potter had been tempted to Stamford Bridge, 'for footballing reasons', which meant Albion's hotseat was empty.

The chairman took his time, and ten days later, De Zerbi signed on the dotted line to become Albion's 38th permanent manager. In just over 18 months on the south coast, the Italian and his staff – Andrea Maldera, Ricard Segarra, Marcattilio Marcattilii, Vincenzo Teresa, Agostino Tibaudi, Marcello Quinto and Enrico Venturelli – gave Albion fans memories to last a lifetime, playing scintillating football and making the entire football world sit up and take notice of little old Brighton. He won 38 of his 89 games, drawing 22, losing 29 – a win ratio of 42.70%. Loads of goals scored, huge club scalps a plenty, sixth place in the Premier League. Oh, and European competition for the very first time.

De Zerbi's public discontent surrounding the club's recruitment strategy was cited as having contributed towards the 'irreconcilable differences', which had formed between him and the club's hierarchy.

On leaving, De Zerbi stated; "I am very sad to be leaving Brighton, but I am very proud of what my players and staff have achieved with the support of everyone at the club and our amazing fans in the past two historical seasons."

What a ride!

Grazie mille, Roberto.

Thursday 19th May 1983

Albion players Chris Ramsey, Jimmy Case, Gordon Smith and Perry Digweed appeared on Top of the Pops. The club's record, The Boys in the Old Brighton Blue, was no. 127 in the charts!

Sunday 19th May 1991

The Division Two play-off semi-final against Millwall kicked off at midday at the Goldstone. Paul Stephenson fired the Lions into a 15th-minute lead. Mark Barham got on the end of a huge hoof by Perry Digweed to level the scores just before half-time. Mike Small fired his side ahead (53rd), set up Clive Walker (55th) and then put through Robert Codner (59th) to make it 4-1 on the hour! Before the match, Dean Wilkins was presented with a gift from the match sponsors for his Man of the Match performance in the vital 2-1 win over Ipswich Town eight days earlier – a kettle!

Tuesday 20th May 1986

Dean Saunders bagged his first Wales goals (2) in the 3-0 win over Canada in Vancouver.

Tuesday 20th May 1997

Kaoru Mitoma was born in Hita, Ōita, Japan. The tricky winger joined Kawasaki Frontale's academy at under-10 level and was eventually offered a chance to step up to under-18s. Believing he wasn't ready for professional football, Kaoru chose to study at the University of Tsukuba, who had also produced Frontale stalwarts Shogo Taniguchi and Shintaro Kurumaya. The forward's thesis was on dribbling. We can only assume he got a distinction.

Wednesday 20th May 1998

"The Albion is an essential part of community life; the club is a source of local pride and enjoyment and provides a common bond for the people of Brighton, Hove and much of Sussex. They need to be back in the Brighton area and if they were to disappear it would be a tragedy for the whole of the county." The conclusion of a Green Party statement supporting the use of Withdean Stadium by the Albion.

Thursday 20th May 2004

Swindon Town were the Withdean visitors for the second leg of the Second Division play-offs. On this very, very wet evening, Sam Parkin ended Ben Roberts' impressive run of clean sheets by netting just nine minutes from the end of normal time before substitute Rory Fallon gave the Wiltshire side the lead seven minutes into extra-time. Albion pushed and pushed but, with Leon Knight off injured, couldn't convert their chances. As the match entered the final minute, the Swindon fans started to celebrate.

Charlie Oatway's throw was flicked on by Danny Cullip for Adam Virgo to force a header past the opposing keeper to send a soaked Withdean into ecstasy. Penalties. Roberts saved Tommy Mooney's kick to earn Mark McGhee's men a trip to the Millennium Stadium. The match was voted by the fans as the best during the club's 12-year tenure at the Theatre of Trees.

Friday 20th May 2011

Albion signed Will Hoskins from Bristol Rovers on a two-year deal. The 25-year-old scored 20 times in 47 appearances in 2010/11 as the Gas were relegated from League One. The Nottingham-born striker, who has represented England at under-18, under-19 and under-20 level, said of the move; "It's wonderful to become a part of a project which is on the up. Everyone knows that things can happen at this club so as soon as I became aware that Brighton were interested in me, I had my heart set on coming here. I've had the chance to play against them and saw how the team moves, passes and works firsthand. That's something I was really impressed with, so I can't wait to get started next season."

Monday 20th May 2019

Graham Potter was appointed head coach of the Albion, on a four-year contract. The Solihull-born former left-back enjoyed a fairly unremarkable playing career and represented Birmingham City, Wycombe Wanderers (loan), Stoke City, Southampton, West Bromwich Albion, Northampton Town (loan), Reading (loan), York City, Boston United, Shrewsbury Town (loan) and Macclesfield Town between 1992 and 2005.

With support from the Professional Footballers' Association, Potter graduated from The Open University in December 2005 with a degree in social sciences working as a football development manager for the University of Hull, and then as technical director for the Ghana women's team at the 2007 FIFA Women's World Cup. After completing an MSc Leadership: Personal & Professional Development, which focused on using emotional intelligence, he took charge of Leeds Carnegie in Northern Counties East League Division One in 2008. Potter was famously poached by Östersund – a few months before Leeds Carnegie folded in 2011 – who plied their trade in the fourth tier of Swedish football. Three promotions, a cup win and European football for the first time certainly escalated his stock and it was no surprise when Swansea City came for him in June 2018. A year later, and Potter took (only) three members of his backroom staff – Billy Reid, Bjorn Hamberg and Kyle Macaulay – with him to join Brighton.

Saturday 21st May 1983

An unforgettable day in the club's history; Brighton & Hove Albion versus Manchester United in the FA Cup Final in front of 100,000 fans at Wembley Stadium, and many millions more worldwide on TV. The team flew into north London courtesy of a British Caledonian (the club's sponsors) helicopter. Tony Grealish led the team out, sporting a white headband in sympathy for the suspended Steve Foster.

On 13 minutes, Gary Howlett floated over a delightful cross for Gordon Smith to head into the bottom of the net – 1-0 Albion in the FA Cup Final! Dreamland! In the second-half Chris Ramsey was injured by a crude Norman Whiteside challenge and forced off, but not before Frank Stapleton had equalised with the right-back limping behind him. Ray Wilkins curled a magnificent shot around Graham Moseley but hadn't reckoned on Gary Stevens. The Man of the Match equalised four minutes from the final whistle, firing in from a short corner.

In the very last minute of extra-time Michael Robinson shrugged off Kevin Moran and passed across the box to Gordon Smith. Commentator Peter Jones famously screamed "and Smith must score" as goalkeeper Gary Bailey saved the Scotsman's low shot with his legs. The final whistle blew 21 seconds later. Both teams embarked on a lap of honour before the Albion flew back to Hove. At the 25th anniversary dinner of the famous game, Smith was asked what went through his mind as the ball came to him. "My immediate thought was to either leather it or dink it; I went with the latter."

Saturday 21st May 1988

Steve Penney netted the second and last of his international goals for Northern Ireland in the 3-0 win over Malta in Belfast.

Sunday 21st May 2023

Albion hosted Southampton in the penultimate Premier League home game of the campaign. Alexis Mac Allister teed up Ferguson, who took a touch to set himself before smashing the ball through the legs of a defender and the keeper to put his side ahead in the 29th minute. The 18-year-old Irishman took his tally to ten for the season just 11 minutes later.

Pascal Gross then equalled Glenn Murray and Neal Maupay's Premier League club record of 26 goals with a fierce left-foot effort. On the final whistle, the ground reverberated to 'We're All Going On a European Tour' as De Zerbi's men celebrated qualifying for European football for the very first time. Words I never thought I'd write as an Albion fan. What a truly remarkable achievement.

Wednesday 22nd May 1991

Albion travelled to the Lions' Den. After a resounding 4-1 first-leg home play-off victory against Millwall, over 3,000 Albion fans headed to south London dreaming of Wembley. An early home strike gave the travelling army the jitters until Robert Codner buried the equaliser. Young substitute John Robinson replaced Garry Nelson and confirmed Albion's victory with a fine effort to make it 6-2 on aggregate. On the final whistle, Millwall fans consoled themselves by nicking policeman's helmets, setting them on fire, and launching them on the East Stand roof. On arrival back in Brighton, the players celebrated at The Event, West Street where Radio One DJ Bruno Brookes was performing in aid of Steve Gatting's testimonial, and Sussex cricketer Tony Pigott's benefit year.

Sunday 22nd May 2011

The exterior stand signage was erected at Falmer. The carpets were laid in the hospitality areas while the perimeter tarmacking outside the stands was finished. The American Express Community Stadium was very close to being open for business. The whole of Brighton & Hove – and beyond – was now starting to get very excited indeed!

Saturday 23rd May 1981

A 3-0 defeat in Poland signified Mark Lawrenson's 14th and final appearance for the Republic of Ireland as an Albion player. The Preston-born defender went on to win 39 caps in total for his country, scoring on five occasions.

Monday 23rd May 1983

There were ugly scenes at the Goldstone Ground as FA Cup Final replay tickets went on sale to non-season-ticket-holders, who were restricted to one ticket each.

Thursday 24th May 1956

Doug Rougvie was born in Fife. The uncompromising defender joined Albion for £50,000 from Chelsea in 1987 after winning seven trophies in seven seasons at Aberdeen. The big Scot made 46 appearances and netted three times during 1987/88. His solitary Scotland cap came at Windsor Park, against Northern Ireland, in 1983.

Tuesday 24th May 2011

After 57 goals in 136 Brighton & Hove Albion appearances, Glenn Murray signed for Crystal Palace on a free transfer after failing to agree terms with Gus Poyet for the new season – after scoring the goals that got the club promoted to the Championship. One of Albion's all-time great forwards was replaced with Craig Mackail-Smith. The irony is that the pair would have worked well together as a strike partnership!

Wednesday 24th May 2023

A few weeks earlier Julio Enciso had scored a Goal of the Season contender at Chelsea. On this day, he managed to secure the accolade – against Premier League champions Manchester City, in a game with effectively nothing to play for as the opposition had already won the league, and Albion had qualified for the Europa League. On 38 minutes, the 19-year-old Paraguayan teenager picked the ball up from Levi Colwill and, in space 30 yards out, unleashed an absolute howitzer of a strike that curled into the top right-hand corner, beyond the despairing reach of Ortega – a truly world-class strike, applauded by sections of the away support. The goal meant teenagers had scored 11 of Albion's Premier League goals in 2022/23, two more than the other 19 clubs combined! And, as if that wasn't enough, the 1-1 scoreline meant Roberto De Zerbi's men had qualified for a European competition for the first time in the club's 122-year history. What an evening!

Monday 25th May 1953

Albion played outside England and Wales for the first time; a 4-4 draw against Belgian side RFC Liège. The teams exchanged tiepins and cufflinks before the kick-off.

Tuesday 25th May 1982

England kept a clean sheet in the 2-0 Wembley win over the Netherlands. Albion's Steve Foster was a rock in the centre of defence. It was Peter Shilton's first game as captain. Tony Woodcock and Paul Mariner were the goalscorers.

Tuesday 25th May 2010

An overhead image of Falmer, on this day, showed: the skeletons of the North and South stands, with terracing being added; an East Stand with the framework of a roof, ready for panelling; and the impressive, and currently roofless, West Stand having its upper tier terraced. It was really happening!

Thursday 26th May 1983

The FA Cup Final replay. On 22 minutes, Bryan Robson scored Manchester United's first, then Norman Whiteside made it 2-0 four minutes later. Albion's best chance came when Jimmy Case's shot was deflected, but Gary Bailey managed to tip it over. Robson scored again just before the break and Arnold Mühren added a fourth from the spot. The Albion fans' spirit was never broken as they out-sang the red masses. A game that doesn't need to be talked about ever again!

Wednesday 26th May 1999

Skint Records, home to Fatboy Slim (Norman Cook), were revealed as Albion's new shirt sponsor.

Saturday 27th May 1911

Albion were registered at Companies House. The company was listed at 129 Church Road, Hove. The club's Articles of Association did not allow any member of the board to receive any remuneration, and included a clause forbidding any board member to make any financial gain should the club fold. The clause was removed by Bill Archer and Greg Stanley in 1995.

Thursday 27th May 1982

Tony Grealish was on the wrong end of a 7-0 scoreline in Brazil. It was the Republic of Ireland midfielder's fourth international appearance while at the Goldstone.

Thursday 28th May 1998

"When I left in 1981 the club was thriving. That has totally gone and that is why it is so important that we get back to Withdean," declared Albion boss Brian Horton on signing a one-year contract.

Thursday 29th May 1997

Crawley's Broadfield Stadium, Coral's Brighton & Hove Greyhound Stadium or Gillingham's Priestfield Stadium? No decision had yet been made on where Albion would play next season.

Wednesday 29th May 2024

Ten members of Albion's women's squad ended the season by heading off on international duty. Most were involved in qualifiers for the 2025 Euros.

Three Norwegians – Guro Bergsvand, Maria Thorisdóttir and Elisabeth Terland – were preparing to face Italy, while Swedes Julia Zigiotti and Emma Kullberg were set to play Ireland. The rest had friendlies to look forward to in Australia, South America and across Europe.

Wednesday 30th May 1979

Nottingham Forest beat Malmö 1-0 in the European Cup Final in Munich. The manager of both clubs had an Albion connection; the English side's boss was Brian Clough, who sat in the Goldstone Ground hotseat for just nine months from November 1973. The Swedish side's gaffer was Bob Houghton, who was with Albion in 1969/70 but never played.

Sunday 30th May 2004

Albion headed to Cardiff to face Bristol City in the Second Division Play-off Final. Pint-sized hitman Leon Knight – the Second Division's leading goalscorer – hit the bar with a first-half free-kick but made no mistake from the spot in the 84th minute. Manager Mark McGhee sent out the unused substitutes – Kerry Mayo, Michel Kuipers and Adam Hinshelwood – to warm-up with instructions to 'gee up' the fans.

Just a few moments later striker Chris Iwelumo played a one-two with Knight and was fouled. Knight converted the penalty to send the 31,000 Seagulls fans – many of whom displayed 'We Want Falmer' banners – into raptures. Championship here we come!

Sunday 31st May 1970

Ian Chapman was born in Brighton. The popular left-back made his debut on Valentine's Day 1987 as a 16-year-old and went on to make 331 appearances, scoring 16 goals, before a move to Gillingham in 1996.

Saturday 31st May 1980

Peter Ward came on in the 85th minute of England's 2-1 win over Australia in Sydney – the shortest-ever international career for an England player up to that date.

Tuesday 31st May 2005

Lifelong fan Aaron Berry won the Albion a £250,000 transfer kitty after triumphing in the Win-a-Player promotion, run by Football League sponsors Coca-Cola. The IT trainer from Worthing registered his vote via the club website every day throughout the 80-day promotion, to see off competition from thousands of supporters of Football League and Scottish Premier League clubs. Manager Mark McGhee spent the money on 18-year-old striker Colin Kazim-Richards from Bury, who would become known as the 'Coca-Cola kid'.

Monday 31st May 2010

Sébastien Carole officially ended the third of his loan Albion spells. The winger arrived at Withdean from Châteauroux in 2005, in time for the second successive season in the Championship that ultimately ended in relegation back to the third tier. His first full campaign saw him on the opposite flank to his compatriot Alexandre Frutos and his energetic displays attracted the interest of Leeds United. Two-and-a-half years later Micky Adams re-signed the Frenchman – he made five starts in five months – before Gus Poyet gave him a further chance to impress in January 2010. Unfortunately, he didn't, and left in May 2010. Carole represented Martinique twice and his last club was Knaresborough Town, in Division One of the Northern Counties East League, in 2017.

Saturday 31st May 2017

The Albion Mag Radio Show, on 1BrightonFM (1BTN), aired in Brighton & Hove on 101.4FM and online. Presenters Dean Kilford and Leon Cox were joined in the studio by ex-Albion youth coach, and former Worthing manager Jon Meaney, and women's captain Sophie Perry.

Saturday 3rd May, 1997 around 4.20ish pm:
Robbie Reinelt scores at Hereford. The most important goal in
Albion's history.

© *The Argus*

JUNE

Saturday 1st June 1940

Albion's only game on this date was a wartime fixture against Watford that finished 2-2 in front of just 857 fans at the Goldstone Ground.

Wednesday 1st June 2011

Albion announced that the building contract works on the new stadium at Falmer had been completed on time by contractor Buckingham Group. Chief executive Martin Perry and construction director Derek Chapman praised the achievement. Chapman said; "I have worked in the construction sector all my life, but as a passionate Albion fan I have never been involved in a job which has given me so much satisfaction or excitement as The Amex. Buckingham has made that process very enjoyable, so I thank them and their subcontractors for all their hard work over the past two-and-a-half years." There was still plenty to do internally, but the stadium was Albion's at last – a day short of 14 years since the bulldozers moved on to the Goldstone site to commence demolition.

Sunday 2nd June 1991

Around 32,400 Albion fans (out of a total of 59,940) were at the Twin Towers, the biggest away following in the club's history, for the Second Division Play-off Final. Wearing the infamous red 'Chewits wrapper' kit, the club's third Wembley visit ended in a 3-1 defeat to Notts County. Dave Regis scored for the Magpies with his midriff and Dean Wilkins netted a consolation close to the full-time whistle.

Monday 2nd June 1997

A very sad – but inevitable – day as the bulldozers moved in to begin the demolition of the 95-year-old, and much loved, Goldstone Ground.

Thursday 2nd June 2016

Brighton & Hove Albion Women had their promotion to the Women's Super League Two approved after meeting the necessary WSL licensing requirements. A week prior, they beat Northern Division winners Sporting Club Albion 4-2 in a play-off at Adams Park. Quickfire second-half goals from Kate Natkiel, Sophie Perry and Amy Taylor, after Natkiel had earlier cancelled out Leigh Dugmore's opener, ended their tenure in the third tier of the women's game. The WSL's on- and off-field criteria included finance and business management, facilities and marketing requirements.

"Brighton thoroughly deserve their promotion after such a fantastic season and for their development off the pitch in recent years. It is great for the league that we now have a club on the south coast, which will help us to develop a wider fanbase," said The Football Association's head of leagues and competitions, Katie Brazier. Albion CEO Paul Barber added; "We are very proud of the achievements of our women's team this season."

Sunday 3rd June 1979

Alan Mullery was sent off during a friendly game against San Diego Sockers in California! One of the home players kicked Peter Sayer and the ex-England captain ran on to the pitch to protest and swore at the officials. He was subsequently sent off, later fined £750, and banned from the touchline.

Thursday 3rd June 1998

Following on from the previous day's 10-2 planning committee vote in favour of Albion's Withdean use, two more council meetings approved use of the stadium, dependent on safety certificates and landlord approval.

Thursday 3rd June 2010

On a sunny day, the stunning white arches that would hold up the West Stand roof were lowered into place at Falmer.

Thursday 4th June 1998

SWEAT (Save Withdean Environment Action Team) rejected Lord Bassam's proposal for the council; club and residents to work together to make the Albion's time there a success.

Monday 5th June 2006

A month after its formation, the Seagulls Party was officially launched. Registered with The Electoral Commission, the party would field candidates at future elections and champion the proposed new stadium at Falmer. Party leader Paul Samrah said of their chances; "We have strong support right across the Lewes district, from Newick to Newhaven and from Seaford to Saltdean. Make no mistake, we are very serious in our aims. Anyone looking for a precedent need look no further than The Valley Party, which 15 years ago attracted over 14,000 votes in favour of Charlton Athletic's stadium when it fought local elections in south-east London." Don't mess with Albion fans!

Monday 6th June 2011

In 1980, the Albion paid £500,000 to Manchester United for the services of young striker Andy Ritchie. In the 31 years that followed, the club did not pay a higher fee for a player – until this day. Midfielder/ second striker Will Buckley arrived in a £1 million deal from Watford. Yes, that's right – a million pounds! The 21-year-old began his career at Rochdale, where he spent two seasons, before joining the Hornets in 2010. The move for the Oldham-born six-footer was precipitated by Elliott Bennett's sale to Premier League Norwich City.

Meanwhile, at Falmer, Albion's new badge was mounted at either end of the West Stand. The roundel design, based on the classic insignia that was used from 1977 to 1998, now features a seagull – with a yellow beak – facing to the right, instead of the left. Perceptual studies have found that humans judge rightward objects as moving faster, and their movements to be more natural, than the same objects going left. Also, our minds represent time as unfolding from left to right, so things facing right give the impression they're moving into the future and making progress. Pretty accurate!

Monday 7th June 1986

Spain got their World Cup revenge for Northern Ireland's victory four years earlier. Albion's Steve Penney did his best but the red and yellows triumphed 2-1 in Guadalajara, Mexico.

Friday 7th June 2024

Pascal Gross scored his first international goal for Germany in their friendly 2-1 victory over Greece in Mönchengladbach. The midfielder was earning his seventh cap and netted a superb late winner in the 89th minute. The Albion legend said; "My journey has been quite unique after moving from Ingolstadt to England [in 2017]."

Tuesday 8th June 1948

After finishing bottom of the Third Division (South), Albion applied for re-election. Chairman Charles Wakeling highlighted ground improvements (extended terracing and an enlarged South Stand) and described the large Goldstone crowds in a letter to the other clubs. Albion received 47 votes, Norwich City 47, Colchester United 2, Gillingham 1 and Worcester City 1.

Wednesday 9th June 1999

David Cameron – not the former Prime Minister – arrived after buying himself out of the Argyll & Sutherland Highlanders. Once called 'useless' by assistant manager Alan Cork, and occasionally 'silky' by supporters – with tongues firmly planted in collective cheeks – the 'striker' donned the stripes 17 times without scoring.

Tuesday 10th June 1947

Jim Walker was born in Northwich, Cheshire. The midfielder was signed from Derby County but never lived up to his £25,000 price tag and left for Peterborough United in 1976. After his playing career ended, Jim become a physiotherapist, working in Kuwait and Blackburn Rovers before joining Aston Villa in 1986.

Saturday 11th June 1988

After the exciting promotion run-in, 1,500 Albion fans wasted no time in snapping up season tickets for the forthcoming Second Division campaign.

Thursday 11th June 1998

One of the best transfers in the history of the Albion; warehouseman Gary Hart arrived from Essex League Stansted for just £1,000. Originally signed as a striker, the popular player featured in many positions in his 300+ Albion appearances and made his last first-team run-out in the stripes in the final home game at Withdean. Also on this day, the government allowed Brighton & Hove Council to make the final decision on Withdean's use.

Friday 12th June 1981

Alan Mullery, the club's most successful manager to that point, shocked the football world by resigning as Albion boss.

Wednesday 13th June 1973

The club lost one of its favourite sons; Charlie Webb passed away in Hove aged 86. Such was the inside-left's love of the Albion that he turned down a chance to manage Tottenham Hotspur before World War II.

Thursday 13th June 2002

Albion fans rejoiced at Hove Town Hall as the city planning committee voted 11-1 in favour, in principle, of a community stadium at Falmer. The application, first submitted in October 2001, caused unprecedented levels of interest in the city. Speaking for Albion as Dick Knight was abroad, Martin Perry told councillors the decision they were taking was equal in importance to approving the marina or The Brighton Centre. Among the opponents of the plan, Green convenor Keith Taylor, who boycotted the meeting on the grounds it was a stitch-up. He suggested the application could run into real trouble if there was a public inquiry.

Thursday 14th June 1905

One-season wonder Hugh Vallance was born in Wolverhampton. The striker scored an amazing 30 league goals in just 37 Third Division (South) games in the 1929/30 season, one more than team-mate Dan Kirkwood. Seven games into the new campaign, Hugh left the Goldstone following a very serious, long-forgotten misdemeanour which was explained when Brighton & Hove Albion Heritage Society published an article in their superb quarterly magazine, *The Albion Chronicle* in 2024.

Tuesday 14th June 2011

Two huge TV screens were erected at Falmer. Situated on the back wall of the South and North stands – either side of the goal – the screens were two of the biggest of their kind in Europe. Albion staff had been in their North Stand offices for a week and the Albion in the Community team were due to arrive sometime in the next fortnight. On the same day, Elliott Bennett left for Premier League Norwich City for an undisclosed fee. The Telford-born playmaker spent two seasons with Albion making 98 appearances – two as substitute – scoring 17 times, including some real humdingers at Oldham, Walsall and the Theatre of Trees. The 22-year-old also contributed an incredible amount of assists, notching well over 20 as Albion romped to the League One title in 2011.

Wednesday 14th June 2023

The first of seven signings for the Albion's first team squad for the 2023/24 season put pen to paper – João Pedro (from Watford). The other six were: Mahmoud Dahoud (Borussia Dortmund), James Milner (Liverpool), Bart Verbruggen (Anderlecht), Igor Julio (Fiorentina), Carlos Baleba (Lille) and Valentín Barco (Boca Juniors).

Saturday 15th June 1991

Pascal Gross (Groß) was born in Mannheim, Germany. The versatile midfielder started his career at TSG Hoffenheim, then played for Karlsruher SC and FC Ingolstadt 04. He also represented the three German club's second sides too. The 26-year-old arrived on the south coast in the summer of 2017, for a fee of £3 million, to a resounding chorus of 'who?!' from the home support. Not at a game, obviously, but in pubs, clubs and front rooms across Sussex. No-one had heard of him. His Albion career started well, and he scored the club's first goal in the Premier League, ending the campaign with seven goals and eight assists. An excellent return when you consider Brighton only hit the net on 34 occasions during 2017/18! No Pascal – no Premier League!

He fell out of favour for a while under Chris Hughton, who switched to a 4-3-3 formation, and suffered with injuries too. Never renowned for his pace, Pascal more than made up for it with numerous other attributes, including the wonderful 'Gross turn'. Initially named after the move's originator, and footballing icon Johan Cruyff, the German gradually made it his own, to the absolute joy of the Falmer regulars. His ability to play literally anywhere on the pitch, his set-piece delivery, assists, goals and consistency has ensured his rightful place in Albion's history. Never one to whinge and moan when he's out of the team, Gross has embedded himself into the Albion furniture with his team ethic and general humility – a huge part of Brighton's Premier League tenure. The excellent wearebrighton.com suggested he could be the greatest player to ever represent Brighton & Hove Albion Football Club – they could well be right. Pascal Gross, we salute you!

Monday 15th June 1998

Albion appointed Martin Hinshelwood as director of youth, a day before his birthday, together with Dean Wilkins as youth-team coach. On the same day, the club announced that they expected Withdean to be ready by the end of September.

Saturday 15th June 2024

Albion appointed Fabian Hürzeler as head coach. The 31-year-old led St. Pauli – based in Hamburg, Germany – to promotion to the Bundesliga in May. Born in Houston, Texas, the youngest manager of the Premier League era played for Bayern Munich's academy in Germany's lower leagues before becoming player-manager of fourth-tier Pipinsried, taking over as St. Pauli's head coach in 2022. Tony Bloom commented on the bold move; "From the start of the process to appoint our new head coach, Fabian was always a standout candidate and one who had caught our attention with his exceptional work at St. Pauli over the past 18 months. He has a style of play that aligns with how we want a Brighton & Hove Albion team to play, and I'm confident it is one our supporters will appreciate and enjoy." Hürzeler told brightonandhovealbion.com: "Brighton have a unique history and a bold vision for the future so I am truly excited to be part of the project. The club has made incredible progress over the last few seasons and the aim is to continue building on that success."

Saturday 16th June 2001

Albion fans congregated at St Peter's Church, Brighton to celebrate the club's 100th anniversary at a special thanksgiving service. Brighton & Hove mayor Harry Steer declared; "God bless you Albion, from the city of Brighton & Hove we congratulate you on your centenary and we wish you every success in the future, going up and up."

Saturday 17th June 1911

Don Barker was born in Derbyshire. The inside-forward was signed, as a 35-year-old, by Charlie Webb for £400 in July 1946 and had to travel to home matches from his Midlands home due to the lack of housing in Sussex at the time.

Friday 17th June 2011

In October 2008, Albion fan Graeme Rolf noticed work commencing at the proposed site of the stadium at Falmer. He decided to take a few photographs and shared them with fellow supporters on internet forum North Stand Chat. Two-and-a-half years later, after at least 125 Friday lunchtime visits, his final shots were posted. An invaluable service to Albionites the world over, his final album showed the pristine interior; boardroom, suites, kiosks, lifts, toilets, press room, supporters' bar, museum and club shop. What a beautiful place!

Thursday 18th June 1931

Peter Harburn was born in Finsbury, London. The big striker scored 65 goals in 133 starts before an £8,000 move to First Division Everton in 1958. The move up a division wasn't a success. After stints at Scunthorpe United and Workington Town, the Londoner ended up at Chelmsford City, where he became coach and manager as well as running the Bird in Hand pub. Harburn was still playing – in goal – in 1984 and passed away in 2010.

Monday 18th June 2012

Paul Barber started his Albion tenure. He was linked to various roles at Premier League clubs, including a return to Tottenham Hotspur, before surprising some football people by joining a Championship club. He oversaw the stadium's expansion to a capacity of just over 30,000 in his first full year, and announced Albion's most valuable sponsorship deal ever, when American Express signed a multi-year agreement to be on the shirt. Now deputy chairman as well CEO, Barber has overseen huge progress – on and off the pitch – as Albion cemented their place in the top division.

Sunday 18th June 2023

Brighton & Hove Albion Blind FC made history by winning the FA Disability Cup for the first time, beating RNC Hereford 1-0. The victory completed a historic league and cup double, after the Albion also finished top of the National Blind Football League. The final, held at St. George's Park, was watched by thousands of fans live on BT Sport. Hamad Ebrahim scored the only goal of the game. Albion's victorious squad: 1 Maciej Kason, 3 Cyril Thomas, 4 Liam Archer, 5 Robin Williams, 6 Saman Ojradast, 7 Hamad Ebrahim, 8 Darren Harris.

Friday 19th June 1931

The founder of Brighton & Hove Albion Football Club, John Jackson, died at the age of 70. The son of a Birmingham master toolmaker, John represented Coventry Rangers between the sticks before coaching at Liverpool and Leicester Fosse, arriving on the coast in 1901.

Wednesday 19th June 2024

In familiar surroundings, Deniz Undav – who had enjoyed a prolific season on loan at VfB Stuttgart – replaced İlkay Gündoğan in Germany's 2-0 win over Hungary at the 2024 European Championships in Stuttgart. Pascal Gross was also on the bench for the Germans.

Wednesday 20th June 1951

Billy McEwan was born in Lanarkshire, Scotland. The midfielder began his career at Hibernian before heading south to Blackpool in May 1973. Brian Clough signed him for £15,000 in February 1974 and despite only making 28 appearances – scoring three times – Billy showed great leadership qualities. He was appointed technical director of the Antigua and Barbuda Football Association in March 2010 and became manager of Antigua Barracuda a month later. Diagnosed with Parkinson's disease in 2014, he died in 2022.

Saturday 20th June 2020

Neal Maupay scored the winner five minutes into added time as relegation-threatened Albion clinched a 2-1 home win over Arsenal – the first match after the 2019/2020 season had been halted due to the coronavirus pandemic. The Frenchman slotted in his ninth and most important goal of the season to give his side their first league win of 2020 – and cap a remarkable comeback. Brighton were the first team to publicly voice opposition to games being played at neutral grounds in the discussion about how the Premier League might conclude during the pandemic. While the Amex was obviously lacking in fervent home support – it was completely empty – this did not hamper Albion's appetite for the fight.

Thursday 20th June 2024

Albion captain Lewis Dunk was on the bench as England played out a disappointing 1-1 draw against Denmark at the 2024 European Championships in Frankfurt, Germany.

Sunday 21st June 1964

Dean Saunders was born in Swansea and began his career at the Vetch Field. Released in July 1985, he arrived in Hove and quickly impressed the Goldstone fans with his pace and eye for goal. After netting 19 times in his first season, Saunders' form dipped and Barry Lloyd replaced him with Richard Tiltman, much to the chagrin of the home support. A paltry bid of £60,000 was accepted from Oxford United in March 1987. In a career spanning almost 20 years, the Welshman also played for Liverpool, Aston Villa, Galatasaray, Nottingham Forest, Sheffield United, Benfica and finally Bradford City at the age of 36.

Monday 22nd June 1998

The club announced a novel, free travel zone extending throughout the Brighton & Hove area. A travel voucher worth £2 would be included with each match ticket for bus and train travel to Worthing in the west, Haywards Heath in the north and Lewes in the east. In 2024, it's still in place.

Tuesday 23rd June 1998

Paul Holsgrove joined on a free transfer from Stoke City and signed a two-year contract. Despite not playing a single competitive game, the 28-year-old midfielder was sold to Hibernian just six weeks later for £110,000! A good bit of business.

Sunday 23rd June 2013

Albion manager Gus Poyet appeared on Match of the Day as a pundit. During half-time of a Confederations Cup match broadcast, presenter Mark Chapman suggested that the Uruguayan had been sacked by the club, and that the production team had printed out the club statement. This was not the case. He had been informed earlier that day.

Thursday 23rd June 2022

The first of 24 transfers out of the club for the 2022/23 campaign was Davy Pröpper, who returned to former club PSV Eindhoven. Other notable departures included José Izquierdo (Club Brugge), Bernardo (Red Bull Salzburg), Viktor Gyökeres (Coventry City), Mathew Ryan (Real Sociedad), Alireza Jahanbakhsh (Feyenoord), Ben White (Arsenal), Percy Tau (Al Ahly), Jürgen Locadia (VfL Bochum), Christian Walton (Ipswich Town), Dan Burn (Newcastle United), Ryan Longman (Hull City), Billy Arce (free agent) and Gary Dicker, who hung up his boots after helping out with the under-23s.

Monday 24th June 1901

The day when it all began... Brighton & Hove Albion Football Club came into being at the Seven Stars public house in Ship Street, Brighton. Founder John Jackson had previously been involved with the town's other two outfits, United and Rangers. The new club was to be christened Brighton & Hove United, but Hove Football Club objected on the grounds that they would lose support as the public may assume United were a merger of the former United and Rangers.

As a result, the Albion was born. The origins of the name are unclear, but two reasons stand out: the town had many businesses with the Albion suffix, or it was because founder John Jackson had close links with West Bromwich Albion.

Either way, it works!

Up the Albion!

Sunday 24th June 2001

Happy 100th birthday Brighton & Hove Albion Football Club! During that time the club had enjoyed seven promotions and endured seven relegations. The next decade would prove to be equally as exciting with a further six divisional movements – four up and two down.

Friday 24th June 2011

One hundred and ten years ago, Brighton & Hove Albion were founded in the Seven Stars pub in Brighton. On this day, the club's Tower Point offices were handed back to the landlord. The Albion were now based at Falmer!

Tuesday 25th June 1982

A great day for Albion. Sammy Nelson came on against Spain in the famous 1-0 World Cup win for Northern Ireland over the hosts in Valencia. The crucial goal was scored by Gerry Armstrong, who would go on to play for the Albion a few years later. Nearly 300 miles away in Bilbao, Steve Foster made his third and last England appearance in the 1-0 win over Kuwait.

Wednesday 26th June 1974

Former Dutch marine Michel Kuipers was born in Amsterdam. After just one appearance for Bristol Rovers, Micky Adams picked up the big keeper on a free transfer in June 2000. Capable of world-class saves, the Dutchman was a crowd favourite at Withdean before moving to Crawley Town in 2010, after a couple of loan spells at Boston United. The fans made up a song for him (to the tune of The Beatles' Yellow Submarine):

'Michel Kuipers the former Dutch marine,
The former Dutch marine,
The former Dutch marine, chef!'

Monday 26th June 2023

Albion announced a couple of important name changes. From 1st August, the American Express Community Stadium would become the American Express Stadium while the club's charitable arm, Albion in the Community (AITC), was to be known as the Brighton & Hove Albion Foundation, which would be housed in Freshfield Road, in the east of Brighton.

Chief executive and deputy chairman Paul Barber said; "These small but important changes are designed to deliver even better value to our main partner, while also more closely aligning and connecting our charity's excellent work and its many participants with our club."

Thursday 27th June 2002

The Society of Sussex Downsmen, the oldest South Downs conservation group, called for a public inquiry into the new stadium plans for Falmer.

Wednesday 28th June 1933

A future Busby Babe was born in Lancashire. Freddie Goodwin first came to prominence at Manchester United in 1953 but was overshadowed by the outstanding Duncan Edwards who would sadly die in the Munich air crash of 1958. After a spell with Leeds United, and short tenures at Scunthorpe United and New York Generals, Freddie took control in Hove in November 1968 transforming a relegation-threatened side into promotion chasers.

Freddie left for Birmingham City in May 1970. Five years later he moved to the US to coach and serve as president of Minnesota Kicks. He then coached Tacoma Stars and started a travel agency on Vashon Island in Washington state. He died in 2016.

Saturday 29th June 2002

Former Stoke City and Icelandic international boss, Gudjón Thórdarson, declared his intention of applying for the Albion manager's job. As of 2024, his last managerial role was at Ungmennafélagið Víkingur, also known as U.M.F. Víkingur or Víkingur Ólafsvík, based on the west coast of Iceland.

Friday 30th June 2006

The Argus reported that the war medals of former Albion chairman Captain William Charles 'Carlo' Campbell were to be auctioned. He was decorated for gallantry while flying more than 20 sorties within a few months during World War I but was best known for an abortive bid to bring cheetah racing to Britain in 1937.

He imported six cheetahs to perk up greyhound racing at White City in west London but the 70mph creatures failed to muster the necessary competitive spirit. An observer recalled that 'they just wandered about'. Greyhounds could be relied on to race an entire track, and through the finish line, and gamblers could get odds on dogs to finish first or second, or to place. Cheetahs, on the other hand, were immune to the demands of the Tote and if one took an early lead, the others would simply stop, sensibly saving their energy.

Monday 30th June 2008

Adam Virgo rejoined the Albion on a free transfer from Celtic, three years after leaving for the Glasgow giants in a £1.5 million deal. The Brighton-born defender enjoyed loan spells at Coventry City and Colchester United before signing a two-year deal. Virgo said; "It feels fantastic to be coming home, now I can't wait to get started. When I knew the club and Micky were interested it was a very easy decision to make."

The oldest known matchday programme to feature the Albion, at Southampton in 1903.

© www.seagullsprogrammes.co.uk

JULY

Monday 1st July 1996

Out-of-contract Albion skipper Paul McCarthy signed for Wycombe Wanderers for a fee that was eventually determined by a tribunal at £100,000 after 217 appearances – and eight goals – for the club. The fan favourite played over 250 times for the Chairboys including the memorable run to the FA Cup semi-final in 2001 and finished his professional career at Ebbsfleet United, where he featured in 110 games, lifting the FA Trophy in 2008. Tragically, the Irishman died, aged just 45, of a suspected heart attack in 2017.

Wednesday 1st July 2015

Tomer Hemed signed for the Albion from Spanish club UCD Almeria for a fee of £1 million. The Israel-born striker had been plying his trade in La Liga but decided to swap facing Messi and Ronaldo a couple of times a season, to guaranteeing trips to Charlton Athletic and MK Dons with his new team-mates. In his first campaign on the coast, the 6ft hitman topped the goalscoring charts with 17, including a hat-trick in a 5-0 home demolition of Fulham which left Albion second in the Championship, a point behind Middlesbrough with four games remaining.

In 2016/17, Glenn Murray joined the attack (again) as Hemed enjoyed another successful season, finishing as the third-highest scorer, behind the returning Cumbrian and Anthony Knockaert. The Premier League proved a bit more difficult for the forward and he went out on loan to Queens Park Rangers for 2018/19. He is fondly remembered for his crucial contribution to Albion's return to the top division after 34 years. Hemed finished his playing career at Maccabi Haifa and, in August 2024, rejoined to the Albion as a mentor.

Saturday 1st July 2017

Undoubtedly one of the most important signings in the history of Brighton & Hove Albion, Pascal Gross signed from Bundesliga outfit FC Ingolstadt 04, where he scored 17 times in 158 games, for just £3 million. The German scored Albion's first in the Premier League – at home to West Bromwich Albion (see 9th September 2017) – to take his total to seven in an ever-present maiden campaign. He has played in every position (except for in goal, but I'm sure he could do a job) for the club and has been the model of consistency during the club's seven-year (so far) stint in the top-flight. His Cruyff turn – now called the Gross turn in the West Stand Upper – is guaranteed to raise a cheer every time. His solid performances were rewarded with his first senior cap for his country (see Thursday 9th September 2023).

Sunday 1st July 2018

The first of 33 Albion players were sent out on loan for the forthcoming season. Notable names on the list for 2018/19 included Robert Sánchez (Forest Green Rovers), Ben White (Peterborough United), Alexis Mac Allister (Argentinos Juniors) and Billy Arce (Emelec, Ecuador). Twenty-five players left permanently including Jiří Skalák, Connor Goldson, Uwe Hünemeier, Niki Mäenpää, Liam Rosenior and Oliver Norwood.

Monday 2nd July 1928

Peter Taylor, the first Albion-related one, was born in Nottingham. He met Brian Clough while at Middlesbrough in the 1950s and the pair's careers were linked for the next 27 years. They strolled into the Goldstone in late 1973 and while Clough would depart just eight months later, Taylor honoured his contract and signed two of the club's all-time great players for ridiculously low fees; Brian Horton for £27,000 and Peter Ward for just £4,000! He re-joined his old friend in 1976 and the two would lead Nottingham Forest to two successive European Cup triumphs and a league title.

They fell out following a dispute over a transfer in May 1983 and Taylor's sudden death in October 1990 robbed Clough of the chance of reconciliation, something he greatly regretted.

Monday 2nd July 2007

The inspector's report into South Downs National Park declared the site at Falmer should not be included as it was already designated for possible development.

Tuesday 3rd July 1883

The first player to score 50 goals for the club, Jack Hall, was born in Hucknall, Nottinghamshire. The centre-forward signed for Albion from Stoke City in 1906 and his prolific form – 54 goals in 93 starts – attracted the attention of First Division Middlesbrough in 1908.

Friday 3rd July 2009

The first concrete slabs that would form the backbone of the East Stand were carefully driven into the ground at the Falmer site.

Sunday 3rd July 2016

Great news for Albion fans everywhere as the club announced the return of striker Glenn Murray on a season-long loan from AFC Bournemouth. The 32-year-old's 23 Championship goals in 2016/17 played a huge part in the club's promotion to the Premier League.

Friday 4th July 1997

The scene of many ups, downs, downright lows and fantastic highs, the Goldstone Ground was finally demolished. The work, which took five weeks, razed the 96-year-old football arena to make way for a retail park. A disgraceful act that fed one man's greed and destroyed the hopes and aspirations of thousands of men, women and children. If you ever read this, Bill Archer, hang your head in shame.

Wednesday 4th July 2007

Following Gordon Brown's ascension to Prime Minister there was a cabinet reshuffle – again – and the stadium decision was moved back to on, or before, 25th July. The hopes of thousands of Albion fans were now in the hands of Hazel Blears.

Monday 4th July 2011

Just under a month earlier, Albion fans wiped their eyes in disbelief as the club spent a million pounds on a player for the first time in their history. On this day goal machine Craig Mackail-Smith arrived for an undisclosed fee, believed to be well over £2 million! The forward scored 27 league goals for Peterborough United in 2010/11 and his signing showed a real statement of intent by the club and its board. 'Exciting times ahead' may prove to be the understatement of the decade.

Monday 5th July 1999

The South Stand seating arrived at Withdean, 19 days before the first scheduled match at the stadium, a friendly against Nottingham Forest.

Thursday 6th July 1876

An eventual Celtic Park favourite, Paddy Gilhooly was born in Scotland. The inside-right was brought to the Goldstone in 1904 after a three-year spell at White Hart Lane and, previously, a successful campaign in Glasgow. Paddy was released in 1905 after scoring five times in 16 starts and sadly died just two years later, aged 31.

Friday 6th July 2012

It was confirmed that England international Wayne Bridge would join the Albion on a season-long loan. The left-back's debut came a month later and his first goal on 25th August, a 5-1 home victory over Barnsley – almost a decade since scoring his last for Chelsea in December 2003. He played 37 league games, including both play-off legs against Crystal Palace, netting on three occasions. One of the finest players to ever wear the stripes, Bridge told *The Independent;* "Brighton have been great to me. I just want to say a big thank you to the chairman and the fans. Gus [Poyet] has revitalised my love for football after I was in the wilderness at Manchester City."

Tuesday 6th July 2021

Zambian international Enock Mwepu joined Albion from reigning Austrian champions Red Bull Salzburg. The 23-year-old midfielder became Graham Potter's first signing ahead of the 2021/22 Premier League campaign. He was nicknamed 'The Computer' by Salzburg fans due to his ability to read the game.

Tuesday 7th July 1931

Alex South was born in Brighton. The centre-half played for Whitehawk Boys Club before joining the Goldstone ground staff. The local lad made 85 starts in eight years.

Wednesday 8th July 1959

FA Cup Final left-back Graham Pearce was born in Hammersmith, London. Just nine months before the big day out at Wembley, the defender was plying his trade with non-league Barnet. Mike Bailey paid £20,000 for Sammy Nelson and Steve Gatting's understudy, and a series of injuries later saw the stocky Londoner run out on 21st May 1983.

Thursday 9th July 1998

SWEAT advised Brighton & Hove Council of their intention to seek judicial review to stop Albion playing at Withdean Stadium.

Friday 9th July 1999

Manager Micky Adams took his squad to Ballygar in County Galway, Ireland. The pre-season 'bonding' trip included a number of newcomers including Paul Watson, Paul Rogers, Ryan Palmer, Jamie Campbell and Charlie Oatway, plus trialists Chris Wilder and Aidan Newhouse.

Wednesday 10th July 2002

Albion joined fellow Football League clubs in a mass protest over the collapsed ITV Digital deal. Representatives of almost all of the 72 league clubs picketed outside the London offices of Carlton and Granada, the parent companies behind the defunct channel. The protest raised awareness of the High Court battle to recoup the £178.5 million lost.

Wednesday 10th July 2024

England faced the Netherlands in a European Championship semi-final in Dortmund, Germany. Albion captain Lewis Dunk was on the bench for Gareth Southgate's side while his club team-mate Bart Verbruggen played the full 90 minutes for the Oranje. In an absorbing contest, the Three Lions dominated the first half, and Netherlands the second. In the last minute, two of the substitutes combined as Cole Palmer slid a pass through to Ollie Watkins, who took a touch and drilled it past the Albion custodian from a tight angle. An excellent finish. England were in their second successive Euros final.

Monday 11th July 1988

Former chairman Mike Bamber died after a two-year battle with cancer. Bamber joined the board in 1970 and became chairman three years later. In November 1973 he persuaded Brian Clough – who always regarded Bamber as the best chairman he worked for – to take over the reins, but it was his appointment of Alan Mullery in 1976 that paved the way for the club's golden years. He once appeared on local television playing the drums in his lounge.

Monday 11th July 2022

An almost full house was in attendance at Falmer to watch England Women's group stage match with Norway in the European Championships. The away side, ranked 11th in the world, were outplayed, outclassed and completely stunned by a home team oozing confidence. Georgia Stanway started the masterclass slotting in a 12th-minute penalty and within half an hour, Lauren Hemp and Ellen White had extended England's lead. Beth Mead bagged a brace and White – to move within one of Wayne Rooney's international record – netted another to make it six without reply by half-time. Russo made it seven (66th) before Mead completed her deserved hat-trick. An astonishing night in Brighton. Final score: England 8, Norway 0.

Thursday 12th July 1962

Brother of future England captain Ray Wilkins, Dean, was born in Middlesex. The midfielder joined the Albion after making two appearances for QPR in 1983 but soon departed for PEC Zwolle in Holland – on the recommendation of Hans Kraay – for three years. The 25-year-old returned in 1987 when Barry Lloyd paid £10,000 for his services. Wilkins became an integral part of the promotion side in 1988, and the Play-off Final losing team of 1991 – making 123 consecutive appearances – with his incisive passing and creativity. Dean re-joined Albion – after 375 appearances and 31 goals – as youth-team coach in 1998 and took over as first-team boss in September 2006.

Thursday 12th July 2001

More than 4,500 Albion fans wrote to the city council asking them to keep the Falmer site in its Local Plan. But roughly the same number, spurred on by environmentalists and Falmer Parish Council, were against the idea.

Monday 13th July 1987

Barry Lloyd sold Danny Wilson to Luton Town for £150,000. New centre-half Doug Rougvie replaced the Northern Irishman as captain.

Wednesday 14th July 1999

New striker David Cameron, who had bought himself out of the Army to become a professional footballer, impressed in the victory over Saltdean United. The Scot was not allowed to travel with the first team on the pre-season tour of Ireland because of defence regulations.

Sunday 14th July 2024

England lost the 2024 European Championships final in Berlin. After winning every game on the way – six in total – to the final, Spain were worthy winners, winning 2-1. Cole Palmer scored England's goal. Albion club captain Lewis Dunk was in the squad but unfortunately didn't feature during the tournament.

Sunday 15th July 1928

Jimmy Leadbetter was born in Edinburgh. The inside-forward had a tough job following in the footsteps of Johnny McNichol but managed a highly credible 33 goals in 133 Albion starts.

Thursday 15th July 2021

The Albion signed Danielle Carter from Reading. The 28-year-old represented England at every age group from under-17s to senior, winning four full caps and scoring six goals (up to March 2024) and can operate anywhere across the front line.

She won the FA Cup three times during her time with Arsenal and scored the winning goal in the 2016 final against Chelsea. Head coach Hope Powell said; "Danielle is a player I have known and admired for a long time, and I'm really pleased she is joining us for the next stage of our journey in the WSL."

Thursday 16th July 1981

Widely regarded as one of the greatest players to ever pull on a blue-and-white-striped shirt, Vicente Rodríguez Guillén was born in Valencia. During his hugely successful 11-year spell with his hometown club – where he won La Liga twice – Vicente was christened 'El puñal de Benicalap' (the dagger of Benicalap), for being a 'spear down the flank'. On 17th April 2014, the midfielder announced his retirement from football and returned to work with Valencia as a member of the technical staff. He described his former boss, Gus Poyet, as "the worst person I've come across in football", "selfish" and "egocentric".

Friday 16th July 2010

Radostin Kishishev signed for the Albion. After a seven-year spell in the Premier League with Charlton Athletic, Kish enjoyed loan stays at Leeds United and Leicester City before returning to his home country in January 2009. Gus came calling and the combative midfielder's experience – he won 88 caps for Bulgaria – played a significant part in the club's peerless 2010/11 season. He returned to play for hometown club Chernomorets Burgas for one more season and managed them in 2018/19.

Saturday 16th July 2011

Club legend Gary Hart enjoyed his last hurrah for the Albion in the Sussex Senior Cup Final against Eastbourne Borough in the inaugural competitive fixture at the American Express Community Stadium. The long-serving talisman opened the scoring to become the very first player to find the back of the net at the new arena; a fitting way to bring down the curtain on a magnificent Albion career.

Sunday 16th July 2023

Albion Women signed the vastly experienced María Victoria Losada Gómez (Vicky) from Roma on a long-term deal. The 32-year-old Spanish midfielder's illustrious career included three stints at Barcelona (292 appearances) where she collected six Primera División winners' medals. Plus, domestic cups with Manchester City and Chelsea and a Serie A title with Roma. An impressive haul.

Wednesday 17th July 1901

Despite the Albion's founders persuading Hove FC that they would not use the 'United' suffix for their new club – so as not to confuse locals who might assume the new club was an amalgamation – the Goldstone's owners still threatened to get The FA involved.

Monday 18th July 1983

The British press reported the Albion were to sign... Kevin Keegan! Meanwhile, Brighton rock shop owner Chris Cattlin was appointed assistant manager under Jimmy Melia – even though the latter was on holiday at the time and knew nothing of the appointment.

Saturday 18th July 1987

After seven years of all-blue shirts (with varying amounts of white trim, and the occasional red stripe), Albion announced – much to the relief of fans worldwide – the return to the famous blue and white stripes.

Friday 18th July 2003

Goalscoring machine Bobby Zamora was sold to Tottenham Hotspur for a club-record fee of £1.5 million. Despite its inevitability, the sale of the 22-year-old, and sixth-highest club goalscorer of all time, devastated Albion fans.

Saturday 19th July 1958

FA Cup finalist Neil Smillie was born in Yorkshire. The winger played a key role on the road to Wembley and scored three times in 98 appearances before a £100,000 switch to Watford in 1985.

Wednesday 19th July 2017

Brighton & Hove Albion announced that Hope Powell had been appointed as first-team manager of the club's women's team. The

51-year-old arrived on the south coast with an impressive CV. She represented England on 66 occasions, scoring 35 times, after making her debut as a 16-year-old. Powell managed her country too – from 1998 to 2013 – straight after hanging up her boots.

Saturday 20th July 1974

Leeds United manager Don Revie was appointed England boss. The Elland Road outfit announced their new manager as… Brian Clough. Only problem was that the outspoken former goal machine – for Middlesbrough and Sunderland – was in charge at the Albion! Chairman Mike Bamber agreed compensation of £75,000 for the remaining four years of his manager's contract, but Leeds reneged on the deal. The Whites eventually paid Albion £45,000 in compensation. Clough lasted 44 days in Yorkshire.

Wednesday 20th July 1994

Solomon Benjamin March was born in Eastbourne, East Sussex. His dad, Steve, was an Albion apprentice in the late 1980s and Solly represented Crystal Palace between the ages of 11 and 13 before moving to his local side, Eastbourne Borough, then Lewes, who recommended the winger to the Albion, who offered the 17-year-old a scholarship. He enjoyed his first-team bow in 2013/14. Steady progress was made on the pitch and Solly has been a mainstay of the Premier League era, ultimately peaking in 2022/23 under the expert tutelage of Roberto De Zerbi, scoring eight times in 39 appearances. It's always great to have one of our own represent the club.

Wednesday 21st July 2004

Former Atletico Madrid reserve Maheta Molango signed for Albion – after netting three times in two trial games – with a warning from Mark McGhee. "We will wait until we've got him signed and sealed before we reveal details like the length of contract," declared the Scot. As of June 2024, Maheta was chief executive officer of the Professional Footballers' Association.

Friday 22nd July 1983

Albion's shirt sponsor, British Caledonian Airways, pulled out of the deal after three years.

Friday 23rd July 1999

The safety certificate for Withdean Stadium was granted at 5.30pm, the day before the first Albion game; a friendly against Nottingham Forest.

Tuesday 24th July 1984

Mike Bamber's reign as Albion chairman came to an end after 11 tumultuous years. Disillusioned directors – not happy with Bamber's running of the club – precipitated Brian Bedson's appointment as head honcho.

Saturday 24th July 1999

After two long years at Gillingham, Albion were finally back in Brighton. The Withdean Stadium welcomed Nottingham Forest for the inaugural friendly match. The Albion players arrived on an open-top bus, while the Brighton Silver Band played Sussex by the Sea as the teams ran out in front of the sell-out 5,891 crowd. There was a streaker (male) during the 2-2 draw, Gary Hart scored the first Withdean goal, and the first of hundreds of supporters' litter patrols began in earnest.

Tuesday 24th July 2007

Secretary of State for Communities and Local Government, Hazel Blears gave the community stadium at Falmer planning approval. Following public inquiries, the then-deputy Prime Minister John Prescott initially approved the plans back in October 2005 before Lewes District Council, among others, announced it would appeal against the decision on planning grounds.

Now, over ten years since a ball was last kicked at the Goldstone Ground, Albion finally looked set to have a home of their own. Manager Dean Wilkins summed up the decision; "I'm so pleased for the supporters who have had the unfortunate situation of travelling to Gillingham for two years and then being stuck at Withdean for such a long time. I am absolutely thrilled for them." It wasn't quite over yet though...

Friday 24th July 2009

The skeleton of the East Stand was beginning to take shape up at Falmer. An overhead shot on this day shows 12 Portakabins in the car park and the yet-to-be-demolished university buildings where the corner of the West and North stands will meet.

Friday 25th July 1969

Due to the lack of pitches in Spain, Albion embarked on a three-match tour of the Republic of Ireland instead. Alex Dawson (2) and Allan Gilliver scored the goals for Freddie Goodwin's men in the 3-0 win at Dundalk.

Monday 26th July 2004

Deputy Prime Minister John Prescott announced that the public inquiry would be reopened, with a view to establishing whether there is a better alternative site in the area. Hindsight is a wonderful thing, isn't it?

Wednesday 27th July 1955

An Albion legend was born in Staffordshire. Considered too small to be a professional footballer, Peter Ward began an apprenticeship as an engine-fitter at Rolls-Royce. He eventually arrived after netting 21 goals in 50 games for Burton Albion. Their manager, Ken Guttridge, then became assistant manager to Peter Taylor, who gambled £4,000 on the slight striker in 1975.

Wardy scored within 50 seconds of his debut at Hereford. Pacy dribbling, speed off the mark, and the ability to turn on a sixpence, lit up the Goldstone in the late 1970s as average crowds of over 23,000 witnessed Albion's rise from the Third Division to the First. Wardy broke the club's season goalscoring record with 36 in 1976/77 and netted 16 in the club's inaugural top-flight campaign. In October 1980, the 25-year-old joined former boss Peter Taylor at Nottingham Forest for £450,000 as part of the transfer triangle that took Garry Birtles to Manchester United and Andy Ritchie to Albion.

Monday 27th July 2009

The steel structure of the East Stand began to emerge. Supporters could watch the construction on the Falmer Webcam, installed to capture time-lapse photography of the long-awaited stadium as it rose from the ground.

Wednesday 27th July 2011

Brighton 'Til I Die was performed at the Theatre Royal, New Road, Brighton. The play, updated from 2001, concentrated on the Albion; from near extinction at the hands of profiteering owners, to the opening of the new stadium at Falmer. Writer Paul Hodson's lively script followed the fortunes of two friends, Southey and Gerbil, whose lives were intertwined with the club's fortunes. The stand-out performance was Mark Brailsford as Mr Albion, an eccentric mine of club information who outlined the club's history with perfect comic timing. *The Argus* commented; "The evening ended on a high with the definite sense that the real glory days of the club are yet to come."

Friday 28th July 2000

The First Deposit Draft of the new Brighton & Hove Local Plan included, as policy SR25; "A new football/community stadium and multi-purpose sports hall is proposed on land adjoining Village Way North together with sports science/sports medicine facilities linked to the University of Brighton." What could possibly go wrong?

Monday 29th July 2002

Marijan Kovacevic enjoyed his first taste of English football, partnering captain Danny Cullip in a pre-season friendly at Leyton Orient. Jamaican culinary queen Rustie Lee was in the main stand with her husband Andreas Hohmann, the Croatian trialist's agent.

Friday 30th July 1915

George Curtis' successor was born in Falkirk, Scotland. Archie Macaulay, one of the best-known names in 1940s and 1950s football, took charge of Albion in April 1963. The Scot enjoyed an illustrious playing career winning a Scottish League title with Rangers in 1935, representing his country, and gained a First Division championship medal with Arsenal, aged 32, in 1948. Responsible for the signing of Bobby Smith, Archie spent five-and-a-half years at the Goldstone but couldn't quite achieve promotion to the second tier.

Thursday 30th July 1998

The battle to 'Bring Home the Albion' took another twist. SWEAT filed papers in the High Court seeking a judicial review into the council's decision to grant Albion planning permission.

Friday 30th July 2021

Ben White moved to Arsenal for a club-record fee of £50 million. The 23-year-old defender joined Albion's academy in 2016 and featured on the first-team bench during his first season. He went on loan to League Two Newport County, playing 51 times during the 2017/18 campaign, and was voted Player of the Season. After spending the opening half of 2018/19 with Albion's under-23s, White was off on loan again, to Peterborough United, in the third tier.

Next season and another step up – this time to Leeds United in the Championship. He excelled in Marcelo Bielsa's promotion-winning side. So much so in fact that, at the end of the season, many Leeds supporters thought he was their player, getting confused that he was on loan from the Albion. In 2020/21, the defender played more minutes for Brighton than any other player which prompted a bid from Mikel Arteta. White has decided not to represent his country but won four England caps during 2021/22.

Tuesday 31st July 1979

Albion launched the club's first standing season ticket, priced at £31.50 for the First Division debut campaign. They were initially confined to the south-eastern corner of the Goldstone Ground.

Monday 31st July 2006

Liberal Democrat MP Norman Baker – who once infamously admitted he'd rather Albion went out of business if it meant a new stadium wouldn't be built at Falmer – suggested improper conduct by John Prescott in newspaper interviews. Baker's claims centred on the visit of the Deputy PM to the offices of Albion director Derek Chapman's Adenstar construction firm in 2002. "Mr Prescott should be removed from hearing the Falmer matter if the court refers it back to him," said Baker. "When I met John Prescott," explained Derek, "I was told not to mention the planning application, so I didn't."

Tuesday 31st July 2007

Lewes District Council announced it was not going to appeal the government's decision to allow Albion's new stadium to be built at Falmer. The council released a statement on this day saying it was frustrated and alarmed at the 'blatantly party-political' decision to award planning consent but, for practical reasons, had decided not to appeal. Nearly there…!

The Seagull Love Review – August 2013:
Mocking the Match of the Day debacle in style.

© TSLR

AUGUST

Saturday 1st August 2009

The first piece of the magnificent white roof girder was slotted in place above the East Stand. The earth slopes, that will support the terracing, were taking shape too. It's all looking good!

Tuesday 1st August 2023

Albion in the Community changed its name to the Brighton & Hove Albion Foundation. From humble beginnings in a Portakabin at the Goldstone Ground when Steve Ford started the scheme in the late 1980s, the community scheme had grown to over 70 core staff with a large team of community coaches working in 35 towns across Sussex, supporting over 5,000 children, young people and adults every week. The core operations were to be moved to the heart of the community, to new headquarters (a former pub) in Freshfield Road, Brighton.

Monday 2nd August 1937

Adrian Thorne was born in Hove. He waited over three years to make his debut and eventually appeared for the first team while stationed in Colchester during his Army national service. On only his seventh league outing, the local lad banged in five goals against Watford to secure Albion's first-ever promotion, to the second division! The forward scored 44 times, in 84 Albion starts, over four seasons. What a player!

Wednesday 2nd August 2000

An historic day for the Albion; Brighton & Hove Council allocated land in its Draft Deposit Local Plan for a new stadium, at Village Way North near Falmer. The development would start with the 10,000-seat West Stand and the temporary 4,000-seat East Stand. A permanent East Stand, then South and North Stands, were to follow at a later date, to give a final capacity – at that point – of 22,438 seats.

Monday 3rd August 1998

Brian Horton's Albion beat Newcastle Town 3-0 – in a game sponsored by the Church of Scientology – thanks to goals from Kerry Mayo, Richard Barker and Stafford Browne.

Monday 3rd August 2015

After 12 years, four clubs – Tottenham Hotspur, West Ham United, Fulham and Queens Park Rangers – and two cup final appearances, Albion legend Bobby Zamora returned to his spiritual home, aged 34.

Thursday 4th August 2005

To emphasise what most Albion fans – and the away supporters – had to endure at the woefully inadequate Withdean Stadium, good sport Des Lynam was thoroughly soaked by a group of fans and the contents of three large watering cans. It was another stunt in the seemingly never-ending sequence of events to highlight Albion's desperate need for a new home.

Wednesday 5th August 1987

George Graham's Arsenal walloped Albion 7-2 at the Goldstone Ground in a pre-season friendly. Steve Penney and new striker Kevin Bremner scored the consolation goals for Barry Lloyd's side. Cries of 'Barry out' and 'Worthing reject' rang out from the terraces.

Friday 6th August 2010

The skeleton of the stadium was completed and the roof panelling work had begun. The road to Stanmer Park was under construction while the concrete flooring was smoothed out in the concourses.

Saturday 6th August 2011

The first league match at Brighton & Hove Albion's new home in Falmer. The American Express Community Stadium, to give it its full name, opened its doors to hordes of ecstatic fans, who had dreamed of this day for over 14 years. Two years playing in the compost heap of England, and 12 at a rundown athletics track in north Brighton, were (almost) forgotten during the emotional build-up to kick-off. Flag-waving home fans, many of whom feared they would never see their side playing in a new stadium they could call home, created a sea of blue and white. A group of fans from the Battle of Trafalgar public house by Brighton Station hired an open-top bus for the occasion, doing three laps of the town centre before heading north! The first opponents – somewhat pertinently as they were also the last at the Goldstone – were Doncaster Rovers, who hadn't read the script as they raced into the lead through Billy Sharp after 39 minutes.

Albion boss Gus Poyet couldn't control his emotions and was sent to the stands by referee Eddie Alderton after being denied a penalty after a challenge on Kazenga LuaLua. The Uruguayan did have a positive influence on the encounter though, replacing Matt Sparrow with Will Buckley who equalised from the edge of the box with seven minutes remaining. Fellow sub Craig Noone then played the galloping forward through – in the eighth minute of injury time – who stroked the ball into the bottom corner to send the vast majority of the 20,219 crowd into raptures. A fitting strike for a monumental day in the history of our football club. Before kick-off, last Goldstone goalscorer, Stuart Storer, and equalising goalscorer at Hereford United, Robbie Reinelt, were introduced to the crowd and received a fittingly rapturous reception.

Saturday 7th August 1999

The day Albion fans everywhere had been waiting for; the end of the two-year exile in Gillingham! Mansfield Town were the first visitors to Withdean Stadium. Appropriately, seven players made their debuts in the 6-0 demolition of the lame Stags; Chris Wilder (future Sheffield United manager), Andy Crosby, Charlie Oatway, Jamie Campbell, Paul Rogers, Aidan Newhouse and Darren Freeman. Newhouse grabbed a brace while Freeman helped himself to a hat-trick, the first Albion player to score three times on his debut since the club's very first game in 1901. The majority of 5,882 fans in attendance went home very happy indeed.

Saturday 7th August 2010

Matt Sparrow, on his Albion debut, scored twice at Swindon Town on the opening day of the season. The former Scunthorpe midfielder unleashed an unstoppable left-footed drive from the edge of the area, which clipped the inside of the post, in the 18th minute after good work from Jamie Smith. The 28-year-old, who had spent 11 years at Glanford Park, completed his brace with 20 minutes left. A classic counter-attack saw Ashley Barnes hold the ball up just inside the Albion half before releasing Sparrow, who swapped passes with Smith, before rounding the advancing Swindon keeper to slot into an open net.

Saturday 7th August 2022

In the opening game of the 2022/23 Premier League campaign, Albion beat Manchester United at Old Trafford for the very first time. The first goal arrived on 30 minutes as Danny Welbeck timed his run to latch on to Leandro Trossard's pass and cross from the left to Pascal Gross, who swept it into an empty net from a few yards out. Just ten minutes later and the German was at it again. A wonderful move, which stunned the home crowd, started with Trossard's back-heel to Moisés Caicedo, who found Gross and via Adam Lallana Albion switched the ball to the right. Solly March then cut inside and his shot was palmed out to Gross, who blasted it in. The Sussex boys ran out deserved winners. The players responsible for the magnificent 2-1 victory were: Sánchez, Veltman, Dunk, Webster, March (Colwill 90), Mac Allister, Caicedo, Lallana

(Mwepu 75), Gross, Trossard (Lamptey 75), Welbeck (Undav 90+1). Thankfully, 73,711 fans were in attendance for this historic occasion.

Wednesday 8th August 1984

Gerry Ryan made his 14th, and final, Republic of Ireland appearance in the 0-0 stalemate with Mexico in Dublin.

Thursday 8th August 2019

Albion signed France international midfielder Léa Le Garrec from Guingamp, subject to international clearance. The 26-year-old became the fourth women's team signing of the transfer window, following the arrivals of Danique Kerkdijk, Matilde Lundorf Skovsen and Megan Walsh. Hope Powell said; "It is a pleasure to welcome Léa to the club. She is someone with plenty of experience of playing at the very highest level in France, and for the national team too."

Wednesday 9th August 2000

After scoring six goals in six games while on loan in the previous campaign, Bobby Zamora signed from Bristol Rovers for £100,000, the biggest deal since John Byrne arrived for £125,000 a decade earlier. The 19-year-old penned a four-year contract and chairman Dick Knight said of the deal; "He's an exciting player and the Albion are definitely going to be the team to watch this season." Understatement of the decade from the chairman there!

Friday 9th August 2002

Planning Minister Lord Rooker announced that the government was to call a full public inquiry on the plans for Falmer. The decision meant fans would have to wait at least until 2004 (!) for the stadium to open. Deputy Prime Minister John Prescott now had the final say on whether the ground should be built at Village Way North. Will it ever end?

Saturday 9th August 2008

Inspired by legendary Albion fanzines *Gull's Eye* and *Scars & Stripes*, *The Seagull Love Review* hit the streets for the first time at Crewe. Incorporating traditional 'zine values of black and white print and unfussy design – 'that will roll up and fit in your back pocket' – *TSLR's* highlights included the magnificent steward posters, wonderful back-cover player illustrations, the possibly borderline obsession with Colin Hawkins, and being nominated for three accolades at the Football Fanzine Awards in their inaugural season.

Friday 9th August 2019

Albion signed a new 12-year sponsorship deal with long-time partners American Express, worth £100 million, according to an industry insider. It represented a 20-fold increase on the existing 10-year arrangement with the financial services firm – Brighton's largest private-sector employer – and secured one of the longest-running sponsorship partnerships in UK football.

Saturday 10th August 2002

Martin Hinshelwood enjoyed a dream start as Albion boss. The 3-1 First Division win at Burnley came courtesy of strikes from Steve Melton, Paul Brooker and Bobby Zamora. The starting line-up – after a virus had swept through the squad – included the manager's 17-year-old nephew Adam for his full league debut.

Tuesday 10th August 2021

Albion signed Japan international Kaoru Mitoma on undisclosed terms from J1 League team Kawasaki Frontale. Technical director Dan Ashworth said of the 24-year-old; "We're delighted to be able to sign Kaoru, who arrives off the back of a couple of really strong seasons in Japan. As part of his development, we have decided to loan him to Union Saint-Gilloise to help him become accustomed to European football, and to test himself in a different environment." In the 2020 J1 League season Mitoma scored 13 goals as Frontale won the title.

Saturday 11th August 1951

Before pre-season friendlies became commonplace, Albion used to warm up with public practice matches between two sides of the club's players: on this day, the Blues beat the Yellows 6-0.

Wednesday 11th August 1999

A night of firsts at Withdean. A League Cup match against former landlords Gillingham; the first under floodlights; first away goals scored – two – resulted in the first defeat at Albion's new 'temporary' home. Unfortunately, Meridian decided to show extensive highlights of the 2-0 reverse.

Saturday 11th August 2001

Former Fulham captain Simon Morgan made his debut in the opening-day 0-0 draw at Cambridge United. The defender went on to make 42 league appearances during the championship-winning campaign.

Monday 12th August 1946

Fred Binney was born in Plymouth. The prolific striker – 44 goals in 85 games – lost his place to Ian Mellor, after two great seasons, in 1976.

Monday 13th August 2007

Melanie Cutress, chair of Falmer Parish Council, announced 'reluctantly' that, following legal advice, they would not challenge the Secretary of State's decision to grant permission for a community stadium at Falmer.

Saturday 14th August 1993

The threat of a winding-up order hung over the club as the league campaign kicked off in Bradford. A Second Division 2-0 defeat to City was notable for the debut of 18-year-old goalkeeper Nicky Rust.

Saturday 15th August 1970

Peter O'Sullivan made his Albion debut in the 0-0 home draw with Torquay United. Joining as a 19-year-old, the Welshman graced the left flank with distinction during his 11 years with the club. A full Welsh international, 'Sully' scored 43 goals in 491 appearances.

Wednesday 15th August 2007

The South Downs Society announced that they would not further challenge the government's decision to allow the building of a community stadium at Falmer.

Friday 15th August 2014

João Carlos Vilaça Teixeira joined the Albion on loan for the season from Liverpool. The attacking midfielder would feature for his temporary club 32 times during 2014/15, finishing top scorer with six goals. Awarded Albion Young Player of the Year, the Portuguese was also Liverpool's Academy Player of the Year.

Popular with the Falmer support for his energetic displays, a broken leg suffered against Huddersfield Town in April prematurely ended his season and resulted in the end of his Albion tenure. Blighted by injuries since, at the time of writing (April 2024), Teixeira could be found playing for Shanghai Shenhua, in the Chinese Super League.

Saturday 16th August 1980

At the risk of incurring the wrath of every Albion fan, Mike Bamber dispensed with Sussex by the Sea in favour of Gonna Fly Now from Rocky, after a visit to San Diego Sockers in the North American League. The crowd of 19,307 saw the team run out in all-blue shirts adorned, for the first time, with a sponsor – British Caledonian Airways.

Saturday 16th August 1997

Albion's first 'home' league game at Gillingham – a 1-1 draw watched by just 2,336 fans – was also Macclesfield Town's first in the Football League. A thoroughly depressing day for everyone connected to the Albion.

Thursday 17th August 1967

John Napier signed for a record fee of £25,000 from Bolton Wanderers. The centre-half was a mainstay in the Albion rearguard for five years – playing on 247 occasions, scoring five times – before moving to Bradford City for £10,000 in 1972.

Thursday 17th August 2006

Ed Bassford took 22% of the vote for the Seagulls Party in the Ouse Valley & Ringmer ward by-election – a very creditable third place. Lewes District Council were getting twitchy.

Saturday 18th August 1979

Albion's first game in the First Division was at home to FA Cup holders Arsenal. Unfortunately, the Gunners hadn't read the script as Republic of Ireland international Frank Stapleton, bubble-permed Alan Sunderland (twice), and future Albion boss Liam Brady all netted in the 4-0 win. Future Brighton players in the Gunners squad included Sammy Nelson and Steve Gatting. The 28,604 crowd was the fourth-highest that season; Manchester United, Liverpool and Spurs attracted 29,000+. Only the visit of Stoke City recorded a sub-20,000 Goldstone gathering.

Tuesday 18th August 2008

Liam Dickinson, with an exquisite volley, scored Albion's first goal of the season at Huddersfield Town – in the fourth game of the campaign – to level the scores at the Galpharm Stadium. Unfortunately, the Terriers then notched another six for a comprehensive 7-1 scoreline. Michel Kuipers was sent off and substitute keeper Graeme Smith's first job, on his debut, was to pick the ball from the net after a penalty, which put the home side two goals ahead. Not the greatest night in the club's history.

Wednesday 19th August 1953

An Albion all-time great made his debut in the 2-1 win at Queens Park Rangers. Much-loved left-back Jimmy Langley missed only five games in his four years at the Goldstone. The Londoner thrilled the big 1950s' crowds with his dribbling and many a tear was shed when Fulham paid £12,000 for his services in 1957 after 16 goals in 178 starts.

Tuesday 19th August 2008

Before he played for the Albion, Ashley Barnes made his international debut for Austria's under-20s, replacing FC Wacker Innsbruck's Julius Perstaller in the 73rd minute, against Switzerland in front of 250 spectators. The match was part of a four-nation friendly tournament that also featured Germany and Italy. Born in Bath to English parents, Barnes qualified to represent Austria due to his paternal grandmother, who was from Klagenfurt, and was initially spotted by officials while on a pre-season tour with Plymouth Argyle a month earlier.

Thursday 20th August 1925

Johnny McNichol was born in Kilmarnock, Scotland. The influential inside-forward signed for a club record £5,000 from Newcastle United and played a pivotal role in the club's resurgence in the late 1940s and early 1950s. Chelsea paid £12,000 – double the previous best – in 1952 and, after scoring 39 times in 165 starts for the Albion, helped the London club to their first league title in 1955.

Wednesday 20th August 1986

Albion Lifeline was launched at The Dome. The fundraising scheme was intended to have 2,500 members who paid a subscription for regular prize draws. The proceeds were initially used to buy a number of players, but the funds were thereafter swallowed up by general costs. The initiative ceased under the chief executive reign of David Bellotti.

Wednesday 20th August 1987

Germaine Hesus 'Kemy' Agustien was born in the Netherlands Antilles. The midfielder signed a two-year contract with Albion after impressing at Swansea City. One performance for the Welsh side, in particular, stood out. In his own words; "I was awarded Man of the Match against Manchester United, with only three hours sleep the night before, as I didn't expect to be playing." This pretty much sums up his time on the south coast. As of 2024, the 37-year-old was turning out for Alvechurch – his 25th club – in the Southern League Premier Division Central.

Saturday 20th August 2005

Albion fans headed to Hull again – the team lost 2-0 – to deliver a giant postcard to John Prescott's constituency office.

Thursday 20th August 2009

The South Stand – the away end – emerged from the ground as the main piles were carefully slotted into place. The curvature of the East Stand was now clearly visible and hinted at the ground's completed contours, designed to be wholly empathetic with its environment.

Saturday 21st August 1948

After finishing bottom of the Third Division (South) in May, Albion kicked off the new season against Swindon Town in all-blue shirts with white sleeves; the first time the stripes had been changed since 1904. The gate was 21,593.

Saturday 21st August 1999

Left-footed right-back Paul Watson made the first of his 215 Albion appearances in the 1-0 Third Division defeat to Torquay United. Supplier of much of Bobby Zamora's ammunition with his pinpoint crosses, free-kicks and corners, Watto left for Woking on a free transfer in October 2005. In the same game, Neville Southall, the 40-year-old former Welsh international goalkeeper, kept Micky Adams' side at bay as the Devonians ran out 1-0 winners at Withdean.

Saturday 21st August 2021

The first Falmer crowd without COVID-19 restrictions for over 18 months were excitedly in place for the visit of newly promoted Watford. Albion continued their best-ever start to a Premier League campaign dispatching the visitors with ease, with their second consecutive victory. Defender Shane Duffy scored the opening goal on 10 minutes, rising highest from Pascal Gross' corner to beat Watford goalkeeper Daniel Bachmann with a powerful header. Neal Maupay doubled the lead four minutes before half-time, taking one touch from an Yves Bissouma pass on the edge of the box before firing past Bachmann. Potter said afterwards; "It was a fantastic header from Duffy, he's a monster in the box. He is so big and strong to stop – it was a great goal." It's good to be back!

Saturday 22nd August 1959

The biggest crowd for an opening-day game at the Goldstone: 31,828 for the visit of Aston Villa, newly relegated from the top-flight. The West Stand was under construction. Record £13,000 purchase, Bill Curry, made his debut in the 2-1 reverse. The striker arrived from Newcastle United and netted 26 times, including three hat-tricks, in his first season. He left for Derby County, for £12,000, in September 1960.

Saturday 22nd August 1964

Just six months earlier, Bobby Smith had been banging in the goals for First Division Tottenham Hotspur, and England. On this day, the big centre-forward made his debut for Brighton & Hove Albion... in the Fourth Division! A Goldstone crowd of 20,058 were not disappointed as the striker bagged a brace as Archie Macaulay's side swept aside Barrow 3-1. The barnstorming hitman had scored 208 goals in 317 senior games for Spurs, 33 of them in the club's double-winning season. He and his strike partner Jimmy Greaves were, at that time, the only Spurs players to have reached the double-century mark for the north London club. Bobby scored 13 times in 15 outings for England, the last run-out coming just a few months before his Albion debut.

Wednesday 22nd August 1979

Teddy Maybank scored Albion's first top-flight goal in the club's inaugural First Division away fixture; a 2-1 defeat at Aston Villa.

Saturday 22nd August 2015

Albion's kick-off with Blackburn Rovers was delayed by 15 minutes due to a crash at the Shoreham Air Show. What no-one realised at the time was the severity of the incident as news gradually filtered through that there had been 11 fatalities when a former military aircraft crashed on to the westbound carriageway of the A27, just a few hundred yards away from Albion's Centre of Excellence at Lancing. The 11 men who tragically lost their lives that day: Anthony Brightwell, 53, Hove; Daniele Polito, 23, Goring-by-Sea; Dylan Archer, 42, Brighton; Jacob Schilt, 23, Brighton; James Mallinson, 72, Newick; Mark Reeves, 53, Seaford; Mark Trussler, 54, Worthing; Matthew Grimstone, 23, Brighton; Matthew Jones, 24, Littlehampton; Maurice Abrahams, 76, Brighton; and Richard Smith, 26, Hove. Matt Grimstone worked as a groundsman for the Albion at Lancing and played for Worthing United, alongside his friend Jacob.

May they all rest in peace.

Wednesday 22nd August 2018

Former Albion midfielder Steve Sidwell returned to the Albion as youth development coach with the under-16s, and as a club ambassador.

Saturday 23rd August 1947

Club legend, Tommy Cook, began an unsuccessful 17-game tenure as Albion boss with a 3-2 Third Division (South) win at Watford.

Saturday 23rd August 1952

A 4-1 home win over Crystal Palace in the Third Division (South) was a great start to the 1952/53 campaign. Both debutants – Jimmy Leadbetter and Les Owens – scored in front of 23,905 Goldstone fans.

Saturday 23rd August 1958

After nearly 30 seasons – straddling two World Wars – Albion finally contested their first fixture in the Second Division. Unfortunately, the trip to Middlesbrough coincided with a prolific Brian Clough firing on all cylinders. The striker scored five times in the 9-0 demolition.

Saturday 24th August 1957

Albion chairman Major Carlo Campbell discussed the club's bonus structure after the 1-0 opening-day win at Gillingham; "This first match had cost us a tidy sum in bonus money, but we don't mind paying this sort of cash." The amount was £4 per player on top of the maximum weekly wage of £17.

Wednesday 25th August 1948

The healthy crowd of 24,432 at Ashton Gate saw Des Tennant make his Albion debut against Bristol City. The big Welshman could play anywhere down the right side and scored 23 of his 47 Albion goals – in 424 appearances – from the penalty spot during his 11 years at the club. An automatic choice, Des was presented with a writing bureau on completion of a decade's service and, after working as chief scout, became landlord of the Allen Arms in Lewes Road, Brighton.

Saturday 26th August 1922

George Moorhead, the first player to represent Albion who was born outside the UK and Ireland – in New Zealand – made his one and only appearance in the 0-0 home draw with Norwich City.

Wednesday 26th August 1998

The battle for Withdean came to a close as SWEAT – the group of local residents opposed to the club's move – informed Brighton & Hove Council that they were withdrawing their application for a judicial review. Surely the Albion would be home soon now…

Saturday 26th August 2006

The Seagulls Party appealed for candidates to fight Lewes District Council wards in May. Albion were trounced 4-1 at home by Crewe Alexandra the following day.

Friday 26th August 2016

Shane Duffy arrived from Blackburn Rovers for a fee of £4.5 million. Just nine days earlier, the Republic of Ireland international contrived to score two own goals at Cardiff and was then sent off in injury time. Thankfully, his five seasons on the south coast proved to be more successful as the 6ft 4in central defender was an integral part of the promotion-winning side of 2016/17, scoring twice in 31 appearances.

Saturday 27th August 1983

Albion returned down to earth with a bump after their FA Cup Final exploits three months and six days earlier. Just 5,750 fans – one seventeenth of the Wembley crowd on that famous May day – were in attendance as Oldham Athletic won 1-0 at Boundary Park in the Second Division.

Tuesday 27th August 1996

A 3-0 defeat at Barnet will perhaps be remembered for the birth of the protest song: Build a Bonfire. It was taken up for the first time on the Underhill terraces and went on to lend itself to the title of a superb book.

Saturday 28th August 1920

Albion lost their first league game 2-0 to Southend United at the Essex town's Kursaal Ground.

Saturday 28th August 1979

Signed from Pompey for £150,000, defender Steve Foster made his (first) Albion debut in the home League Cup second-round first-leg win over Cambridge United. One of only three Albion players to gain senior

England honours – thus far – he played in three matches in 1982; one of which was against Kuwait in the World Cup. A short spell at Aston Villa in 1984 was followed by a League Cup triumph with Luton Town in 1988 and one more transfer to Oxford United before returning home to Hove for three more seasons from 1992. Arguably one of the club's finest players, the Portsmouth-born stopper netted 15 times in a total of 332 Albion appearances.

Saturday 28th August 2010

In what turned out to be the most inspired signing of the season, Liam Bridcutt arrived from Chelsea on an initial five-month contract. The holding midfielder's Albion move was precipitated by Alan Navarro's unfortunate knee injury at Northampton Town a fortnight earlier and the 21-year-old arrived at Withdean after loan spells at Yeovil Town, Watford and Stockport County, respectively.

The Reading-born player gradually became a fixture in the first team with some solid performances and scored one of the best goals ever seen at Withdean; the last-minute left-foot-volley winner in the 4-3 victory over Carlisle United on 5th March 2011.

Saturday 29th August 1981

The 1-1 First Division draw at West Ham United kicked-off the third successive First Division campaign. The game marked Mike Bailey's first game as manager following the 39-year-old's resignation from Charlton Athletic and saw the debuts of Jimmy Case, Don Shanks and Tony Grealish.

Saturday 30th August 1919

One of the most important men in the club's history, Charlie Webb, began his managerial career with a 2-1 defeat at Brentford in the Southern League First Division. The Irishman played three times for his country during a seven-year Goldstone playing spell that saw 79 goals in 275 appearances at inside-left.

On demob after World War I in 1919, Charlie took on the immense task of re-building the Albion. In the proceeding 28 years, the great man built many a fine team on a shoestring budget and turned down the chance to take charge of Tottenham Hotspur to stay at the club he loved.

Monday 30th August 1972

Former England international Barry Bridges was signed for a club-record fee of £29,000 by Pat Saward from Millwall. The 31-year-old striker never quite reached the heights of his earlier career and only managed 14 goals during his 71-game two-year stint on the coast.

Saturday 31st August 1921

Northern Ireland international Jack Doran grabbed a hat-trick in the 3-0 Third Division (South) victory at Exeter City. The centre-forward scored the club's first 12 goals of the season!

Saturday 31st August 1946

The *Evening Argus* reported that the Albion's headquarters should be known as 'HMS Goldstone, so resplendent are the stands and fencing painted in battleship grey'.

Tuesday 31st August 2010

One for the future as Torbjørn Agdestein signed for Albion. The 18-year-old Norwegian under-19 international agreed a one-year deal after impressing boss Gus Poyet during a trial. The striker arrived from Stord FC – a Second Division outfit in Norway – where he scored 36 goals in 75 appearances.

Dogma – September 2022:
Iain Budgen's homage to Albion stickers old and new.

© Dogma

SEPTEMBER

Thursday 1st September 1898

Albion forefathers Brighton United won their first game, 8-0, away against Southwick. The friendly fixture kicked off at 6pm.

Saturday 1st September 1979

Albion enjoyed their first win in Division One. Peter Ward, Paul Clark and Brian Horton were all on target as Bolton Wanderers were dispatched 3-1 at the Goldstone Ground. The programme featured pen pal requests from an Ipswich Town fan and an 18-year-old locksmith who supported SV Nufringen in West Germany.

Wednesday 2nd September 1908

Right-half Billy Booth made his debut in Albion's 3-1 home defeat to Southampton. The Sheffield-born defender was part of the successful side that won the Southern League Championship, FA Charity Shield and the Southern Charity Cup in the club's early golden age.

Despite a career interrupted by World War I, Billy managed 12 goals in 369 appearances before leaving for his native Yorkshire as Albion became founder members of the Third Division (South) in 1920.

Tuesday 2nd September 1997

One of the biggest results in the Albion's history came off the pitch as the despised regime of Bill Archer, Greg Stanley and David Bellotti were finally replaced by Dick Knight, Bob Pinnock and Martin Perry, after two years of bitter fighting. Things were looking up.

Friday 2nd September 2011

Vicente Rodríguez Guillén joined Albion on loan from Spanish side Valencia. In a scintillating spell on the coast, the midfielder treated the Falmer faithful to some virtuoso performances, gliding past many poor Championship defenders as if they weren't there. He netted five times in 32 appearances and will be fondly remembered by all that saw him play.

Saturday 3rd September 1904

The 2-2 draw at New Brompton (now Gillingham) was notable for the change of shirt. Replacing the all-blue numbers, Albion wore the famous blue and white stripes for the very first time.

Saturday 3rd September 1983

Chelsea fans in the 20,874 crowd celebrated their 2-1 Second Division victory by snapping the North Stand crossbar at the Goldstone. Opposition full-back Chris Hutchings was arrested for refusing to leave the pitch on police orders. By the time he was convicted by Hove magistrates he was an Albion player! It would be the last 20,000+ crowd for a home league fixture until the first game at Falmer in 2011.

Monday 4th September 1950

Described as a 'chunky little player' in Tim Carder and Roger Harris' excellent *Albion A-Z, A Who's Who of Brighton & Hove Albion FC*, Frankie Howard made his debut in the 1-1 Third Division (South) draw at Millwall. The outside-left – who was rejected for national service because of his flat feet – was one of the quickest players to wear the stripes and notched 31 goals in 219 appearances.

He became groundsman in 1962, after ligament injury prematurely ended his career aged 28, and tended to the highly regarded Goldstone turf for 31 years until a cold-hearted David Bellotti savagely made the stalwart redundant in 1993.

Wednesday 4th September 1991

A very strange night at The Den began with Perry Digweed injuring himself during the warm-up. His replacement, defender Gary Chivers, performed admirably between the sticks for eight minutes until Mark Beeney, who had been sitting in the stand, was ready to enter the fray.

John Byrne and Robert Codner scored the goals in a 2-1 victory, but the contest will be remembered for the pitch invasion... by a 14-year-old boy! Millwall striker Chris Armstrong, on the ground facing the away end, incited the Albion contingent and fans surged to the front of the terrace. A youngster then vaulted the fence in the adjacent main stand, ran down the touchline and karate-kicked John Robinson in the back before being wrestled to the ground by Beeney!

Sunday 4th September 2022

In what turned out to be Graham Potter's last game as Albion manager, his side annihilated Leicester City at Falmer. A final score of 5-2 was flattering to the visitors as the home side fired in 35 attempts on goal, with 11 on target, in a scintillating display.

Monday 5th September 1910

The Albion were crowned 'Champions of All England'. Before Premiership winners faced that season's FA Cup winners in the traditional football season curtain-raiser, the Southern League champions would face the Football League title winners for the Charity Shield.

The season had already kicked-off when Aston Villa – league champions six times in the previous 16 years – faced Albion at Stamford Bridge. In the 72nd minute Bill Hastings threaded a pass through to Charlie Webb who jinked past two Villa defenders before powering home a rising cross shot. The Midlanders didn't win the league again until 1981. So, when opposition fans chant 'Champions of England, you'll never sing that,' they're wrong!

Monday 5th September 1987

Barry Lloyd's transfer dealings were listed as: 13 incoming players at £357,000 and four outgoing – Terry Connor, Danny Wilson, Dean Saunders and Eric Young – for a total of £470,000 received.

Friday 6th September 1901

The *Evening Argus* announced Albion's election into the Southern League Second Division. "It is hoped that football enthusiasts will turn up in large numbers, and to show the executive that their efforts to improve the class of football in the district are appreciated." Seventy-six years later the Goldstone hosted an England under-21 game against Norway. Peter Ward scored a hat-trick in a 6-0 win on his international debut!

Thursday 6th September 2007

After years of marches, lobbying, letter-writing, protests, sit-ins, lock-outs, flower-sending, political party-forming, leaflet-dropping, celebrity-soaking, postcard-distributing and petition-signing, Albion fans could finally, unequivocally, without question or chance of appeal, celebrate planning permission for the community stadium at Falmer. It had been a very long wait!

Saturday 7th September 1901

Albion played their first-ever fixture on a training pitch on Dyke Road. The club were due to host Shoreham at Sussex Cricket Club's County

Ground in Eaton Road, Hove, but the fixture clashed with a cricket match. Albion, playing in 'fisherman's blue' shirts and white 'knickers', won 2-0 in front of a 'fair attendance' with Clem Barker notching the club's first-ever goal. Over the other side of town, the Hove Football Club launched their new venture – 'the well-appointed private ground which they named the Goldstone Ground' – with a 3-0 friendly defeat to Clapton.

Wednesday 7th September 1966

In the programme versus Bournemouth, the 'Postbag' section dealt with two issues: a fan asked why supporters don't use 'the Shrimps' as a nickname to which the club replied; "Albion is the word we use – short, easy and it just suits us." Several letters arrived at the Goldstone Ground concerning the 'use of horns, rattles, bells, whistles and trumpets during the Swindon match'. The club replied; "Noise is all part of the soccer scene, but we feel certain our followers will co-operate in not making an unnecessary disturbance."

Tuesday 7th September 1982

Albion registered their first Division One victory of the campaign. Gerry Ryan scored in the 1-0 Goldstone triumph over Arsenal.

Monday 7th September 1987

Tommy Elphick was born in Brighton. The centre-back began his football career at Woodingdean FC before signing for the Albion as a teenager. He made his debut in December 2005, alongside his brother Gary – who was sent off – in a 5-1 defeat at Reading. His sibling was released in 2006 and Tommy made his first start the following year, establishing himself in a side full of local lads.

He scored one of the penalties in the League Cup shoot-out win against newly rich Manchester City in 2008 (see Wednesday 24th September 2008). Elphick's last season saw Albion lift the League One title in 2011 but the 23-year-old didn't feature in the Championship as Gus Poyet sold him to AFC Bournemouth where he was to enjoy a season of Premier League football in 2015/16.

Short stints followed at Aston Villa, Reading, Hull City and Huddersfield Town before he hung up his boots in 2021. At the time of writing (April 2024) he can be found next to Andoni Iraola in the dugout at Dean Court as the Cherries' assistant manager.

Friday 7th September 2007

Dean Cox fired Albion two up – either side of strikes from Dean Hammond and David Martot – at home to Millwall in what turned out to be Goal of the Season for 2007/08. The diminutive winger sent a sublime chip over Chris Day from 25 yards to register a final score of 3-0 to the Albion.

Monday 8th September 1997

Ian Baird scored his last Albion goal in the rearranged game at Colchester United which was moved due to Princess Diana's funeral. The 3-1 loss left the Seagulls 22nd in the Third Division.

Saturday 8th September 2006

Former first-team coach Dean Wilkins took charge of his first game at Millwall's New Den. Despite Richard Carpenter's opening-period dismissal, ten-man Albion battled and earned the points when Dean Cox's 88th-minute free-kick deflected in off Marvin Elliott.

Thursday 8th September 2022

After three years and four months in charge of Brighton & Hove Albion, Graham Potter left for Chelsea – and all their lovely money. Sorry, I meant for football reasons. The former Swansea manager took his backroom staff – who were also all given a huge amount of cash to join him.

Most managerial departures are met with disappointment by supporters, but this was different. Many felt he could have achieved greatness with the club and taken us to the next level. Thankfully, Roberto De Zerbi did just that.

While his exit left a very bitter taste in the collective mouths of Albion fans across the world, what Potter achieved on the pitch is unquestionable. Here's how he described his desired 'philosophy' for his new club; "I want a tactically flexible, attacking, possession-based team. Players that are brave, that aren't afraid to make mistakes.

That can get on the ball and show courage and really try to enjoy their football. If the players are enjoying their football, there's a chance that the supporters will enjoy it as well. That's how you grow and develop as a club. Styles of play don't make you win games. The challenge is having players believe in it and how it works."

Wednesday 9th September 1970

Kurt Nogan was born in Cardiff. The striker arrived on a free transfer from Luton Town in 1992 and became the first player to score more than 20 goals in consecutive seasons since Albert Mundy in the 1950s. The Welshman moved to Burnley for £250,000 in February 1995 – having scored 60 times in 120 Albion run-outs – despite enduring a 20-game goalscoring drought before his departure. After a couple of seasons he moved to the Clarets' rivals Preston North End.

Saturday 9th September 1972

Albion moved up to 15th place with their first Division Two win for a decade; a 2-1 home victory over Fulham. A goal from John Templeman, plus a penalty from Bert Murray, secured the points after five games without a win.

Saturday 9th September 1989

A quite extraordinary Second Division fixture at Bramall Lane. Albion went three down to Sheffield United only to come back, through a couple of braces from Kevin Bremner and Paul Wood, to lead 4-3! The Blades sharpened up their act to run out 5-4 eventual winners with future Albion assistant manager Bob Booker on the scoresheet for the home side. Three days later Albion scored four on the road again, this time in a 4-2 victory at Wolves.

Saturday 9th September 2017

Brighton & Hove Albion Football Club enjoyed their first win in the Premier League; the first in the top-flight for 34 years. Two goals from Pascal Gross, and a strike from Tomer Hemed, helped Chris Hughton's men to a victory over West Bromwich Albion. Gross scored the opener just before the break, converting Solly March's cross from close range, before making it two, sending a tame strike past the reach of Ben Foster just after half-time. Hemed got in front of the defender to convert a Gross centre for the third. Albion's first goals of the Premier League era, in a 3-1 win.

Thursday 9th September 2023

Albion legend Pascal Gross made his Germany national team debut against Japan at the Volkswagen Arena in Wolfsburg. Head coach Hansi Flick brought on the Albion man in the 64th minute as a substitute to replace former Liverpool midfielder Emre Can. Kaoru Mitoma starred in a 4-1 victory for the visitors.

Wednesday 10th September 1980

Dublin was the venue for this World Cup qualifier against the Netherlands. Mark Lawrenson scored his second goal for the Republic of Ireland in the 2-1 win.

Friday 10th September 1982

David López Moreno was born in La Rioja, Spain. After two Copa del Rey defeats during his five years at Athletic Bilbao, he signed a one-year contract with the Albion. He scored nine times in his first season, including a memorable free-kick against Crystal Palace in 2013. He played a total of 67 games for the club, scoring 12 goals. Fondly remembered as Spanish Dave, as of April 2024, the 41-year-old was still playing, for UD Caravaca in the regional Spanish leagues.

Saturday 10th September 1988

In the middle of an eight-game losing run, AFC Bournemouth visited the Goldstone. Goalkeeper Perry Digweed was caught in traffic and failed to make kick-off so John Keeley, despite having his injured fingers strapped, deputised. The former taxi driver couldn't stop the Cherries winning 2-1 in a game that marked recent Barnet capture – for £115,000 – Robert Codner's first Albion appearance.

Friday 10th September 2021

An historic day for Brighton & Hove Albion's women's teams. Costing £8.5 million, a brand-new facility at the American Express Elite Football Performance Centre (training ground) opened in Lancing. Chairman Tony Bloom said; "It provides the women's teams with unrivalled, world-class facilities and underpins our ambitions for the club on the pitch." The new area will house the women's first-team, academy and staff, and provide a changing facility for Albion in the Community's community pitch.

Saturday 11th September 1981

Albion led the way in recycling. Glass bottle banks appeared in the area carrying a club advert.

Tuesday 11th September 2001

The Twin Towers disaster in New York dominated everyone's thoughts at Withdean Stadium. In an understandably muted atmosphere, Albion lost 3-0 to Southampton in the Worthington Cup second round.

Saturday 12th September 1981

Steve Gatting made his debut in the 1-0 First Division defeat at Everton. Born in Middlesex, the defender's brother Mike captained England at cricket and his son Joe was a forward with Albion, scoring five goals in 52 appearances (most as substitute) between July 2005 and January 2009. Left-footed Gatts played in the 1983 FA Cup Final, at right-back in the replay, and was an ever-present as Albion won promotion in 1988. Steve made 369 appearances, scoring 21 times, and his last game for the club was the 1991 Play-off Final defeat to Notts County.

Tuesday 12th September 1989

Albion beat Wolverhampton Wanderers for the ninth successive time. Garry Nelson, Kevin Bremner (2) and Robert Codner scored at Molineux in a 4-2 Division Two victory to keep the 100% record intact.

Saturday 13th September 1975

Albion began a club-record run of 14 consecutive home victories with a 6-0 thrashing of Chester City. The crowd of 7,924 saw goals from Fred Binney (2), Peter O'Sullivan, Ian Mellor and Gerry Fell (2) to get the club back to winning Goldstone ways after two straight defeats.

Saturday 13th September 1997

Darlington fan Paul Heeny became new Albion fanzine *Scars & Stripes'* first-ever customer at Priestfield. From humble beginnings, the publication dramatically improved after the first handful of issues and was soon outselling the official matchday programme. *Scars & Stripes* proved to be the launching point of many Albion-related ventures and during the two-year sojourn in Kent, it raised nearly £10,000 before the final edition in early 2000. Founder members include Paul Camillin (Albion's head of media in 2024), Paul Hazlewood (Albion club photographer in 2024), Darren McKay (owner of North Stand Chat) and me, author of this book!

Tuesday 14th September 1886

Albion hero Charlie Webb was born at Curragh Camp, Ireland.

Tuesday 14th September 2010

The West Stand exterior panelling began – in the centre of the structure – in earnest while, at either end, the breeze-block brickwork was laid.

Saturday 15th September 1979

Gary Stevens made his full Albion debut as a 17-year-old in a First Division game at the Goldstone Ground versus Ipswich Town. The accomplished defender scored the equaliser in the 1983 FA Cup Final and went on to score three times in 152 appearances. Sold to Tottenham Hotspur as a 21-year-old for £300,000, Gary won the UEFA Cup in his first season and represented England seven times. Stevens signed for Portsmouth in 1990 but persistent injuries forced him to retire in 1992. He never fully recovered from a knee injury suffered in November 1988 when contesting possession of the ball with Wimbledon's John Fashanu near the touchline. 'Hardman' Vinnie Jones scythed Stevens down in what was an horrendous tackle, or should I say assault.

Wednesday 15th September 2021

On the fourth issue, the *Dogma* fanzine was fully launched, with paying subscribers. The publication's core editorial and design team were in place and the result was a stunning print product packed full of well-written articles and high-quality artwork. In a model unique to *Dogma*, distribution is via a season subscription model, and not from sellers outside stadiums.

Tuesday 16th September 1969

With a scoreline of 1-1 at Orient, the referee abandoned the match due to a muddy pitch and worsening weather conditions. The 5,518 spectators were not happy and the official had to be escorted from the pitch by the Metropolitan Police.

Saturday 16th September 1989

Barry Lloyd's side beat West Ham United 3-0 at the Goldstone with first-half efforts from Kevin Bremner, Robert Codner and Garry Nelson. The win, in front of 12,689 supporters, moved Albion up to second in Division Two.

Saturday 16th September 2023

A fortnight earlier, an Evan Ferguson hat-trick had seen off Newcastle United in Sussex and now Roberto De Zerbi's men travelled to Old Trafford to face Manchester United to see if they could continue their fine early season form. In what was a byword for the day, a delightful passing move in the 20th minute started with Danny Welbeck, with his back to goal. The forward found Simon Adingra, who broke down the right. Adam Lallana then dummied his cross and Welbeck directed a low left-footed shot past the keeper from six yards.

Eight minutes into the second period, Kaoru Mitoma found Tariq Lamptey on the left, who squared it for Pascal Gross, who delightfully sidestepped Argentina international Lisandro Martinez to place a right-foot shot from 12 yards into the bottom corner. A fantastic finish in front of 73,000 people. Pedro made it three on 71 minutes. Manchester United 1, Brighton & Hove Albion 3. The Seagulls were fourth in the Premier League. A very good day at the office.

Saturday 17th September 1983

Local press reported that an Anglo-American syndicate were to join the board. The club denied all knowledge and assured fans that the current board would 'continue to work for the good of Brighton & Hove Albion – the supporters come first'. Also in the programme for the 1-1 draw versus Carlisle United, Gordon Smith recalled the time he went to Paul McCartney's house and had the privilege of a private gig by the ex-Beatle.

Saturday 17th September 2005

Albion's BODS undertook a wheelchair push from Falmer to Withdean in 'Push for Falmer'.

Sunday 17th September 2006

Yet another supporters' rally against the Liberal Democrats as 2,000 fans turned up outside The Brighton Centre.

Saturday 18th September 1926

The most goals in an Albion Football League match, as of June 2024, is 12: a 9-3 home win over Swindon Town. Sam Jennings scored four, England forward Tommy Cook netted twice, while Andy Neil, Jack Nightingale and Wally Little (pen) grabbed one each.

Sunday 18th September 1938

Charlie Livesey was born in London. The clever forward scored 37 times in 146 Brighton appearances between 1965 and 1969. Such was his ability that England manager Alf Ramsey had the West Ham-born attacker watched just a few months before the World Cup finals in January 1966 – Albion were mid-table in the Third Division at the time!

Tuesday 18th September 2001

In reaction to the appalling events at the Twin Towers a week earlier, a group of supporters got together to set up the Robert Eaton Memorial Fund (REMF), in memory of the Albion fan who lost his life in New York.

Sunday 18th September 2010

Bobby Smith died at an Enfield hospital, aged 77. The forward's move to the Goldstone Ground in 1964 shocked the football world; just a few months earlier Bobby had been playing for Tottenham Hotspur in the First Division and was a full England international. Bobby finished his career with an impressive total of 218 goals in 376 league appearances.

Sunday 18th September 2022

After Graham Potter left the club and took the entire backroom staff with him to Chelsea, it's fair to say most Albion fans were utterly devastated. Thankfully, it was absolutely nothing to do with money, so at least there's that. What we didn't know was that an exceptional young manager was to take over the hotseat and revolutionise the way we played football. Roberto De Zerbi's appointment engendered a faint chorus of 'Who?' when he arrived at Falmer.

The Italian had achieved consecutive eighth-place finishes with Sassuolo in Serie A before moving to Ukraine in 2021. The war with Russia meant the league was suspended, which meant he was effectively out of work. Fortunately for the Albion, Tony Bloom knows a good boss when he meets one and Roberto signed a four-year contract before taking charge of his first game, at Anfield. In his first season his Albion team qualified for European competition for the very first time. What a start!

Saturday 19th September 1925

A brace from Wally Little, and a single strike from Tommy Cook, earned the points in the 3-2 Division Three (South) victory over Crystal Palace at the Goldstone.

Wednesday 19th September 1990

South-coast rivals Portsmouth were the visitors for this Division Two clash. Mike Small, Robert Codner and Dean Wilkins scored the goals in the 3-1 win to move the Seagulls up to sixth place in front of 9,117 fans at the Goldstone.

Saturday 20th September 1919

Bandy-legged Wally Little made his first Albion start in the 3-1 Southern League Division One victory over Bristol Rovers at the Goldstone Ground. The Middlesex man switched from left-back to left-half, becoming a crowd favourite, and holds the record for penalties scored; 26 of his 36 Albion goals – in 332 appearances.

Thursday 20th September 1984

Andrew Whing was born into an Aston Villa-supporting family in Birmingham. Dean Wilkins initially brought the right-back in on a two-month loan from Coventry City in October 2006, making the deal permanent in June 2007. In his second season, the popular Brummie collected the Player of the Year award. He fell out of favour soon after Gus Poyet arrived – Íñigo Calderón made the position his – but always acted in a professional manner. Unfortunately, his 125 first-team appearances were not accompanied by a goal but Whingy can be sure of a warm welcome should he ever return to Sussex.

Friday 20th September 1985

David Stockdale was born in Leeds. After a handful of Premier League appearances over six years for Fulham, manager Sami Hyypiä signed the goalkeeper on a three-year deal. The Yorkshireman quickly established himself as club number one and became popular with fans for his wholehearted displays. He made 45 appearances in the promotion-winning 2016/17 campaign, saving a penalty in a 2–1 win over Fulham and kept 20 clean sheets, but the team's poor finish to the season, including Stockdale scoring two own goals in a defeat at Norwich City – both were incredibly unlucky rebounds off the woodwork – meant Albion finished as runners-up to Newcastle United. He was named in the 2016/17 PFA Championship Team of the Year, and was runner-up to Anthony Knockaert as Albion's Player of the Season. In total, Stockdale played 139 times for the stripes before signing for Birmingham City in 2017. As of 2024, he played for York City, working under former Albion defender – and father of Jack – Adam Hinshelwood.

Monday 20th September 2004

Brian Clough died of stomach cancer aged 69. Best remembered for winning successive European Cups with Nottingham Forest in 1979 and 1980, the outspoken manager famously joined Albion after taking Derby County to their first league championship in 1971/72. Clough spent only eight months on the coast before leaving for an infamous 44-day stint as Leeds United boss in July 1974. He oversaw home humiliations to Bristol Rovers (8-2) and non-league Walton & Hersham, in the FA Cup, 4-0.

Saturday 21st September 1901

Brighton & Hove Albion played their first-ever competitive game; a preliminary FA Cup 6-2 win over Brighton Athletic, a local amateur side, at the Sussex County Cricket Ground.

Wednesday 21st September 1994

Liam Brady's men beat Premiership Leicester City 1-0 in this League Cup second-round tie at the Goldstone. Kurt Nogan's strike was watched by an 11,481 crowd.

Thursday 21st September 2023

A momentous occasion at the American Express Stadium – Albion's first-ever game in European competition. AEK Athens were the visitors in the Europa League in a group which also included two former European Cup winners, Olympique de Marseille and Ajax. Albion made seven changes from the 3-1 win at Old Trafford a few days earlier with Igor Julio and Ansu Fati making their full debuts. James Milner became the first player to feature in European competition for five different clubs. The 1,500 AEK fans were celebrating after 11 minutes when Sidibe powered a free header into the top corner. João Pedro slotted home a penalty on the half hour before Gacinovic flicked past Steele to make it 2-1 to the visitors on 41 minutes. Albion were awarded a second spot-kick on 66 minutes and Pedro sent Stankovic the wrong way to level the scores. AEK went back in front with six minutes to go when substitute Ponce netted the winner. Despite 13 minutes of added-on time, Albion couldn't find an equaliser.

Thursday 22nd September 1910

Fans gathered at The Dome for a 'smoking concert' to celebrate the Albion's FA Charity Shield triumph.

Saturday 22nd September 1928

Bobby Farrell made his Albion debut in the 3-1 Third Division (South) defeat at Norwich City. The diminutive Scot joined after a failed trial along the coast at Portsmouth and was a huge favourite at the Goldstone Ground. A great character, the outside-right netted 95 goals in 466 appearances for the club.

Saturday 23rd September 1922

Albion legend Tommy Cook made his debut in the Division Three (South) 0-0 draw at Queens Park Rangers.

Wednesday 23rd September 1992

David Beckham made his competitive debut for Manchester United as a substitute at the Goldstone Ground. Matthew Edwards scored for Albion in the 1-1 League Cup draw. The gate was 16,649. If you listen carefully in the YouTube clip, you can hear a special North Stand greeting for the future England captain.

Saturday 23rd September 2006

Meridian TV broadcast a helpful programme about a 'secret hotel' report at Falmer.

Saturday 24th September 1949

Bournemouth and Boscombe Athletic's Dean Court was the venue for Glen Wilson's Albion debut. The County Durham-born left-half joined the club after being spotted by player-coach Jack Dugnolle playing for Fareham Town against Albion's 'A' team. The defender, who began his career at Newcastle United, once featured in a league XI that beat the Dutch national side 6-1 in 1956! Glen – who made 436 appearances, netting 28 times – was a member of the backroom staff for nearly 20 years until his untimely departure as part of an economy drive in 1986. For the record, a 17,391 crowd witnessed the 2-2 draw in Dorset.

Wednesday 24th September 2008

Withdean's biggest crowd during Albion's 12-year tenure – 8,729 – was in attendance for the visit of the world's richest football club, Manchester City, for a League Cup second-round tie. The Citizens took the lead after 64 minutes and, with time running out, Glenn Murray beat Kasper Schmeichel to force extra-time. The Theatre of Trees was rocking and the roof would have been raised – if there was one – five minutes into the extra period when Dean Cox fed on-loan striker Joe Anyinsah who showed great composure to tuck the ball past the goalkeeper's outstretched left hand. Stephen Ireland equalised and it was down to penalties. First up for Albion was David Livermore, who scored, Ched Evans levelled then Tommy Elphick fired home. Brazilian Elano squared things before Murray restored the home side's advantage. Vincent Kompany maintained the 100% record from the spot, as did

Adam Virgo. Then it was time for Michel Kuipers' heroics as the Dutchman got down low to block Michael Ball's kick. On-loan – his third such spell – left-back Matt Richards stepped up to clinch a third-round tie with Derby County.

Sunday 24th September 2017

The ninth and final edition of *The Albion Mag* hit the streets of Brighton & Hove. Featuring cult hero Jeff Minton, Albion fans at the summit of Mount Kilimanjaro, Mark McGhee and Bob Booker, young film-maker Elliott Hasler, a potted Brighton history in a thousand words, Shoreham Football Club, showbiz fans and a piece by a New York Mets commentator, the free 68-page, full-colour publication was a welcome addition to the Albion media landscape.

Sunday 25th September 1938

Wally Gould was born in Yorkshire. The 23-year-old winger joined from York City for £4,000 in 1964 and played a vital role in Albion's Fourth Division championship a year later, top scoring with 21 goals and missing only three games. A fixture for four seasons, Wally was reluctantly released and went on to enjoy a successful spell in South Africa.

Sunday 25th September 1983

Glenn Murray was born in Maryport, Cumbria. The striker originally joined the Albion in 2008 from Rochdale, firing the club to promotion to the Championship in 2011. Great in the air, with excellent close control, Murray stood out in the third tier and fans were devastated when he moved to Crystal Palace for the start of the 2011/12 campaign. But, thankfully, the football gods did the right thing and he came back on loan in 2016, signing permanently for the club's first-ever Premier League season in 2017. In eight seasons, over two spells, Murray netted 111 times in 287 appearances to sit second in the club's all-time top goalscorer list, 12 behind Albion legend Tommy Cook.

Saturday 25th September 2010

After four wins and one defeat in their opening seven League One fixtures, Albion reached the summit for the first time with a 2-1 win over Oldham Athletic at Withdean Stadium. Fran Sandaza – soon to be affectionately christened 'the horse' by the South Stand faithful – made an immediate impact on his debut after 71 minutes. Replacing Glenn Murray, the Spanish striker – who had scored against the Old Firm for

Dundee United in the previous season – popped up on the goal-line in the sixth minute of injury time to smash home a loose ball to send the home crowd wild. Gus Poyet's men would not be moved from their lofty perch for the rest of the season.

Tuesday 26th September 1995

On-loan Gary Bull scored twice in the 4-1 win at Cambridge United in the Auto Windscreens Shield. The game also marked the debut of former England international Russell Osman. After 18 months without first-team action, it was no surprise that the defender couldn't live up to his distinguished reputation during his 11 run-outs on the south coast.

Monday 26th September 2005

At least 10,000 fans – including Des Lynam, Norman Cook, local celebrities plus countless ex-players and current squad members – marched on the Labour Party Conference at The Brighton Centre. The procession started from Madeira Drive and snaked along the seafront as the vociferous throng showed their support for a new stadium at Falmer, hoping that Deputy Prime Minister John Prescott would take notice of the huge groundswell of support from the people of Sussex.

Wednesday 26th September 2018

Albion appointed Dan Ashworth, 47, as the club's new technical director. He had undertaken a similar position at The FA and was due to begin the following spring. Tony Bloom said; "There is no doubting Dan's standing within the game, and we are absolutely delighted that he will be joining us as our technical director." Ashworth commented; "I am delighted to be joining Brighton & Hove Albion, one of the country's most progressive clubs. This is a huge opportunity for me and I have taken a lot of time to talk to Tony Bloom, Paul Barber and Chris Hughton before making the decision to make the move."

Saturday 27th September 1997

Mark Morris and Stuart Tuck both found the target during the first 'home' victory in Kent. The 2-1 win over Rochdale moved the Seagulls up to 22nd in the basement division.

Monday 27th September 2004

Later referred to as 'March 1', thousands of Albion fans – blowing whistles, banging drums, waving banners and placards, with very loud voices – congregated on the seafront by the Palace Pier to march peacefully to the Labour Party Conference at The Brighton Centre. Joined by manager Mark McGhee and most of the first-team squad, the protesters' message was conveyed through banners and placards, pledge cards in restaurants and hotels, and huge sticks of rock, all in the peaceful and unbreakable spirit now associated with the Albion and their long-suffering supporters. Falmer for All campaigners, Tim Carder and Paul Samrah, personally hand-delivered pledge cards to Tony and Cherie Blair, rather appropriately, at The Royal Albion Hotel. Brighton Pavilion Labour MP David Lepper said; "We have got to look no further than Falmer. It is the best site. This march shows the support for it."

Tuesday 27th September 2011

Unfortunately, the first home league defeat at our lovely new home was against... Palace in the Championship. To rub salt into the wounds, the previous season's leading scorer for the Albion, Glenn Murray, netted the third to make it 3-1.

Monday 27th September 2021

Albion fans eagerly awaited kick-off at Selhurst Park knowing a victory could take Graham Potter's men to the top of the Premier League for the very first time. Albion nemesis Wilfried Zaha's penalty – his eighth goal against us – near half-time looked to have given Palace the three points as the seconds ticked down towards the final whistle.

Keeper Vicente Guaita passed the ball straight to Joël Veltman on the halfway line who lofted the ball over the top for Neal Maupay to chase. The Frenchman delicately lifted it over Guaita into the net to cue pandemonium in the away end. 'Why did you let it bounce?' can clearly be heard on a YouTube clip from a frustrated home fan. Maupay, in a magnificent show of sh*thousery, cupped his ears in front of the Sainsbury's Stand to spark confrontations between the two sets of players that continued down the tunnel as the home fans joined in, taunting the visitors.

"Football is nothing without fans and some involvement with players," said Maupay. "The atmosphere was really tough and when I scored, I looked at Zaha and smiled at him because when he scored his penalty he celebrated and he gave some to our fans. I won't say what he said and what I said but you know how it is on the pitch with players sometimes. You give banter on the pitch sometimes and it was the perfect time to give him something."

Saturday 28th September 1935

Albion's indifferent start to the Third Division (South) season continued. After a 5-0 loss at Coventry City a week earlier, a 'revenge' was wreaked in a 7-1 mauling of Newport County at the Goldstone Ground! Billy Richards and Bert Stephens both registered a brace while Buster Brown grabbed a hat-trick. Brown's name is written into Albion folklore due to his amazing goal record: 45 in 66 appearances. He was signed to replace Arthur Attwood in March 1934 and, despite playing only ten games, finished top scorer with 15, including two hat-tricks. The big and bustling striker continued in the same vein for the 1934/35 campaign, despite missing pre-season due to the tragic death of his wife.

Wednesday 29th September 1926

Albion finally purchased the Goldstone Ground on a 99-year lease from the Stanford Estate after originally sub-letting from Alderman Clark since 1904. Fast-forward just over 90 years and Bill Archer sold it, without securing a new home, to Chartwell for £7.4 million.

Saturday 29th September 1962

'Mr Reliable' Norman Gall made his Albion debut in the 2-0 Third Division defeat at Watford's Vicarage Road; a day before his 20th birthday. Born in Wallsend, the defender was signed from Gateshead, where he played as an amateur. Winning Player of the Season twice – in 1971 and 1974 – Norman went on to play 488 times for the Albion, netting four goals. He summarised on Albion games for many years on BBC Sussex.

Wednesday 30th September 1936

The wartime years' greatest stalwart, Stan Risdon, pulled on an Albion shirt for the first time. Having made only 21 league starts before the outbreak of World War II, the utility player started an incredible run of appearing in 216 of the 243 wartime fixtures. On the re-introduction of league football in 1946, the Devonian was 33 and featured on just three more occasions.

Saturday 30th September 1972

Richard Carpenter was born in Sheppey, Kent. The midfielder achieved promotion with Gillingham, Fulham and Cardiff City before winning two divisional titles and a play-off final after joining the Albion in 2000. The antiques collector made 252 appearances, scoring 20 times, for Brighton and will be fondly remembered for his committed displays and wonderful goals.

Saturday 30th September 1978

Two own goals, by the same player – Mick Baxter – helped Albion to a 5-1 victory over Preston North End at the Goldstone Ground. Gerry Ryan, Peter Ward and Paul Clark notched a strike apiece in front of 19,217 fans to move the Seagulls up to third place in the Second Division.

Saturday 30th September 2023

A star of the future made his full Albion debut at Aston Villa. The versatile Jack Hinshelwood became a first-team regular and would score three times – in wins against Brentford, Tottenham and Crystal Palace – during the season. Unfortunately, in what was a baptism of fire for the youngster, Albion came away from Birmingham with a 6-1 defeat.

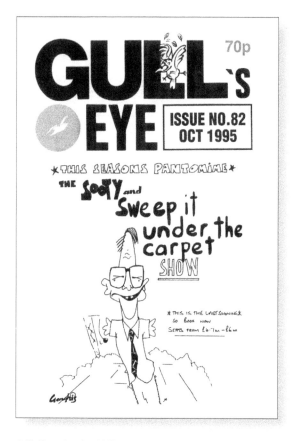

Gull's Eye – October 1995:
The natives were getting very restless at the Goldstone.

© Gull's Eye

OCTOBER

Saturday 1st October 1932

Club secretary Albert Underwood famously forgot to register Albion for exemption from the four qualifying rounds of the FA Cup! As a result, County League Shoreham visited the Goldstone and were promptly hammered 12-0! Arthur Attwood plundered a double hat-trick. The Musselmen shellacking precipitated an incredible ten-game run in the competition, culminating in a fifth-round replay defeat against West Ham United at the Goldstone Ground in front of 36,742 fans, just five less than the record crowd set 26 years later. Worthing, Hastings & St Leonards, Barnet, Crystal Palace, Wrexham (one replay), Chelsea and Bradford Park Avenue were also dispatched.

Wednesday 1st October 1980

Bruno Saltor Grau was born in Spain. He started his career at Espanyol and arrived on the south coast in 2012, via spells at Gimnàstic, Lleida, Almería and Valencia. Adored by Albion fans for his class on and off the pitch, the right-back retired from playing in 2019, aged 38, and joined the coaching staff under Graham Potter. When the aforementioned left for 'footballing reasons', Bruno followed, much to the chagrin of Seagulls fans across the globe.

Saturday 1st October 1983

The 11,517 fans present at the Goldstone Ground couldn't believe their eyes; Albion led Charlton Athletic 5-0 at half-time! The incredible final score of 7-0 included a Jimmy Case hat-trick. Gerry Ryan (2), Gordon Smith and Terry Connor were also on the scoresheet. Despite the magnificent result, rumours abounded that coach Chris Cattlin was picking the team (instead of manager Jimmy Melia).

Tuesday 1st October 1996

Before the home fixture with Lincoln City, chairman Bill Archer completely rejected the proposed consortium takeover, much to the annoyance of the 4,411 Goldstone spectators. When the Imps opened the scoring in the 25th minute, a pitch invasion by desperate fans resulted in the players leaving the pitch, holding the game up for 13 minutes.

The suspended points deduction imposed following the abandonment of the York City game the previous April would now be brought in. The 3-1 scoreline left Jimmy Case's men in second-to-last spot in Division Three. Peter Smith scored Albion's only goal.

Thursday 1st October 1998

The month began with Albion fans being asked to write to the Local Plan team urging them to include a stadium. This later became known as 'Letter One'!

Saturday 1st October 2022

Roberto De Zerbi's tenure in the Albion hotseat got off to a good start at Liverpool. A Leandro Trossard hat-trick helped the Italian's charges to a 3-3 draw after being two goals up.

Tuesday 2nd October 1990

The club revealed that Harry Enfield's 'Loadsamoney' character filmed a sketch for his new TV comedy programme behind the North Stand goal with groundsman Frankie Howard as an extra! It's not known if any of the players featured in the 'Charles Charlie Charles' sketch.

Friday 2nd October 2020

Aimed at a new generation of younger fans, the Seagulls Social podcast was set up by Ryan Adsett, Ben Spalding and Maz Mirzadeh during the COVID-19 pandemic. Regular special guests from the Albion world make this one of the club's most popular pods.

Thursday 3rd October 2006

Lewes District Council agreed to sign a government consent order to allow the quashing of planning permission for the stadium at Falmer – the day before the issue was to be heard in court.

Tuesday 4th October 2005

Probably the most amazing headline ever connected with Brighton & Hove Albion Football Club was in *The Argus*; 'Maradona Eyes Up Albion'! It was reported that the Argentinian – probably the best footballer of his generation – was lining up a takeover bid with his compatriot Ossie Ardiles. Chairman Dick Knight said of the revelation; "I believe it is distinctly probable that all sorts of people would be interested in the Albion when we get our stadium." You know what they say about hindsight...

Tuesday 5th October 2010

The distinctive blue hue of the stand roofs at Falmer was evident as the last of the panelling was put in place. The impressive West Stand central glass façade was now finished and internal fitting works were in full swing. The new bridge over the track at Falmer Station was also taking shape. Never a dull moment at the site of Brighton & Hove Albion's new home.

Saturday 5th October 2019

Irish striker Aaron Connolly scored twice on his first Premier League start against Tottenham Hotspur. Neal Maupay also netted in the comprehensive 3-0 victory at Falmer.

Thursday 5th October 2023

Brighton & Hove Albion's first away game in a European competition. Olympique de Marseille were the hosts as 2,800 visitors descended on the south of France. The club set up a ticket collection point by La Joliette square where Albion fans were advised to congregate before being shuttled to the ground. 'For our own safety', the authorities decided to take us on a scenic tour of the French city, which added over 30 minutes to the otherwise short journey.

The home side surged into a two-goal lead after 20 minutes through Chancel Mbemba and Jordan Veretout. In a raucous Stade Velodrome, De Zerbi's men rallied and on 55 minutes Pascal Gross calmly converted past Pau Lopez to give Albion a fighting chance. The crowd of over 60,000 was relentless in its support of the home side with the competing ultra groups behind each goal creating a deafening atmosphere. This only encouraged the Albion fans in the corner who could sense their team could snatch a late equaliser. Tariq Lamptey slalomed into the box with a few minutes left on the clock, the referee pointed to the spot which João Pedro duly dispatched to make it 2-2. An otherwise amazing experience was somewhat dampened by the police keeping over a thousand Albion fans in an underground car park for three hours post-match without food, water or sanitation.

Saturday 6th October 1984

Big Mick Ferguson – who would net seven times in 21 run-outs – made his Albion debut in the 2-0 Second Division Goldstone win over Birmingham City.

Tuesday 6th October 2020

Albion signed Polish international midfielder Jakub Moder from Lech Poznan. The 21-year-old was initially loaned back. Moder – who had represented Poland at junior levels from under-16s to under-21s – made his senior international debut as a substitute against the Netherlands in the UEFA Nations League. He has his own song:

'Tony Bloom,
Went to Europe,
In a brand-new Skoda,
Brought us back a magic man,
Jakub, Jakub Moder...'

Sunday 7th October 1973

Sami Tuomas Hyypiä was born in Porvoo, Finland. After an illustrious playing career – including a decade at Liverpool – the tall Finn moved into management. After a promising two years at Bayer Leverkusen, the former defender was snapped up by the Albion board after Óscar Garcia had offered to leave after the play-off semi-final defeat to Derby County in May 2014.

Fast-forward six months and another Albion manager had tendered their resignation, this time after Hyypiä had presided over one win in 18 games. His final record read: six victories in 26 outings (three in cups), ten draws and ten defeats. Tony Bloom was reluctant to accept Hyypiä's gracious decision to step down but it did enable the chairman to recruit Chris Hughton a few weeks later.

Saturday 7th October 1978

The largest crowd ever to witness an Albion/Palace clash, 33,685, was at Selhurst Park as the Eagles continued their unbeaten run against the Seagulls with a 3-1 win at Selhurst Park. Brian Horton scored the consolation for Alan Mullery's side to make it eight games since an Albion victory over their fiercest rivals.

Sunday 7th October 2018

Albion defender Lewis Dunk was called up to the England squad by Gareth Southgate for the Uefa Nations League fixtures away to Croatia and Spain. The Brighton-born 26-year-old – who had signed a new five-year deal with the club two days earlier – was the first Albion player to be called up since Steve Foster was part of Ron Greenwood's squad for the 1982 World Cup in Spain. Albion manager Chris Hughton said; "We are absolutely thrilled for Lewis, he fully deserves this call up. He has shown his quality in the Premier League and his progression has been a steady and consistent one."

Saturday 8th October 1985

Bradford returned to their city, for the first time following the tragic fire at Valley Parade, to host Albion in a League Cup tie at Odsal Stadium, home of rugby league outfit Bradford Northern. Chris Cattlin's men won 2-0.

Monday 8th October 2001

Albion submitted stadium-related planning applications to Brighton & Hove Council.

Tuesday 8th October 2002

Martin Hinshelwood moved upstairs, after 11 straight league defeats, as Dick Knight appointed Steve Coppell as manager. "Steve Coppell will bring a level of experience we feel is vital at this time. I have made him fully aware that no increase in the playing budget will suddenly be made available, but he understands the club's position. He is now eager to get started," proclaimed the chairman.

Saturday 9th October 1993

An injury crisis necessitated Barry Lloyd fielding the youngest Albion line-up in history in the 1-1 draw with Stockport County at the Goldstone. The average age was just 21 years and 153 days and the team (with ages) was: Nicky Rust (19), Stuart Myall (18), Stuart Tuck (19), Ian Chapman (23), Stuart Munday (21), Paul McCarthy (22), Danny Simmonds (18), Simon Funnell (19), Kurt Nogan (23), Robert Codner (28) and Matthew Edwards (22). Kurt Nogan scored the Albion goal.

Friday 9th October 1998

The day after becoming the club's second 'People's Player', Rod Thomas scored just 22 minutes into his Albion debut in the 3-2 win at Cambridge United. The winger joined from Chester City in a £25,000 deal and most of the fee was raised by the fans.

Monday 9th October 2000

Letter number four. Albion fans were again asked to write, this time in support of the stadium planning application.

Saturday 10th October 1964

Witnessed by a 14,261 gate, Albion enjoyed a third home win in seven days. Wally Gould, Jimmy Collins (2), Jack Smith (2) and Bobby Smith scored in the 6-0 drubbing of Notts County. The fixture also saw the debut of former Welsh international full-back Mel Hopkins.

Monday 10th October 2022

It was reported that Enock Mwepu had to retire from professional football at the age of 24. The midfielder fell ill on a flight to link up with his Zambia team-mates. The previously unknown hereditary cardiac condition was so severe that Mwepu would be extremely likely to suffer a 'fatal cardiac arrest' should he continue to play.

"A boy from a small Zambian township called Chambishi has news to share," wrote Mwepu on Twitter (X). "He stood strong to follow his dreams of playing football at the highest level, and by grace of God, he lived his dream by reaching the Premier League. Some dreams, however, have an end, so it is with sadness that I announce the need to hang up my boots because of the medical advice I received. This is not the end of my involvement in football, I intend to stay involved to some degree. I would like to take this opportunity to thank everyone who supported me in my football trip including my wife and family. The Zambian FA, all my past team-mates and coaches, especially everyone at Brighton & Hove Albion."

Mwepu played six times for Albion in 2022/23 – before falling ill during the September international break – and on 21 occasions during 2021/22, scoring three goals.

"We are all absolutely devastated for Enock," said Tony Bloom. "He and his family have had a traumatic few weeks and while we are just thankful he has come through that period, he has seen such a promising career cut short at such a young age. As a club we will give him all the love, help and support we possibly can to make a full recovery, and then as he decides on the next steps in his life."

Saturday 11th October 1986

Goalkeeper John Keeley's debut was in a 1-0 defeat at Ipswich Town. The Essex-born stopper arrived for just £1,500 from Chelmsford City in 1986 and was sold four years later to Oldham Athletic, after 160 starts, for £240,000.

Wednesday 12th October 1983

Despite Albion's relegation from the top-flight, Tony Grealish was still good enough to represent his country in a European Championship qualifier. The midfielder couldn't do anything to stop a 3-2 Netherlands victory in Dublin.

Tuesday 12th October 1999

'Let's have a winner' Danny Cullip signed for £50,000 from Brentford after impressing during a four-match loan spell. The inspirational defender led from the back in his five years on the coast and was much-loved by the Withdean faithful. Cullip moved to Sheffield United – after 239 appearances and 10 goals – for £250,000 in 2004 and was twice Albion Player of the Season.

Tuesday 12th October 2004

Early Day Motion 1712, regarding the stadium application, was tabled in Parliament. Thirty-three MPs signed up to the second EDM.

Monday 13th October 2003

Jake Robinson became Albion's youngest goalscorer, aged 16, when he slotted home a pass from Nathan Jones in the 88th minute against Forest Green Rovers in the second round of the LDV Vans Trophy at the Withdean Stadium.

Saturday 14th October 1933

Len Darling made the first of 341 appearances – he scored 14 times – in an Albion shirt in the 1-0 win at Aldershot. He played 113 matches during World War II in the Football Leage (South).

Saturday 14th October 1961

In the programme – priced sixpence – versus Luton Town, *News of the World*'s Harry Ditton wrote about the new European Cup competition; "Many of these continentals carry gamesmanship to the point of downright cheating – time-wasting, shirt-pulling and obstruction tactics – and matters are not helped by the importation of foreign referees who, by our own standards, are often incompetent."

Wonder what Harry would make of the Premier League now?

Wednesday 14th October 1998

Scars & Stripes hosted 'Fans and Bands United' at the Paradox, West Street, Brighton. England's 3-0 win over Luxembourg was shown downstairs in Club Barcelona before The Levellers, who performed their own version of Abba's SOS (Save Our Seagulls), Buster Bloodvessel and the Fish Brothers entertained over 1,200 Albion fans. The memorable event raised over £4,000 for the club which was presented to Dick Knight on the pitch at Gillingham.

Saturday 14th October 2006

MP Norman Baker was challenged by Falmer For All (FFA) campaigners on a Southern Counties Radio phone-in.

Thursday 14th October 2009

Albion schoolboy Jake Caskey – who later added the prefix 'Forster' in recognition of his step-dad Nicky's part in his career development – made his international debut in the England under-16s win against Wales in the Victory Shield clash at Yeovil's Huish Park. The 15-year-old midfielder started the game and was eventually replaced nine minutes before the end. Albion director of football Martin Hinshelwood travelled to Somerset and was delighted to see one of the club's future stars represent their country. "As a football club we were pleased that he was selected for the squad, and really proud that he made his debut," said the former Crystal Palace midfielder. As of early 2024, the midfielder is playing for Stevenage, under Steve Evans, in League One.

Saturday 15th October 1955

Striker Peter Harburn started an amazing goalscoring run – 12 goals in eight games – in the 3-0 Third Division (South) victory at Watford. By a quirk of fixture-list computer fate, it was the second of three games between the two teams on this date. The first, in 1921, finished 1-1 at the Goldstone and the third, in Hertfordshire, ended with the same scoreline in 1988.

Tuesday 15th October 1996

The fourth-tier 1-0 defeat to Hereford United was memorable for the mass walkout with 15 minutes of the game remaining by fans disillusioned with the board. Most of the 3,444 spectators left when a rocket was set off from behind the East Terrace. The result, on the pitch, kept Albion four points adrift at the bottom of the basement division.

Thursday 15th October 2009

The demolition of the university buildings began in earnest. The steel mesh, ready for the concrete to be pumped on it, was laid to form the floors in the East Stand.

Sunday 15th October 2023

Former Republic of Ireland and Albion legend Gerry Ryan died at the age of 68. The Dubliner landed on the south coast from Derby County in 1978 and went on to make 199 appearances, scoring 39 times. The forward scored the goal which sealed Albion's promotion to the top-flight in 1979 and came on as a substitute in the 1983 FA Cup Final against Manchester United. He was a pivotal player in the club's original golden period and later returned to the Goldstone Ground as assistant to former manager Liam Brady, his friend and international colleague. Brady told the club's website; "Gerry was a wonderful team-mate. He was a very quick winger, very brave, and he took people on. Off the pitch Gerry was just a really nice guy. He was affable and unassuming, and got on with everyone he came in contact with. He'll be sadly missed by everyone who knew him." RIP Gerry.

Sunday 15th October 2023

Away from their normal home at Crawley Town's Broadfield Stadium, Albion Women entertained Tottenham Hotspur at Falmer. A record crowd of 6,951 watched their team go down 3-1, with an Elisabeth Terland strike not enough to see off their opponents from north London.

Friday 16th October 1970

Peter O'Sullivan started the first of 194 consecutive first-team Albion appearances in the 1-0 Division Three defeat at Torquay United.

Saturday 16th October 1984

Winger Steve Penney made his Northern Ireland debut in the 3-0 victory over Israel in Belfast.

Saturday 16th October 2010

Unbelievably, some Albion fans had been voicing their displeasure – despite being top – at Gus Poyet's style of play; patient build-up from the back, short passes, utilising the full-backs and using the goalkeeper as a sweeper. All the dissenters were sent scurrying for their Wimbledon videos – circa late 1980s – after the astonishing show at Charlton Athletic on this day. In possibly one of the most comprehensive, commanding and skilful away performances ever witnessed by Albion fans, the team absolutely destroyed their hosts playing 'tippy tappy' football. The 3,394 fans from Sussex were rubbing their eyes in disbelief as their heroes recorded the biggest win on the road since 2000, adding to the best start to a season for 84 years.

Calderón began the rout converting a Dicker cross (26th minute), Murray (62nd) sidestepped the keeper, LuaLua thumped one in from the edge of the box (81st) before Sparrow completed the demolition in injury time with an acrobatic header. The home fans clapped Albion players from the pitch. A great game of football.

Saturday 17th October 1981

Albion drew 3-3 with Liverpool at the Goldstone. Ray Kennedy, Kenny Dalglish and Terry McDermott were on target for the Reds. Steve Foster, Jimmy Case and Andy Ritchie replied for the Seagulls.

Friday 17th October 1997

An Albion delegation descended on Woking Football Club to investigate the possibility of a groundshare arrangement with the Conference side.

Wednesday 17th October 2001

The second Peter Taylor to manage the Albion took control of the club. A winger in his playing career, he represented England four times while playing for Crystal Palace – in the Third Division!

Saturday 18th October 1902

Albion enjoyed the biggest away win in the club's history. Shoreham FC were humbled 12-0 in an FA Cup second qualifying round fixture at Oxen Field. The goals: Ben Garfield, Barney Lee (2), Sid Thair (3), Frank Scott (4), an own goal and Alf Harland.

Tuesday 18th October 2005

On-loan Manchester United defender Paul McShane 'scored' the only goal of the game, with 12 minutes remaining, to give the Seagulls their first win over Crystal Palace at Selhurst Park since 1983. The 3,500-plus visiting supporters were on tenterhooks as Clinton Morrison stabbed a loose ball home in the final seconds only for the referee to rule the effort offside. The result helped to banish the mauling from three years earlier.

Friday 19th October 1980

Albion legend Paul Mooney passed away, aged 79, in Brighton.

Wednesday 19th October 1983

Jimmy Melia resigned as manager of Brighton & Hove Albion. The Scouser had led his team out at Wembley just five months earlier. His record read: played 39; wins 9, draws 13 and losses 17.

Friday 20th October 1967

Due to a railway guards' dispute, a convoy of four cars ferried Albion players to a Nottingham hotel in readiness for the following day's fixture with Mansfield Town.

Saturday 20th October 1984

The day many Albion fans had been waiting for... a new roof on the North Stand! The crowd of just 10,000 didn't exactly 'raise' the new £200,000 structure during a turgid 0-0 stalemate with Barnsley. The first thousand entrants to the stand were given a free foam hand, leftovers from the FA Cup Final appearance 18 months earlier.

Gary Howlett, provider of the first goal on that memorable day, made his last appearance for the club. The game was so poor that manager Chris Cattlin fined himself a week's wages!

Tuesday 20th October 2009

The first part of the Falmer Arch was followed – storm-chaser style – down the A23 by 'Jack Straw' (aka Graeme Rolf). The intrepid amateur photographer had been documenting the stadium's construction since the first sod was dug in December 2008 and posted his images on fans' forum North Stand Chat.

Friday 20th October 2017

Albion's first away win in the Premier League, and the first in the top-flight since a 2-1 victory at Swansea City on 1st March 1983. A stunning curler into the top corner from José Izquierdo was sandwiched between a brace from Glenn Murray as Albion thrashed West Ham United 3-0 in east London to pile on the misery for home boss Slaven Bilić. Chris Hughton's men climbed to tenth in the table.

Saturday 21st October 1922

Ernest 'Tug' Wilson made his Albion debut in the 2-1 home win over Brentford. Rejected four years earlier by Sheffield Wednesday for being too small, the little Yorkshireman dominated the left flank for 14 years. Notching 71 goals in an incredible 566 appearances – a record unlikely to ever be beaten – Tug was much-loved by the Goldstone faithful and missed just 29 games in 12 seasons. He set up a bookmaker, on his retirement, with former team-mate Frank Brett and passed away, aged 56, in 1955. A true Albion legend.

Wednesday 21st October 1998

A Football League Appeals Tribunal awarded Albion more than £1 million compensation from Aston Villa for 17-year-old Gareth Barry. The schoolboy from Hastings attended the club's Centre of Excellence. A few months later a salty John Gregory (Villa boss) said; "Dick Knight wouldn't recognise Gareth Barry if he stood on Brighton beach in an Albion shirt with a ball tucked under his arm and a seagull on his head.

We are being asked to pick up the bill for a football club so badly run that it nearly went to the wall." Part of Knight's retort; "John Gregory's cheeky chappie quips speak volumes for themselves. By his own admission he previously told the national press that Aston Villa had stolen Gareth Barry from Brighton." Knight 1, Gregory 0.

Saturday 22nd October 1977

An all-ticket Goldstone crowd of 28,208 witnessed a thrilling 1-1 draw with Crystal Palace. Ian 'Spider' Mellor put Albion ahead (40th minute) only for Paul Hinshelwood – brother of Martin and father of Adam – to equalise with eight minutes remaining.

Saturday 22nd October 1983

Chris Cattlin's first game in charge. The former left-back took over from Jimmy Melia and his shrewd dealings resulted in Albion finishing just a game away from a top-flight return in 1985. The club's second FA Cup sixth-round appearance the next season wasn't enough, and the rock shop owner was shown the door – much to the disgust of many fans – for the return of Alan Mullery. You know what they say about 'going back'…?

Saturday 23rd October 1920

Jack Doran – who scored 55 goals in just 85 Albion starts – made his international debut for Ireland against England at Roker Park in Sunderland. The Belfast-born hitman failed to find the target in the 2-0 Home Championship defeat.

Saturday 23rd October 1982

A hero returned… Peter Ward, who had moved to Nottingham Forest two years earlier, came home for four months on loan and played in the 3-1 First Division victory over West Ham United.

Saturday 24th October 1925

Paul Mooney made his debut in the 2-1 Third Division (South) win over QPR. The dependable stopper, who represented the Albion 315 times, scoring 11 goals, was great in the air and once scored a header from the halfway line at Walsall! 'Cast Iron Head' joined County League Vernon Athletic in 1936.

Saturday 25th October 1952

Denis Foreman scored on his Albion debut; a 4-2 home win over Aldershot. The South African-born left-sided attacker managed 69 strikes in 219 games before a bad injury in 1958 slowed down his last years at the Goldstone. He also represented Sussex at cricket from 1952 to 1967.

Saturday 26th October 1996

Over 1,000 Albion fans marched from Brighton Station – accompanied by many Fulham supporters – via Western Road and Church Road to the Goldstone Ground in a peaceful demonstration against Bill Archer, Greg Stanley and David Bellotti. The latter was forced from his seat after a firework was thrown during the 0-0 draw with the west Londoners.

Tuesday 26th October 2010

Two Albion Girls' Centre of Excellence players were selected for the England Women's under-15s training camp. Zoë Cross, 12, from Crawley, and Selsey's Leah Samain, 13, were chosen after attending the FA CoE London and South-East Regional Talent Camp, after impressing in the Albion under-14s.

Thursday 26th October 2023

Albion hosted four-times European Cup winners Ajax at Falmer. Incredibly, the Amsterdam club – and serial Dutch champions – were bottom of the Eredivisie after a calamitous start to the season. Despite the away side's appalling domestic form they were unbeaten in 11 European outings.

In a boisterous atmosphere, João Pedro tapped in (42nd minute) after Kaoru Mitoma had cut inside and had a shot parried to the onrushing Brazilian forward. Ansu Fati rolled a low shot through a defender's legs and past Ramaj into the far corner to complete the scoring eight minutes into the second half – an exquisite finish from the Spaniard. Brighton & Hove Albion's first-ever victory in European competition. Manager Roberto De Zerbi said; "It is a great day for our fans, our club, our owner and we are very proud to give them this day."

Tuesday 27th October 2009

The Justin Campaign – named in memory of the former Albion player Justin Fashanu, an openly gay footballer, who tragically took his own life in 1998 – in association with the Albion and KickItOut, hosted an evening of talk and debate around homophobia in football at Withdean Stadium.

The debate included Paul Hayward, *The Observer* sports editor; Alison Vaughn, KIO campaign manager; Charlie Oatway and Darren Ollerton, campaign director for The Justin Campaign. The evening, also attended by supporters and club officials, proved open and honest, the consensus being that professionals and fans alike were ready to see an end to homophobia in football.

Saturday 27th October 2018

Albion's third successive victory moved them up to 11th in the Premier League. Glenn Murray, who was a doubt for the game after suffering concussion the previous weekend, instinctively directed the ball inside the post – from a mis-hit Bruno effort – from seven yards to earn Albion the points against Wolverhampton Wanderers at Falmer. The 48th-minute effort was the striker's 100th for the Albion, taking the Cumbrian-born forward to second in the all-time leading scorer list behind Tommy Cook on 123. "I've had some special moments here at the Amex," said Muzza. "I've been here a long time and I'm immensely proud of scoring 100 goals for the club."

Saturday 28th October 1995

George Parris scored a cheeky goal against Bristol Rovers, earning him an Albion nickname that will last a lifetime. As the opposition keeper gathered the ball as an Albion attack ended, the former West Ham United man's momentum kept him going off the pitch, so he waited, with his hand on the post, until the unsuspecting Pirate stopper rolled the ball out. He then robbed the ball off him and slotted it into an empty net! Sneaky George was born.

Friday 28th October 2005

Deputy Prime Minister John Prescott's letter arrived at Albion HQ regarding the Falmer decision: it's a 'yes'! Surely it's full steam ahead now?

Tuesday 28th October 2008

Former Welsh international midfielder Robbie Savage completed his seven-game loan spell from Derby County against his former club, Leicester City. The Foxes were two up by half-time, when the Welsh midfielder and Kevin McLeod were replaced by Kevin Thornton and Dean Cox, respectively. The changes made all the difference as another loanee, Leeds United's Bradley Johnson, fired in two sweet left-foot strikes from distance. With less than two minutes remaining, Albion completed a remarkable comeback as Joe Anyinsah broke in the right channel before crossing low into the six-yard box. Leicester defender Jack Hobbs could only turn the ball past his own keeper to make it 3-2.

Saturday 29th October 1910

'Pom Pom' Bob Whiting ended his record of five straight clean sheets in the 2-1 Goldstone victory over Queens Park Rangers. The result was also the last triumph in a fine run of nine consecutive wins where only three goals were conceded, and 18 scored. The next game was a 2-1 defeat at West Ham United.

Saturday 29th October 2005

The day after Prescott's letter, the club laid on champagne before the Ipswich game for ecstatic fans at Withdean Stadium. Surely that would be it now?

Thursday 29th October 2020

The club and Albion in the Community extended their help to local charities by paying for 2,000 meals for families across the city of

Brighton & Hove over the winter months. The commitment was to provide funding for the meals through the months of October, November, December and January, with a regular monthly contribution to Brighton-based food charity Chomp. Club captain Lewis Dunk explained; "As players and as a club we really wanted to show our support for the brilliant campaign being led by Marcus Rashford. What he has done is amazing and has highlighted such an important issue in modern-day Britain."

Saturday 29th October 2022

After leaving the Albion to become Chelsea manager – for football reasons you understand – Graham Potter was 'welcomed' back at Falmer by a bubbling and partisan crowd as he strolled to the other dugout. Leandro Trossard's calm finish, and two calamitous own goals, fired Albion into a three-goal lead by half-time. Pascal Gross completed the scoring in injury time to give Roberto De Zerbi a memorable first win (4-1) – their first over Chelsea in the league – as Albion boss. Post-match, Potter said that he had "nothing to say sorry for" after his hostile reception. His opposite number suggested that "our fans were the best player". Good work, Roberto.

Monday 30th October 1989

Ashley Barnes was born in Bath, Somerset. After initially joining on loan from Plymouth Argyle, the striker signed a two-year deal for the start of the 2010/11 campaign. Barnes finished his first season as Brighton's second-top goalscorer behind Glenn Murray, with 20 goals in 49 appearances, helping Albion secure promotion to the Championship. In 2011/12, Barnes remained first-choice striker, finishing the season as leading goalscorer with 14 goals in all competitions. Burnley paid £700,000 for his services during the January transfer window of 2014, and he represented the Clarets for ten seasons, including seven in the Premier League. His final figures for the Albion were as follows: 53 goals in 170 appearances.

Saturday 30th October 2010

Table-topping Albion – six points clear – battered their hosts at London Road thanks to a brace from birthday boy Ashley Barnes. Peterborough had George Boyd sent off for violent conduct early on as the away side's dominance began to frustrate the Cambridgeshire outfit. Albion took an early lead when Barnes glanced home from an Elliott Bennett free-kick on 16 minutes. The assist king then missed a penalty before Iñigo Calderón notched from close range – his third in as many games.

Home goalkeeper Joe Lewis was in outstanding form keeping Albion's rampant attack at bay. But, he couldn't do anything to deny Barnes' second, a penalty (62nd minute). The scoreline did not do justice to the absolute control Gus Poyet's men had on the contest and the 21-year-old Barnes could have made it more convincing, hitting the crossbar twice late on. Gus said of the demolition; "I'm not putting anything in Calde's tea to make him score! I said when we got him from nowhere that it was a lucky day for the Albion. We had 15 shots on target and we scored three goals. I pay massive credit to their goalkeeper Joe Lewis because he was outstanding." Peterborough United 0, Brighton & Hove Albion 3.

Saturday 31st October 1903

Alan Haig-Brown made the first of his three Albion appearances in the 4-0 defeat at West Ham United. The outside-right was also an accomplished writer, penning articles for *The Times*, and other newspapers, more than a thousand poems and three books; *Sporting Sonnets*, *My Game Book* and *The OTC and the Great War*.

Wednesday 31st October 1973

It was not announced officially until the following day; Brian Clough and Peter Taylor had signed a five-year contract to take control of the team. The move shocked the football world.

Monday 31st October 2022

Albion Women's boss Hope Powell stepped down as manager after an 8-0 home defeat by Spurs. The former England Women's boss joined the club in July 2017, leading them to their best Women's Super League finish of sixth in 2021. The hammering by Tottenham left Albion second-bottom with one win and four defeats from the opening five league games.

The Seagull Love Review – November 2012:
TSLR nailing Ashley Barnes' accent.

© TSLR

NOVEMBER

Thursday 1st November 2001

The month saw fans sending letters (Letter Five) to individual councillors requesting their support for the new stadium.

Saturday 1st November 2003

New manager Mark McGhee took charge of his first game; the 2-2 Division Two draw at Peterborough United. The month also began with fans being urged to write a letter (Letter Eight) in support of University of Brighton's plans for redevelopment, which were linked to the stadium scheme.

Sunday 1st November 2009

After the amazing feat of keeping his side in League One the previous May, Russell Slade was sacked as Albion boss. The cap-wearing miracle worker's season had not started well – just three league wins in 15 outings – and chairman Tony Bloom acted quickly to stop the rot. He was only at the club for eight months, but Slade's achievements will live long in the memory. He's guaranteed a warm reception at Falmer.

Monday 1st November 2010

Former Albion goalkeeper Harry Baldwin passed away, aged 90. The Birmingham-born custodian started his league career with West Bromwich Albion in 1937 before moving to Albion two years later, on the recommendation of former Baggies and England inside-forward Eddie Sandford, a nephew of Bill 'Bullet' Jones.

He competed with Jack Ball for the number one jersey over six seasons reaching his peak during 1947/48, when he saved seven penalties out of nine, including an incredible run of five in succession. He made 215 appearances for the club.

Tuesday 2nd November 1993

Gull's Eye appealed for fans to attend what might be the club's last-ever game against Wrexham in Division Two. Just 5,530 turned up.

Saturday 3rd November 1973

New manager Brian Clough, and his assistant Peter Taylor, were applauded as they took to their seats in the directors' box. The crowd of 16,017 for the Third Division visit of York City was nearly 10,000 up on the previous attendance.

Tuesday 3rd November 1993

Albion were in the High Court to fight off a winding-up petition from the Inland Revenue and Customs & Excise.

Friday 4th November 1960

Albion splashed out a record £15,000 for 22-year-old Tony Nicholas from Chelsea. The nippy forward topped the goalscoring charts at the end of his first season – 13 in 27 starts – but was part of George Curtis' cull in 1962 after relegation to the Third Division.

Saturday 4th November 2017

Man of the Match Glenn Murray's 29th-minute close-range finish was enough to take all three points in Wales. The victory at Swansea City saw Albion move up to eighth in the Premier League, their highest position all season. Since the start of 2016/17, Harry Kane (37) was the only English player to have scored more goals in the top two tiers of English football than Glenn Murray (27 – level with Tammy Abraham).

Wednesday 5th November 1997

Just 1,025 – the lowest-ever for an Albion 'home' fixture in the Football League – were at Priestfield to witness the fourth-tier 3-0 defeat to Barnet which left Steve Gritt's men in 23rd spot, just six points above doomed Doncaster Rovers.

Saturday 5th November 2016

Steve Sidwell scored an outrageous goal – from just inside the opposition's half! The ball fell to the midfielder inside the centre circle and after a quick look up to see where the keeper was, the former Chelsea, Fulham and Aston Villa man struck with his left foot, lobbing the stranded custodian who slipped over tracking back. Sidwell ran straight to the bench to hold an Anthony Knockaert shirt aloft. The French winger was unavailable as his dad had recently passed away.

Saturday 6th November 1982

Unbeaten in their first six home Division One fixtures of the season, Albion hosted Manchester United. The record continued as Peter Ward volleyed home the only goal of the contest.

Wednesday 7th November 1906

Right-sided forward Bert Longstaff made his debut in the United League 2-2 draw at Crystal Palace. Born in Shoreham-by-Sea in 1885, he went on to net 86 times in 443 starts and was in the top-ten highest appearances list. He could have joined Tottenham Hotspur in 1903 but his mother wanted him to remain at home!

Friday 8th November 1957

Alan Curbishley – real name Llewellyn – was born in East Ham. After spells at Birmingham City, Aston Villa and Charlton Athletic the midfielder moved to Albion in 1987. Curbs scored 15 times in 132 appearances before a move back to The Valley in 1990.

Sunday 8th November 1992

Rohan Greg Ince was born in Whitechapel, east London. The midfielder failed to live up to his earlier promise having scored a Goal-of-the-Season-winning-volley at Swindon Town in the League Cup in 2014. In six seasons, he made 91 appearances, scoring on four occasions. As of March 2024, Ince was enjoying his third campaign at National League side Woking.

Saturday 8th November 1997

Albion organised a double-decker bus to Gillingham, for £4.50 a head, boosting the attendance for the fourth-tier clash with Rotherham United to 1,950. A perfect reflection of the mood at the time, the bus broke down and arrived back in Sussex around 9.30pm. Albion lost 2-1 with Stuart Storer scoring the 'home' side's goal.

Tuesday 8th November 2016

In a remarkable show of solidarity for their bereaved team-mate, Albion boss Chris Hughton and several first-team players travelled to France to support Anthony Knockaert at the funeral of the winger's father, Patrick. "Coming all the way from England it's just unbelievable. My dad had the best tribute ever," Knockaert, 24, tweeted. Goalkeepers David Stockdale and Niki Mäenpää, defenders Bruno, Gaetan Bong, Lewis Dunk, Connor Goldson and Liam Rosenior, midfielder Dale Stephens and winger Jamie Murphy made the trip to Leers, on the outskirts of Lille. "I will never forget that day! The respect of this football club is too much. You are not just my team-mates but my friends forever," added the Frenchman.

Saturday 9th November 1962

Terry Connor was born in Leeds. The striker joined Albion in a direct exchange that took Andy Ritchie to Leeds United in a record deal worth £500,000 in 1983. The 20-year-old was cup-tied for the big day at Wembley but made his mark the following season back in Division Two scoring 17 times. Terry top-scored on three occasions – 59 times in 174 run-outs – before being sold to Portsmouth for £200,000 in 1987.

Saturday 9th November 1996

Albion fans made the ultimate sacrifice by boycotting the home game against Mansfield Town in an effort to bring down the hated regime of Bill Archer, Greg Stanley and David Bellotti. The official attendance was just 1,933, the lowest home gate ever recorded by Albion in the Football League at the time. A gate mysteriously opened on the East Terrace just before half-time and hundreds flooded into the ground and took over the directors' box during the interval. The game ended 1-1.

Friday 9th November 2001

In a great example of why football can be such an inspiring sport, Albion supporters played a match against their Crystal Palace counterparts in memory of Robert Eaton, who tragically died in the Twin Towers disaster on 11th September.

The game at Southwick, organised by the Robert Eaton Memorial Fund (REMF), finished 4-4 after normal time and our friends from Croydon triumphed on penalties. The only time when it is acceptable to politely applaud a Palace victory!

Thursday 9th November 2023

The Johan Cruyff Arena in Amsterdam was the setting for Albion's second away fixture in the Europa League. After their convincing victory in Sussex a fortnight earlier, Roberto De Zerbi's men were confident ahead of kick-off.

The 2,500 fans in the ground, and the many more in hundreds of bars around the city, had something to celebrate after just 15 minutes when Simon Adingra fed the flying Ansu Fati who calmly slotted into the corner from ten yards. The diminutive striker returned the favour for his Ivorian team-mate – eight minutes into the second half – who hit a rising shot across the keeper to make it two without reply for Albion's first-ever competitive victory on foreign soil.

Monday 10th November 1947

It was a sad day at the Goldstone as two club legends departed. Team manager Tommy Cook left after seven months in the hotseat while Charlie Webb ended his 38-year involvement by quitting as general manager.

Saturday 10th November 1990

The programme included a centre-page spread of the proposed new stadium. The 25,000 all-seater has space for 5,000 cars with an adjacent full-size Astroturf pitch. A site had yet to be found. Commercial director Ray Bloom said; "We are currently losing £1,000 a day and are very nearly £3 million in debt. It's not feasible to convert the Goldstone Ground."

Tuesday 10th November 2009

The dawning of a new and exciting era for Brighton & Hove Albion – Gus Poyet became first-team boss. It was the former Uruguay international's first time in the managerial hotseat after winning the League Cup as assistant to Juande Ramos at Tottenham Hotspur in 2008. He was joined by his old Spurs team-mate Mauricio Taricco in the assistant manager's role.

Monday 11th November 2002

Steve Sidwell made his Albion debut on loan from Arsenal, as a 19-year-old, in the 1-1 televised First Division draw at Wolverhampton Wanderers.

Saturday 11th November 2006

Northwich Victoria visited Withdean for this FA Cup first-round tie. The Nationwide Conference side didn't stand a chance as Albion turned on the style and rattled in eight. Unsurprisingly, this was the biggest win at the Theatre of Trees during Albion's 12-year tenure.

Sunday 12th November 1994

In front of 3,815 fans, Albion were humiliated 2-1 by Diadora Isthmian League side Kingstonian in south London. The day will be remembered, by some fans, for the pre-match entertainment in the Sir Robert Peel in Kingston!

Saturday 12th November 1995

A quite appalling game of football occurred, below sea level, in Canvey Island. The FA Cup first-round 2-2 draw at the Isthmian League Division Two outfit resulted in an interesting post-match interview. At the end of the tunnel at Park Lane, BBC Southern Counties reporter John Lees interrogated beleaguered Albion boss Liam Brady.

Lees; "Liam, time running out and Alan Harding bore down into the penalty area, if he scored…" Brady; "I don't really wanna talk about it. Nicky Rust is paid to make saves like that." Lees; "If it had gone in, you'd probably have gone out."

Brady; "If me granny had balls, she'd be my grandad."

Saturday 13th November 1965

Albion romped to their largest cup (proper) victory to date. Southern Division One outfit Wisbech Town were the visitors in this FA Cup first-round tie. Albion were three up at the interval with strikes from Charlie Livesey, Jack Smith and an own goal. Then the floodgates opened. Goodchild, Collins, Cassidy (2), Smith again, Gould and a Livesey hat-trick made it 10-1 to the Albion!

Saturday 13th November 1976

Albion legend Steve Foster scored his first 'goal' in professional football for Portsmouth; a 20-yard header against Bury, into his own net!

Saturday 13th November 2004

It's reunion time with Bobby Zamora at Upton Park in a First Division clash. Steve Claridge – 38-years-old – made his Albion debut as Guy Butters headed home with 20 minutes remaining to give his side the three points.

Saturday 13th November 2010

After illuminating Albion performances for the first few months of the season, Kazenga LuaLua broke his ankle in the 3-1 reverse at Hartlepool United. The Congolese winger had been on fire in his ten previous outings, scoring four memorable goals and generally terrorising League One defences. He would not appear in the stripes – not the blue and white variety anyway – again in 2010/11.

Saturday 14th November 1931

Arthur Attwood began an amazing scoring sequence – 14 goals in eight games – netting in the 2-1 win at Thames FC. The east London outfit only lasted four years – from 1928 to 1932 – and played at the 120,000-capacity West Ham Stadium in Custom House. They struggled to compete with other local clubs, including West Ham United, Charlton Athletic and Millwall, and hold the record for the lowest-known attendance for a Saturday Football League fixture; just 469 fans paid to watch them play Luton Town in 1930. Not to be confused with Thames Ironworks, who later became West Ham United.

Monday 14th November 2016

Issue 2 of *The Albion Mag* was available – free of charge – in the pubs and shops of central Brighton & Hove, and further afield. Its 44 pages were full of articles from fans of all ages, and from different sections of society, celebrating and discussing what it is to be an Albion fan.

Sunday 14th November 2021

Graham Potter, his assistant Billy Reid and first-team coach Bruno joined The Big Sleep Out in the centre of Brighton to raise awareness, and vital funds, for the city's homeless people. They joined others at St Peter's Church as part of the event organised by local charity Off the Fence, who run Project Anti-Freeze each winter.

Potter said; "We had an easy version of sleeping rough, but it still gave us an insight into the challenges the homeless community face on a daily and nightly basis. Having experienced just one night out on the street, I cannot imagine what it would be like suffering in this way with no idea of what the future holds, or where the next meal might be coming from." Fortunately, it's something Potter – who was paid tens of millions of pounds for just six months' work at Chelsea two years later – will never have to face.

Wednesday 15th November 1967

Gustavo Augusto Poyet Domínguez was born in the Uruguayan capital of Montevideo. The midfielder started his playing career at Grenoble in the French Second Division. After a season he returned home to River Plate Montevideo for a year before Real Zaragoza snapped up the 23-year-old. Gus enjoyed a successful seven-year spell in Spain, winning the Copa del Rey in 1994 and the UEFA Cup Winners' Cup – when Nayim famously lobbed David Seaman from the half-way line

– a year later, scoring a total of 63 goals in 239 league appearances. He joined Premier League Chelsea on a free in the summer of 1997 and spent four years at Stamford Bridge, lifting the European Super Cup and UEFA Cup Winners' Cup in 1998, and FA Cup in 2000. Gus' prolific stint in west London saw him claim 49 goals in 145 games (all competitions), a fantastic ratio for a midfielder.

Surplus to requirements, Claudio Ranieri received £2.2 million from Tottenham Hotspur in 2001 – a healthy sum for a player who was nearly 34. He hung up his boots after a further three seasons playing top-flight football – following 23 strikes in 98 matches – for a go at management alongside former team-mate Dennis Wise, at both Swindon Town and Leeds United, before helping Juande Ramos win the League Cup for Spurs in 2008, as assistant manager. In November 2009, Gus took the reins at Withdean and the transformation was nothing short of miraculous. Cantering to the League One title in his first full season, the Uruguayan had his charges playing some of the finest passing football ever witnessed by Albion fans.

Saturday 15th November 1997

Revenge was on the cards after Albion had relegated Hereford United back in May. The FA Cup first-round tie at Edgar Street was the main game on Match of the Day. The drama – thankfully – wasn't as intense as six months earlier as Stuart Storer fired the away side into the lead. It didn't last as a Neil Grayson double sent the Bulls through.

Sunday 15th November 2009

Gus Poyet's first game in charge of the Albion – on his 42nd birthday. Albion were at Southampton in front of the Sky cameras and gave their hosts a footballing lesson in the comprehensive 3-1 victory. Two Glenn Murray strikes, and an amazing Andrew Crofts finish from outside the box, wrapped up the points.

Thursday 15th November 2018

Club captain Lewis Dunk made his full England debut, playing the whole 90 minutes in the 3-0 victory over the USA at Wembley Stadium – the fourth Albion player to represent the Three Lions, and the last since Steve Foster in 1982. For the first time, England honoured one of their greatest players by giving Wayne Rooney a final appearance. He came on in the 58th minute ending his international career with a total of 53 goals in 120 appearances.

Monday 16th November 1953

Graham Moseley was born in Lancashire. The keeper featured just 44 times for Derby County in six years and was signed by Alan Mullery for £20,000 in November 1977 to compete with Eric Steele. In a topsy-turvy Albion career, Graham was in and out of the side and was considered a bit clumsy – after incidents with a hedge-trimmer and a glass window.

Despite this, the stopper was immensely popular and played in both FA Cup Final appearances. He won Player of the Season in 1984/85 as Albion came close to regaining their First Division status. A free transfer to Cardiff City beckoned before a car crash ended his career in 1988.

Tuesday 16th November 2010

Woking's Kingfield Stadium was the venue for this FA Cup first-round tie. The game, live on Sky TV, will probably not be remembered for the 2-2 scoreline, but for Cristian Baz's cheeky spot kick. The game had gone to penalties and the young Argentine stepped up to gently side-foot his left-foot effort home. The ball only just crossed the line to set up a second-round contest with FC United of Manchester.

The game was also notable for assistant manager Mauricio Taricco's first professional appearance for six years since tearing his hamstring on his West Ham debut. The full-back immediately offered to terminate his contract and Hammers boss Alan Pardew commented that it was one of the most honest things he had ever known a footballer to do.

Thursday 16th November 2023

Albion striker João Pedro made his international debut for Brazil in a World Cup qualifier against Colombia in Barranquilla. The 22-year-old replaced Real Madrid forward Vinícius Júnior after 27 minutes in a 2-1 defeat. 'Albion', 'Brazil' and 'Real Madrid' in the same paragraph. This is how we roll these days!

Saturday 17th November 1979

League runners-up the previous campaign, Nottingham Forest, hosted the Albion at the City Ground. The Tricky Trees hadn't lost at home in the league for over two seasons: 49 games! The visitors had never won an away fixture in the First Division – you can guess the rest! Gerry Ryan's first-half goal earned two points to lift the Seagulls off the bottom.

Monday 17th November 2020

Following in the footsteps of legendary Albion fanzines, *Gull's Eye, Scars & Stripes*, and *The Seagull Love Review*, the first issue of *Dogma* was published. The 12-page DIY publication - put together in a front room in Fiveways - featured stencilled lettering, photocopied sheets, hand-written headings and was bound by staples. It was created as a COVID-19-era project, principally as a fun way to pass the time during periods of lockdown (and the cancellation of professional football matches). Copies were distributed to a readership of about 15 friends and family members. Inauspicious beginnings.

Saturday 18th November 1972

Local boy Steve Piper donned the stripes for the first time. The 1-0 home defeat to Burnley – the start of a 13-match losing streak – didn't bode well for the Brighton-born defender/midfielder. Steady performances endeared him to his fellow Sussex folk and he was ever-present during the promotion campaign of 1976/77. Steve moved to Portsmouth for £20,000 in February 1978.

Saturday 18th November 2006

The programme reported on the visit of Albion in the Community's Jacob Naish to Tanzania for the Coaching For Hope Conference. The project used football to educate people on the dangers of HIV and Aids across Africa.

Tuesday 19th November 1996

Just 58 intrepid Albion fans headed west to Swansea. The 1-0 defeat for Jimmy Case's men secured bottom spot in the Football League's basement division.

Wednesday 19th November 1997

An *Evening Argus* phone-poll declared a small majority of readers were against the Albion's potential return to Brighton at the Withdean Stadium.

Saturday 20th November 1976

Just under 30,000 fans crammed into the Goldstone to see Peter Ward and Ian Mellor score in Albion's 2-2 FA Cup first-round draw with Crystal Palace.

Sunday 20th November 2022

The 22nd FIFA World Cup began in Qatar. Albion were represented by eight players at the tournament: three for Ecuador, Jeremy Sarmiento, Pervis Estupiñán and Moisés Caicedo, who exited at the group stage; Tariq Lamptey (Ghana – group stage); Kaoru Mitoma (Japan – round of 16); Robert Sánchez (Spain – round of 16); Leandro Trossard (Belgium – group stage); and, of course, Alexis Mac Allister – World Cup winner with Argentina! Albion received a combined total of £1,259,802 'compensation' for their players' appearances in the tournament. The club also received nearly a quarter of a million pounds for ex players' contributions; Maty Ryan (Australia), Ben White (England) and Alireza Jahanbakhsh (Iran).

Thursday 21st November 1991

A great day in Albion's history – Lewis Carl Dunk was born in Brighton. The defender was at Wimbledon when the club moved to Milton Keynes, cancelling their youth set-up in the process. He joined Albion's youngsters and went on trial at Crystal Palace. Our friends up the road offered him a contract, but our future captain saw the light, citing 'school commitment' and that he 'couldn't travel three times a week up to London'.

He then signed a scholarship with the Albion and was promoted to the under-18 squad, aged 16, in November 2007. Dunk's debut was in May 2010, and he featured five times as Albion stormed to the League One title in 2011. A mainstay of the first XI for over a decade, and a virtual ever-present during the stripes' seven years in the Premier League, Dunk has been one of the most consistent and important performers in the club's long history.

Club captain and England international, at the end of 2023/24, Lewis had made 459 appearances for his hometown club, scoring 31 times. Unequivocally, a Brighton & Hove Albion legend. Someone, somewhere is making a statue.

Tuesday 21st November 1995

Jimmy Case's Albion managerial career peaked in his first game in charge! Canvey Island were brushed aside 4-1 in the FA Cup replay but the team eventually succumbed to relegation to the basement division as off-the-pitch goings-on went from bad to terrible. The former player was sacked in December 1996 after 32 defeats in 57 games.

Tuesday 21st November 2006

Interested parties received an invitation to make submissions on various aspects of the planning case, especially Sheepcote Valley.

Saturday 22nd November 1975

The dawn of a new era – a specially chartered train took 584 Albion fans to Watford for a first-round FA Cup tie. It was the first of the Seagull Specials that would transport supporters across the country. Neil Martin and Fred Binney (2) were on target in the 3-0 victory.

Saturday 23rd November 1957

Dave Sexton notched a hat-trick as Albion disposed of Crystal Palace 4-2 in front of 15,757 fans at Selhurst Park

Saturday 23rd November 1996

Carlisle United beat Albion 3-1 at the Goldstone in front of a pitiful crowd of just 4,155. The game marked the first appearance of Kerry Mayo. The local lad came up through the ranks and began his career during the club's lowest ebb, culminating in him scoring an own goal during 'that' game at Hereford. Mayo is the only Albion player to have worn the stripes on the Goldstone, Priestfield and Withdean turfs and celebrated his testimonial season in 2006/07.

Saturday 24th November 1973

A full-house of 6,500 were present at Walton & Hersham's Stompond Lane for Albion's FA Cup first-round visit. Brian Clough's professionals could not overcome the amateurs. The 0-0 draw meant a Goldstone replay.

Thursday 24th November 2005

Lewes District Council mounted their legal challenge to the Falmer 'yes' decision.

Wednesday 25th November 1908

In front of 1,500 spectators at the Goldstone Ground, Albion beat Crystal Palace 2-0 with goals from Tom Stewart (pen) and Jack Martin.

Saturday 25th November 1950

Don Welsh's Albion side – having conceded 13 goals in their previous two league games – faced a potential FA Cup first-round banana skin at Tooting & Mitcham United. Thankfully, the majority of the 10,000 crowd went home disappointed as Jack Mansell, Des Tennant and Johnny McNichol were on target in a 3-2 triumph.

Saturday 25th November 1961

Bobby Baxter made his first Albion appearance in the 0-0 home draw with Preston North End. The left-back was a consistent fixture for six seasons after scoring 30 times in 67 run-outs as a striker for Darlington. Bobby arrived in a swap deal for Dennis Windross in August 1961 and appeared 220 times for Albion, netting on seven occasions, before he headed west to Torquay United in 1967.

Monday 26th November 1990

Daniel Nii Tackie Mensah Welbeck was born, to Ghanaian parents, in Manchester. While never prolific for his clubs – Manchester United, Preston North End and Sunderland (loan), Arsenal and Watford – Danny was for England, netting 16 times in 42 appearances. Initial reservations among the Albion faithful were soon quashed as the club's supporters got to see why he is so revered at his former employers with his selfless running, excellent hold-up play and superb heading ability.

Saturday 26th November 1994

Ade Akinbiyi's first appearance in an Albion shirt was in the 2-1 defeat at Brentford. The 20-year-old striker netted four times in seven starts. His total career transfer fees added up to nearly £16 million and the last of his 14 clubs was Colwyn Bay in 2015.

Tuesday 26th November 1996

An awful night for the Albion. The club's last FA Cup tie at the Goldstone – a replay against Sudbury Town – was lost 4-3 in a penalty shoot-out after a 1-1 extra-time scoreline. In Jimmy Case's programme notes, the three-times European Cup winner said; "Thank you for your attendance this evening and I'm sure you'll all be 'dreaming of Wembley' come the final whistle." Sudbury's goalkeeper, Steve Mokler, had other ideas, bagging the winning spot-kick to send the 500 away fans – in a poor crowd of just 3,902 – back to Suffolk happy.

Sunday 26th November 2000

The official campaign to win council support for the Falmer plans was launched. Des Lynam and Norman Cook were among 700 supporters in attendance at Hove Town Hall to see a presentation of the proposed

£44 million new stadium at Falmer, and how the future of the club depended on it.

Fans were urged to write to local councils in support, as well as the Countryside Agency to ask for the site of the proposed stadium not to be put within the boundaries of the proposed South Downs National Park. Albion chairman Dick Knight showed computer-generated designs of the proposed new home for the Albion declaring; "It will be a sporting beacon of excellence on the south coast."

Mr Knight told supporters Falmer was the only viable site in the boundaries of Brighton & Hove. "That is why we are sticking with Falmer, and we will win Falmer." The eventual cost was closer to £100 million and was underwritten by Tony Bloom.

Saturday 27th November 1965

Albion thrashed Southend United 9-1 in a home Third Division clash; just a fortnight after putting one more past Wisbech Town! The goals, in front of 11,124 fans, came from Jimmy Collins, Johnny Goodchild (2), Wally Gould, Jack Smith (3) and Charlie Livesey (2).

Sunday 27th November 2005

Falmer for All announced a week of action as posters appeared in Lewes declaring 'Wanted' above a picture of local councillor Ann De Vecchi.

Thursday 27th November 2008

Another momentous day in Albion history. Representatives from the club and the Buckingham Group signed the construction contract for the new stadium. Project director Martin Perry and construction director Derek Chapman put pen to paper for the club, while Buckingham Group chairman Paul Wheeler and project director Kevin Underwood signed on behalf of the contractors. Perry said; "Construction contracts are now in place ready for work to proceed. The stadium is on its way!" Music to Albion fans' ears!

Saturday 27th November 2010

Football Club United of Manchester visited Withdean in the FA Cup second round. The Northern Premier League side, formed in 2005 by disgruntled Manchester United supporters following Malcolm Glazer's takeover, filled the Worthing End with noise and colour for their first appearance at this stage of the competition. In the 40th minute, Nicky

Platt – not the one from Coronation Street – gave the visitors the lead. Scott McManus was sent off for violent conduct on the hour as Albion struggled to break down the spirited ten men. Fran Sandaza converted Mauricio Taricco's header in the 83rd minute to bring the scores level before Elliott Bennett stepped up to take a last-minute penalty. Sam Ashton pulled off a great save to take the tie back to Gigg Lane.

Wednesday 28th November 1973

Named after the 1973/74 Queens Park Rangers squad, Anthony Philip David Terry Frank Donald Stanley Gerry Gordon Stephen James Oatway was born in Hammersmith, London. When his aunt was told of the proposed name she proclaimed; "He'll look a right Charlie," and the nickname stuck.

The tough-tackling midfielder arrived from Brentford for a £10,000 fee in 1999 and played a huge part in the successive championships of 2001/02 and 2002/03. A broken ankle, ironically at home to QPR on Boxing Day 2005, eventually ended the popular player's career – after nearly two years of trying to battle back to fitness – in August 2007. Charlie featured 224 times for Albion, scoring nine times and went on to work as a coach under Gus Poyet at Brighton, Sunderland, AEK Athens, Real Betis and Shanghai Shenhua.

He didn't follow the Uruguayan to Bordeaux, instead deciding to join his Albion in the Community mentor, Dr Alan Sanders, who had become director of education, sport and health for Charlton Athletic Community Trust.

Saturday 28th November 1981

The 2-0 defeat at Manchester United was the Albion's 100th game in the top-flight.

Saturday 29th November 1969

News that Albion's home game with Torquay United had been postponed because of a blizzard reached British Rail and notices were posted at Brighton and Hove stations. They were wrong! The 5,640 fans – nearly 6,000 down on the average – saw the teams fight out a 2-2 draw in the snow.

Tuesday 29th November 2005

A mailshot, including posters and petitions, was sent to 1,500 supporters in the Lewes District Council area.

Saturday 30th November 1901

Albion enjoyed their first meeting with a team destined to become a fellow Football League side as Fulham were the visitors to the County Ground. Clem Barker and Frank McAvoy scored the goals to take the Southern League points in front of 1,900 fans.

Saturday 30th November 1996

Another day, another protest. This time London was the location as around 800 Albion fans marched from Victoria Station to Marble Arch to deliver a 5,726-name petition to The FA calling for chairman Bill Archer and chief executive David Bellotti to be charged with misconduct likely to bring the game into disrepute. A few hours later Albion lost 2-0 at Fulham's Craven Cottage.

Thursday 30th November 2023

Just over 1,600 Albion fans headed to Athens for the third away group game in the Europa League. In the first of six matches in the four-team division, AEK had won 3-2 in the reverse fixture in October and Roberto De Zerbi's injury-ravaged squad had a tough job on their hands at the Greek champions. On a balmy evening, João Pedro netted his fifth goal in the competition, from the penalty spot, in the 55th minute. AEK dominated the contest and the victory left Albion in second, with a game to go against leaders Olympique de Marseille on 14th December.

Scars & Stripes – December 1997:
New ground rumours kept appearing.

© Scars & Stripes

DECEMBER

Saturday 1st December 1973

Albion were the first team to put two past Bristol Rovers in the 1973/74 season, in a Third Division fixture at the Goldstone Ground. Unfortunately, the Gas got eight! The Pirates were flying in the league and coming to the end of a 22-match unbeaten run. It was Brian Powney's last time between the sticks and the ITV Big Match cameras were on hand to record the humiliation for posterity.

Monday 1st December 1997

Adrian Newnham launched the Bring Home the Albion campaign. In the proceeding weeks, blue and white ribbons adorned statues, lampposts, cars, railings etc to elicit support from the people of Brighton & Hove.

Monday 1st December 2003

Albion fans had written many letters by this point in time, and the ninth was delivered to Downing Street on this day. A total of 6,200 of this particular letter dropped through No. 10's letterbox.

Saturday 1st December 2007

While Albion were winning 2-0 at Torquay United in the FA Cup, contractors moved on to the Falmer site. Over 11-and-a-half years since vacating the Goldstone Ground, this was the moment everyone connected with the club had been waiting for.

Saturday 2nd December 2000

Another wonder strike from Bobby Zamora – this time at Withdean Stadium. The ball was sliced high into the air in Halifax Town's area. The prolific forward anticipated, kept his eye on the ball, and smashed in an unstoppable volley, a foot off the ground, across the goalkeeper and in off the far post; a quite stunning strike. A crowd of 6,595 were in attendance to witness the 2-0 Third Division victory.

Tuesday 3rd December 1968

Bustling centre-forward Alex Dawson signed from Bury. Freddie Goodwin's first acquisition – and former Busby Babe – was born in Scotland and scored 29 times in 65 Brighton appearances, and 212 in a career total of 393 outings.

Tuesday 3rd December 1996

Loathed chief executive David Bellotti was driven from the West Stand directors' box for the last time as fans surged across the pitch from the North Stand. It made no difference as Albion lost 3-2 at home to Darlington – in front of just 2,709 supporters – to go nine points adrift at the bottom of the basement division. Truly the worst of times.

Wednesday 3rd December 1997

Albion lost 1-0 at home to Notts County, in front of just 1,279 hardy souls at Gillingham.

Wednesday 4th December 1996

A legend on the pitch, Jimmy Case was sacked as manager following the disastrous 3-2 defeat at home to Darlington the previous evening. George Petchey took temporary charge.

Tuesday 4th December 2018

What a game at Falmer! Albion produced one of the best Premier League performances of the season to demolish Crystal Palace, despite only having ten men for 62 minutes. Just minutes after Glenn Murray stroked home a penalty to make it 1-0, Shane Duffy was shown a red card for nudging his head into Patrick van Aanholt, who went to ground as if he'd been punched by Mike Tyson in his prime.

Pascal Gross was immediately replaced by the more defensive-minded Leon Balogun, whose first touch was to launch a stunning half-volley into the net. But, the best was yet to come! Just before the interval, a hoofed clearance from Bernardo saw Florin Andone – who'd replaced the injured Murray – in a foot race with a Palace defender from deep inside his own half. Full pelt, they flew down the touchline and, after about 30 yards, Andone got a touch taking the ball towards the area. Now pursued by another defender coming across the box, the Romanian managed to cut the ball back and somehow squeeze a shot into the bottom corner. One of the finest goals ever seen at the stadium. Final score – 3-1.

Saturday 5th December 1981

Despite being unbeaten at home in the league since the first game of the season – a run of eight games – only 14,251 fans were at the Goldstone for the 2-1 First Division victory over Sunderland. Gordon Smith and Andy Ritchie were the scorers.

Thursday 5th December 2019

Albion's first-ever victory at Arsenal, at the ninth attempt. Adam Webster and Neal Maupay scored the goals as Graham Potter's men ran out 2-1 winners in front of 60,164 fans in north London.

Saturday 6th December 1919

George Zillwood March, 'Zach' – no relation to Solly – bagged a hat-trick in the 3-2 Southern League Goldstone victory over Watford. The little Sussex-born winger gained notoriety shortly before his passing, aged 101, in 1994 when he was identified as the country's oldest surviving former professional footballer.

Monday 6th December 1965

Albion fans listened to their team's exit from the FA Cup at Bedford Town in the West Stand at the Goldstone Ground. The 2-1 defeat was relayed – in sound only – from the opposition's ground, The Eyrie. Bedford Town applied for Football League membership every season between 1965 and 1973, and after a hiatus in 1974, made their eighteenth and final bid in 1975.

Monday 6th December 1976

At the third time of asking, the first-round FA Cup tie between Albion and Crystal Palace was resolved at Stamford Bridge. The south Londoners took the lead before referee Ron Challis awarded Brighton a penalty. Skipper Brian Horton converted the spot-kick, only for Challis to order a retake, which was subsequently saved by Paul Hammond. The Croydon outfit were through. At the final whistle, Alan Mullery famously became embroiled in a heated debate with the ref (who became known as 'Challis of the Palace' thereafter). After being covered in coffee by a belligerent opposition fan, Mullery made a two-fingered salute towards the Palace fans, flinging money in a puddle shouting; "You're not worth that, Palace!" He was fined £75 – and became an instant legend to Brighton & Hove Albion fans across the planet.

Saturday 7th December 1985

The programme for the Barnsley match congratulated 14-year-old Albion fan Simon Rodger from Shoreham on winning a Bobby Charlton Soccer Skills competition. His prize was a trip to show off his skills before Manchester United's Old Trafford contest with Ipswich Town. Almost 17 years later – after playing nearly 300 games for Crystal Palace in 12 years – Simon made his debut for his boyhood heroes in the 5-0 mauling at Selhurst Park! A game erased from the minds of the 6,000 Albion fans in attendance.

Saturday 7th December 1991

As Albion were losing 2-1 at Southend United, Christopher Grant Wood was born in Auckland, New Zealand. The big striker played a pivotal role in Albion's League One title-winning push in 2011, netting nine times in 31 games.

Wednesday 7th December 2005

This week saw signature collections in Lewes, Newhaven, Peacehaven and Seaford and on this day saw a 5,165-name petition presented to Lewes District Council.

Monday 7th December 2020

Albion lost 2-1 at home to Southampton in front of 2,000 fans. It's not 1997, and the club are no longer playing in Gillingham. It was the first time supporters had been allowed back into the stadium – socially distanced – since the COVID-19 pandemic began.

Saturday 8th December 1973

Peter Grummitt donned the Albion goalkeeper's jersey for the first time at Tranmere Rovers. Brian Clough took drastic measures after his side had shipped 12 goals in just two matches! Peter arrived after a decade – and 313 First Division appearances – with Nottingham Forest, and his great agility and adept handling helped Albion to promotion to Division Two in 1977. Sadly, a knee injury ended his career, aged 34, after 158 starts for the stripes.

Tuesday 8th December 1981

A first victory in Southampton for 25 years was reward with strikes from Andy Ritchie and Steve Gatting. The 2-0 win moved Mike Bailey's side into sixth place in the First Division, a UEFA Cup spot and the club's highest-ever league position, thus far.

Friday 8th December 1995

Headteacher Philip Lawrence was fatally stabbed outside his school, St George's, Maida Vale in London. He'd rushed to intervene when one of his pupils was being attacked by a gang. The first person on the scene to help his dying friend was Adrian Thorne, who famously scored five times as Albion won promotion for the first time, against Watford in 1958. The former striker taught science and physical education after retiring as a player. "I went out to try and help the bloke, took his coat and put it under his head, mopped him down, and he was dying. Terrible."

Wednesday 8th December 2010

After almost becoming the victim of a giant-killing in the first game at Withdean, Albion turned on the style to easily dispatch FC United of Manchester in this FA Cup second-round replay at Bury's Gigg Lane. The highest crowd in the fledgling club's history – 6,731 (exactly 7,000 in some publications) – saw the visitors dominate proceedings with Fran Sandaza (25th minute), Iñigo Calderón (45th), Elliott Bennett (86th) and Matt Sparrow (90th) registering to set up an intriguing home tie with south-coast rivals Portsmouth. The game marked the last of Gary Hart's 16 appearances in the competition for Albion.

Monday 9th December 1996

An FA commission deducted two points from managerless Albion's meagre total as a result of the pitch invasion during the Lincoln City game on 1st October. The club was now 11 points adrift of Hartlepool United at the foot of Division Three (fourth tier). It can safely be said that 'things were looking bleak' was a significant understatement. A thoroughly depressing time to be an Albion supporter.

Tuesday 9th December 1997

Five senior and high-earning professionals – Craig Maskell, Paul McDonald, Mark Morris, Denny Mundee and John Humphrey – were paid off as chairman Dick Knight struggled to keep the club afloat due to the poor attendances at Gillingham. On the same day, the Brighton & Hove Albion Supporters' Club invited Withdean residents to meet them at The Sportsman, next to the stadium, and discuss Albion's potential residency. Only one turned up.

Monday 10th December 1990

Kazenga LuaLua somersaulted into the world in Kinshasa, Zaire. A player who could make fans rise from their seats, the flying winger arrived at Withdean Stadium after Gus Poyet followed up a recommendation from his old team-mate Dennis Wise. He scored a rocket 25-yard free-kick on his debut and celebrated with his famous double backflip. An unfortunate leg break saw a return to parent club Newcastle United for convalescence before helping Albion to the League One title. After three loan spells, he signed a permanent deal in November 2011. In eight years at the club, LuaLua – hampered by injuries – struggled for consistency but was capable of astonishing moments of pace and skill. As at early 2024, he could be found bombing down the wing for Levadiakos, in the Greek Super League.

Friday 10th December 1999

A night exemplifying why Withdean Stadium was not a suitable venue for professional football; it absolutely chucked it down! The soaked-to-the-skin fans, including over 30 members of various local bands who had performed at a fundraising concert a few weeks earlier, were treated to a 4-3 scoreline but, unfortunately, the result favoured visitors Rochdale.

Friday 10th December 2021

There was a COVID-19 update for Albion fans. The new 'Plan B' measures were due to come into force with Covid Vaccine Passes expected to be required for entry to sports venues. All fans aged 18 or over had to be able to prove their vaccine status or display proof of a negative lateral flow test. A period in history we'd all rather forget.

Thursday 11th December 1958

Widely regarded as one of the finest managers in Albion's history, Christopher William Gerard Hughton was born in Forest Gate, London, to an Irish mother and a Ghanaian father. Originally a winger, the eventual right-back joined Tottenham Hotspur's youth system in 1971, signed as a part-timer in 1977, and trained as a lift engineer, becoming a full-time pro in July 1979.

In total, Hughton played 398 games for Spurs, winning the FA Cup in 1981 and 1982, and the UEFA Cup in 1984. He retired in 1993 after also representing West Ham and Brentford, and the Republic of Ireland (53 caps).

He gradually earned his coaching stripes, spending 14 years on the staff at Tottenham Hotspur before taking his first full-time position at Newcastle United in 2009, confirming promotion back to the Premier League in his first season. Steady stints at Birmingham City and Norwich City followed before Hughton arrived on the coast on New Year's Eve 2014.

After a couple of play-off near misses, Chris masterminded promotion to the Premier League in 2017. He guided Albion to 15th place in the first season and in May 2019, despite leading the club to safety again finishing 17th, Hughton was sacked. He's assured a warm reception whenever he returns to Falmer.

Saturday 11th December 1982

Albion beat Norwich City 3-0 in the First Division in front of a season-low 9,994 at the Goldstone. Later that evening, Republic of Ireland international Tony Grealish and his wife Pip hosted a party at their Peacehaven home. It was decided all guests should wear green, otherwise they would be refused admittance. Most players wore green pullovers or shirts while Steve Foster wore one green sock. Gerry Ryan's wife Simeon came dressed as a Christmas tree.

Wednesday 11th December 1996

Steve Gritt, the 39-year-old former Charlton Athletic player, was unveiled as new Albion boss. Incorrectly spelt graffiti – 'Grit believes Belotti bullsh*t' – welcomed the Londoner to the Goldstone Ground. Under his leadership, Albion recorded an incredible nine victories and two draws in the last 11 home games.

Saturday 11th December 1999

The first Falmer for All meeting took place. The previous evening, Albion fans were soaked to the skin at Withdean as a torrential downpour accompanied a 4-3 defeat to Rochdale.

Saturday 12th December 1987

In the Chester City programme 'Goldstone News Desk' announced; "Steve and Joy Gatting are celebrating the birth of their first child on 26th November. Joe Gatting weighed in at an impressive 7lb 14oz and is set to follow in the footsteps of his footballing dad and cricketing uncle, Mike." Joe would go on to score five goals for the Albion during 2006/07, including one in the 8-0 rout of Northwich Victoria in the FA Cup in a side of predominantly homegrown players.

Wednesday 13th December 1978

Two Seagull Special trains broke down en route to Nottingham Forest and missed Albion's first-ever appearance in the fifth round of the League Cup. The 1978 Football League champions ran out 3-1 winners.

Tuesday 14th December 1954

Andy Rollings was born in Somerset. Brian Clough paid £25,000 for the central defender – together with team-mate Steve Govier – in April 1974. He made his first-team debut, aged 19, in a 1-0 victory over Crystal Palace six months later. He lost his place to future England international Steve Foster three games into the inaugural First Division campaign in 1979 and eventually moved to Swindon Town for £75,000 – after 192 appearances and 12 strikes – in May 1980. He famously ran the Preston Park Café for many years.

Sunday 14th December 1980

Gordon Greer was born in Scotland. After only 33 games for Clyde, the big centre-back was snapped up by Premier League Blackburn Rovers for £250,000 in 2001. He made just a single appearance for the Ewood Park club and headed back north to Kilmarnock, via a brief loan spell at Stockport County. Short spells at Swindon Town and Doncaster Rovers preceded a permanent move to the Albion, for the start of the final season at Withdean, in 2010. Gus Poyet made 'GG' club captain and the Scot led his team to the League One title in 2011. Greer performed admirably over the next five campaigns and left the Albion in 2016, after 233 run-outs and five goals. A fine servant for the club, he finished his career with Killie in 2019, aged 39.

Tuesday 14th December 1982

Steve James Sidwell was born in Wandsworth, London. The midfielder joined the Albion on loan, from Arsenal, in 2002 scoring five times in just 12 second-tier appearances. His form secured a move to Reading, then Chelsea, Aston Villa, Fulham and Stoke City, before returning to the coast to play a pivotal role in the Albion's promotion to the Premier League.

Monday 14th December 1987

Albion midfielder Mike Trusson was beaten by David Gorton in an eye-balling contest at the Junior Seagulls Christmas Party at The Brighton Centre.

Saturday 15th December 1990

WBO middleweight champion Chris Eubank paraded his champion's belt before the Goldstone crowd, prior to the game with Barnsley, to promote his forthcoming fight with Dan Sherry at The Brighton Centre.

Tuesday 15th December 1992

Jesse Ellis Lingard was born in Warrington. After failing to establish himself as a regular starter at parent club Manchester United, the midfielder was signed on a 93-day loan by Óscar García in February 2014. In 17 appearances, the future England international scored on four occasions.

Monday 15th December 1997

A public meeting at Hove Town Hall formally launched the campaign to secure the use of Withdean Stadium as a temporary home. It would be another 19 months before a ball was kicked.

Tuesday 15th December 2015

In the 22nd game of the season, Albion lost for the first time, going down 3-0 at home to Middlesbrough. Chris Hughton's men failed to deal with crosses, with all three of the opposition's goals coming from centres into the box. Jason Roberts on BBC Radio 5 Live said; "Brighton could have been a bit more decisive. Make no mistake, they've come up against a really strong, well-oiled unit."

Wednesday 16th December 1992

The High Court judge granted the Albion a stay of execution against a winding-up order brought by the Inland Revenue and Customs & Excise. Later that evening, goals from Robert Codner and John Crumplin, with a long-range header, secured a 2-1 FA Cup replay victory at a very wet Woking.

Friday 16th December 2005

John Prescott was greeted with enthusiastic applause from the Withdean Stadium faithful after approving the Falmer Stadium decision. Albion beat the Deputy Prime Minister's team, Hull City, 2-1 with goals from Seb Carole and Charlie Oatway. In the matchday programme, fan Gus Nunneley was pictured receiving a signed shirt to commemorate watching 500 consecutive Albion matches.

Tuesday 16th December 2008

Albion travelled to Shrewsbury Town for an Associate Members Cup semi-final. The much-maligned competition was a realistic route to Wembley for Micky Adams' men. *The Seagull Love Review* handed out the full words to Sussex By the Sea, on a songsheet, to the away support at New Meadow. It was the only highlight of the evening. The game finished 0-0.

Wednesday 17th December 2008

An early Christmas present for long-suffering Albion fans: the ground-breaking ceremony at the Falmer stadium site in front of 100 or so lottery-winning supporters. The dimensions of the pitch were marked into the mud, complete with corner flags, goalposts and a penalty spot. Sompting-born goalkeeper John Sullivan strolled over from the training ground the other side of the A27 to face penalties – in a goal fashioned by two diggers – from Martin Perry and Dick Knight, who 'scored' the first goal at the new stadium. The chairman commented; "It is a testament to the efforts of thousands of people who just didn't give up. No other football club has been through what we have, but that just shows the spirit of the Albion."

Saturday 17th December 2011

Albion started the day with the Championship's poorest disciplinary record – and it soon became even worse. In just the fifth minute, utility player Romain Vincelot was shown a red card for an off-the-ball incident. The Frenchman appeared to thump a Clarets midfielder in the stomach. The Falmer faithful had barely had time to compose themselves before another Albion man headed for an early bath. Ashley Barnes reacted to an unpunished challenge by Chris McCann after 11 minutes.

Needless to say, the home crowd were incensed, none more so than manager Gus Poyet when Craig Noone was sent sprawling in the box on 28 minutes. The Uruguayan threw his coat to the ground in frustration and then disappeared down the tunnel. The game will be remembered for how Albion fans responded to the nine-men setback, turning the volume up to 11. The players reacted with a spirited performance, twice going close to grabbing an unlikely equaliser.

Poyet summed up the match perfectly; "It was a really bad day at the office."

Saturday 18th December 1880

Tommy Charlesworth Allsopp was born in Leicester. The outside-left arrived in Hove from Leicester Fosse in 1905 and missed just eight games out of 111 during his two seasons on the coast.

Sunday 18th December 1988

Elliott Bennett entered the world, in Telford, Shropshire. The right-winger enjoyed two years on the south coast – plus a short loan spell in 2014 – and played in every league game as Albion romped to the League One title in 2011. A crowd favourite, he's perhaps best remembered for netting a spectacular volley as Gus Poyet's men secured the trophy at Walsall.

Friday 18th December 2009

Against a snow-covered backdrop, the main stadium arch was being delicately pieced together underneath low-level floodlights, to maximise time. A year and a day since work on the site began, significant progress had been made. The East Stand's frame, terracing and floors were complete while the South Stand's skeleton was rapidly progressing.

Sunday 18th December 2022

Alexis Mac Allister left mid-season to play for Argentina in the World Cup. After defeat to Saudi Arabia in their first match, head coach Lionel Scaloni started the midfielder and he became an ever-present as La Albiceleste made it to the final. Lionel Messi gave Argentina the lead from the penalty spot in the 23rd minute, making him the first player in the tournament's history to score in the group stage, last 16, quarter-final, semi-final and final.

He then contributed a delicate touch in a counter-attack that ended with Mac Allister setting up Angel Di Maria for the second 13 minutes later. Then Kylian Mbappe decided to get involved, netting a penalty (80th) and a stunning volley just a minute later. Messi bundled his side back in front in extra-time only for Mbappe to complete his hat-trick from the spot two minutes from the end of extra-time.

Penalties. Gonzalo Montiel scored the winning kick from 12 yards to make it 4-2 on pens. Alexis made every Albion fan burst with pride as he became the first player to lift the famous trophy while representing the club.

Saturday 19th December 1981

Match of the Day's 45 staff packed up their equipment and hot-footed it to Stamford Bridge after Albion's home fixture with Leeds United was postponed.

Tuesday 19th December 1984

Manager Chris Cattlin stepped in to help after Hove 13th Scouts lost their kit! The former left-back replaced the old green kit out of his own pocket, with the help of David Rose Sports.

Saturday 20th December 1958

After a record 9-0 humiliation on their Division Two debut, Billy Lane's Albion side welcomed Middlesbrough to the Goldstone Ground. In a game shown later on BBC TV, Brian Clough, who had scored five in the last encounter, grabbed a hat-trick for the visitors while Johnny Shephard netted his second consecutive brace as Brighton went down 6-4!

Sunday 20th December 2020

Albion had won only one of their past 12 Premier League matches. In front of 2,000 fans, Danny Welbeck smacked home a deserved equaliser against Sheffield United after controlling Chris Basham's attempted clearance with his chest just three minutes from time to make it 1-1. COVID-19 conditions restricted the attendance.

Sunday 21st December 1986

Albion tried to attract a bigger crowd for this Division Two game with Shrewsbury Town. Nearly 1,700 senior citizens and youngsters were admitted free to boost the gate to 8,220 and they were rewarded with a 3-0 win. Barry Lloyd revealed, in the programme, that people said his music taste was boring. His favourite artists were George Benson and namesake Manilow. They may have had a point, Barry!

Thursday 22nd December 1887

Gunner Higham entered the world in Daventry. After initially performing in the reserves, the left-back made his Albion debut in 1908. As a reservist, Gunner was the first Brighton player to be called up on the outbreak of the Great War and subsequently missed the whole of the 1914/15 season. He survived the hostilities and played one more season, 1919/20, before hanging up his boots after one goal in 159 starts.

Sunday 22nd December 1996

Former England goalkeeper Peter Shilton celebrated his 1,000th Football League appearance – against Albion – at Leyton Orient. Live on Sky TV, the visitors gave the veteran very little work to do, as the Os ran out 2-0 winners. Hundreds of away fans protested against the board.

Saturday 23rd December 1972

Albion lost for the seventh consecutive time. High-flying QPR won 2-1 at the Goldstone to keep Pat Saward's men bottom of the Second Division. The side lost the next six games too.

Saturday 23rd December 2006

The start of a six-game losing streak, Albion conceded twice at Port Vale. Tommy Fraser scored at the club he would sign for in 2009.

Monday 24th December 1900

Dan Kirkwood was born in Scotland. The striker, signed for £500 from Sheffield Wednesday in 1928, formed the most prolific goalscoring partnership in Albion's history, linking up with Hugh Vallance to score a total of 63 goals in 1929/30. Given a free transfer to Luton Town in 1933, he netted 82 times in just 181 starts.

Saturday 24th December 1955

The last time Albion played on Christmas Eve was over 60 years ago, against Northampton Town. Dennis Gordon, Albert Mundy, Peter Harburn and Glen Wilson were full of festive cheer, scoring in the 4-0 Goldstone triumph.

Thursday 24th December 1998

Alexis Mac Allister was born in Santa Rosa, Argentina. His father, Carlos, who is of Irish/Italian ancestry, played three times for Argentina, and is currently a politician in his home country. Alexis signed for the Albion in 2019 and, after playing for Argentinos Juniors and Boca Juniors on loan, made his Seagulls debut at Wolves in March 2020, the last game before the COVID-19 pandemic halted all football across the planet. He scored sporadically in his first couple of seasons in England, but it was in 2022/23 when the midfielder really made a name for himself, scoring 12 times in 40 appearances. He signed for Liverpool in the summer of 2023 but is guaranteed a warm welcome whenever he visits the south coast.

Monday 25th December 1922

Albion enjoyed their best win on Christmas Day. Eddie Fuller (2), Abe Jones, Wally Little (pen), Tommy Cook (2) and Andy Neil were on target in a 7-1 thrashing of Portsmouth in front of 15,000 spectators at the Goldstone Ground.

Wednesday 25th December 1940

With World War II raging, football continued under the auspices of the Football League (South) and the team – all five of them, one senior player, three juniors and (as a guest) Bolton's Jimmy Ithell – travelled to Carrow Road. After borrowing some Norwich City juniors and servicemen from the crowd, Albion let the Canaries flap to a rather unflattering 18 goals without reply!

Wednesday 26th December 1979

Albion entertained Crystal Palace for the first time in Division One. It was a happy Christmas for the south coast faithful among the 28,358 crowd. A Brian Horton penalty – and strikes from Peter Ward and Gerry Ryan – made it 3-0 to the home side. The result left Brighton 19th on 17 points, while the Londoners sat 11 places higher on 23. Three points for a win wasn't introduced until 1981.

Wednesday 26th December 1990

The match with Bristol Rovers was played in torrential rain at the Goldstone. The visitors won 1-0. The programme identified a new member of the board – 46-year-old Bill Archer: "It's a great honour to be asked to join the board and I am really looking forward to becoming involved in professional sport again [he was instrumental in Liverpool's 1979 shirt sponsorship deal with Crown]. Brighton have terrific potential and I am here to develop a greater sponsorship input for the future." Unfortunately, the benefit of hindsight was unavailable at the time.

Friday 26th December 1997

The Seagulls drew 4-4 – after being 3-0 down – against Colchester United at Gillingham. On-loan Paul Emblen scored a hat-trick in front of 2,647 fans.

Sunday 26th December 2021

Albion entertained Brentford on Village Way and recorded their first win in 12 Premier League encounters. Leandro Trossard's lob and Neal Maupay's fantastic curling strike, both in the first half, saw Graham Potter's men move up to ninth in the table. The official 'attendance' was 30,141. The actual attendance was nearer half that amount. No trains and no buses didn't help, but 2,000 visiting fans managed it. The Premier League's insistence on announcing tickets sold instead of the amount of actual people inside the ground – i.e., those 'attending' – had reached an embarrassing new low.

Saturday 27th December 1958

Promotion contenders Fulham visited Hove with former fans' favourite Jimmy Langley in their line-up. The largest crowd in Goldstone Ground history, 36,747, enjoyed a 3-0 win. Tommy Dixon (2) and Adrian Thorne were on target in Albion's inaugural Division Two campaign.

Saturday 27th December 1980

In an enthralling First Division encounter, Albion beat Crystal Palace 3-2 at the Goldstone. Peter O'Sullivan and Michael Robinson (2) were the goalscorers in front of 27,367 fans.

Tuesday 27th December 1983

'The Dirtiest Player in Europe' made his debut against Fulham at the Goldstone Ground. Dutchman Hans Kraay arrived in Hove with a somewhat tarnished reputation after pushing over a referee while playing for former club NAC Breda. Hugely popular with the home crowd, Kraay was sent off twice in just 23 appearances and will be fondly remembered for his pogo-jumping routine in front of opposition goalkeepers at corners. In 2003, he reached number 3 in the Netherlands charts with 'Er Zal D'r Altijd Eentje Winnen', a track recorded with fans of various Dutch football clubs as a reaction to the violent meeting of hooligans from Ajax and Feyenoord.

Monday 28th December 1998

A brace from Richie Barker secured the points in a 2-1 victory at Peterborough United. Bizarrely, 365 days earlier the teams, the score and the venue were exactly the same!

Monday 28th December 2009

A sublime performance at Adams Park saw Albion trounce their hosts Wycombe Wanderers 5-2. The undoubted hero of the day was Glenn Murray, back in the first team to replace the suspended Liam Dickinson. The Cumbrian-born hitman became the first Brighton player to bag four goals in a game since Bryan Wade's amazing Goldstone debut against Newcastle United in January 1991.

Thursday 28th December 2023

Albion completed a momentous calendar year with an invigorating 4-2 victory over Tottenham Hotspur. In a magnificent performance by Roberto De Zerbi's men, 18-year-old Jack Hinshelwood bagged his second league goal early in the first half, followed by a João Pedro penalty before half-time. Albion hit the woodwork twice and Richarlison missed a few chances. Pervis Estupiñán replaced Igor at the start of the second period.

The Ecuadorian announced his return from injury with an absolute howitzer of a strike to make it 3-0. Pedro scored another penalty and Albion were 4-0 up. Then a calamitous five-minute spell resulted in two Spurs goals (81st and 85th minutes) and a big case of the jitters in the stands at Falmer. A wonderful game of football and the 5,468th competitive match in the club's history – and only the 41st 4-2 victory.

Saturday 29th December 1979

The matchday programme versus Manchester City described a recent visit to Hove by world darts champion Eric Bristow; "Among the gathering were Peter Ward and a young Gary Stevens. As Eric beat all 16 opponents, they looked on with amazement at the skill of a man reputed to earn £1,000 a week from a sport renowned for the beer capacity of its participants. Peter and Gary restricted themselves to a small lager and a bitter lemon, respectively."

Monday 29th December 2014

After Sami Hyypiä's recent sacking, managerless Albion won 2-0 at Fulham to secure only their second win in 20 league games and climb out of the Championship drop zone. It was the last of caretaker boss Nathan Jones' two games in charge.

Friday 29th December 2023

The club announced that long-serving board members, and lifelong fans, Derek Chapman and Marc Sugarman were to step down as non-executive directors of the Albion in June 2024. Derek played a huge part in Albion's recent history, utilising his vast expertise of the construction industry to ensure efficient delivery of the stadium at Falmer, and the Elite Football Performance Centre in Lancing. He joined the board during the Gillingham years, helped fund the move back to Withdean, and keep the club afloat during the early 2000s.

Marc, a chartered accountant, became a board member in 2009, using his background in banking, as an analyst for Morgan Stanley, Goldman Sachs and Citigroup, to provide the club with invaluable insight into sports media rights. He also served as a trustee for Albion in the Community (now Brighton & Hove Albion Foundation) stepping down in the summer of 2022, after 12 years. Tony Bloom said; "On behalf of everyone at the club, I'd like to place on record my thanks to both Derek and Marc for the tremendous service they've given to the club, and on a personal note, the excellent support they've given to me in my time as chairman."

Saturday 30th December 1911

Jimmy Smith, who was born in the Potteries, scored all four goals as Albion beat Southern League newcomers Stoke 4-0 at the Goldstone. The prolific striker – 40 goals in 67 Albion appearances – served as a gunner in the Royal Field Artillery and was tragically killed in action on the Western Front in 1918, just a few weeks before he was due to be married.

Saturday 30th December 2023

Albion legend Brian Horton rang the bell in hospital after successful pancreatic cancer treatment. The 74-year-old former player and manager was diagnosed a few months earlier after a free League Managers Association (LMA) medical on the advice of Wrexham's Steve Parkin.

Saturday 31st December 1927

Micky Kavanagh was born in Dublin. The little forward travelled to Hull for a trial but no-one met him at the train station. A friendly policeman let him spend his first night in a police box. After an unsuccessful try-out, he arrived in Hove in 1948. The Irishman managed seven strikes in 27 starts then severed his knee ligaments to prompt a very early retirement at the age of just 22. He stayed in Sussex and died in Rustington, aged 88, in 2016.

Friday 31st December 2010

Albion completed the signing of 23-year-old winger Craig Noone – on a three-and-a-half-year deal – from Plymouth Argyle. Gus Poyet said; "Craig is a player who has been on our radar for a while, and he impressed against us when we played at Home Park earlier in the season.

Since then, we have kept a close eye on his performances, with Zigor and our scouts continuing to monitor his progress." Capable of changing a game, the Liverpudlian soon endeared himself to the Withdean Stadium faithful with some dazzling displays. 'Nooney!'

Sunday 31st December 2023

The calendar year of 2023 was officially the best in the 122-year history of Brighton & Hove Albion Football Club. In 53 matches, the club enjoyed 27 wins, 13 draws and 13 losses. An incredible 105 goals were scored – four or more on eight occasions – and 70 conceded. A dramatic FA Cup semi-final defeat – the only goalless draw of 2023 – on penalties was hard to take but it's surely only a matter of time before the club reach a major final.

The highest-ever league position, sixth, was secured in May to ensure European football for the very first time. Unbeaten in the first three Europa League group away games, winning two – Ajax (2-0), AEK Athens (1-0) – Albion won two at home too – Ajax (2-0), Olympique de Marseille (1-0) – to top the table and earn a place in the last 16.

Roberto De Zerbi's men performed in front of a total attendance of 1,931,206 in 2023, and only failed to find the net in just four matches.

A monumental year.

Bibliography

Websites

wearebrighton.com
dogmabrighton.com
bbc.co.uk
brightonandhovealbion.com
seagullsprogrammes.co.uk
theathletic.com
theseagulllovereview.blogspot.com
toffeeweb.com
theguardian.com
inparallellines.wordpress.com
thegoldstonewrap.com
northstandchat.com
mirror.co.uk

Books

Eric & Dave – Spencer Vignes (Pitch Publishing)
Albion A to Z – A Who's Who of Brighton & Hove Albion FC –
Tim Carder and Roger Harris (Goldstone Books)
Brighton & Hove Albion Miscellany – Paul Camillin (Pitch Publishing)
Build a Bonfire – Paul Hodson, Steve North (Transworld)
We Want Falmer! – Paul Hodson, Steve North (Stripe Publishing)

About the author

A lifelong Albion fan, Dan Tester has written about the club – on and off – for nearly three decades. After 20 years as a copywriter, he's now a contract content designer. This is his fifth book.

He owns and runs englishfootballbooks.com, an affiliate website collating the best titles on the English game. Away from his desk, Dan can be found co-hosting two monthly radio programmes – Family Funktunes and The Adam & Dan Show – on 1BTN and playing other people's records at venues across the south, and further afield.

ENGLISH FOOTBALL BOOKS

Welcome to English Football Books

We love football books!

Working alongside our affiliate partners, we've hand-picked our favourite titles, to save you the hassle of trawling through other sites.

Whether you're looking for a paperback on your favourite player, or an up-to-date hardback on your club, we're confident you'll find it here at English Football Books.

www.englishfootballbooks.com